Map of Horace Greeley's Route by RAILROAD and OVERLAND STAGECOACH from New York to San Francisco in the Summer of 1859

Atlantic Ocean

NEW YORK
Departed by
Rail May 9, 1859

0   100   200   300   400
SCALE OF MILES

METZIG

NEW EDITIONS

of Classic Commentaries on America's Past

William Bradford—OF PLYMOUTH PLANTATION
with an introduction and notes by Samuel Eliot Morison

Richard Burton—THE CITY OF THE SAINTS
with an introduction and notes by Fawn M. Brodie

Dan De Quille (William Wright)—THE BIG BONANZA
with an introduction by Oscar Lewis

Horace Greeley—AN OVERLAND JOURNEY
with an introduction and notes by Charles T. Duncan

Frances A. Kemble—JOURNAL OF A RESIDENCE ON A
GEORGIAN PLANTATION IN 1838–1839
with an introduction and notes by John A. Scott

Frederick Marryat—A DIARY IN AMERICA
with an introduction and notes by S. W. Jackman

Frederick Law Olmsted—THE COTTON KINGDOM
with an introduction by Arthur M. Schlesinger

"Dame Shirley" (Louise A. K. S. Clappe)—
THE SHIRLEY LETTERS
with an introduction and notes by Carl I. Wheat

Alexis de Tocqueville—DEMOCRACY IN AMERICA
*with an introduction, notes, and bibliographies by
Phillips Bradley*

Anthony Trollope—NORTH AMERICA
*with an introduction and notes by Donald Smalley and
Bradford Allen Booth*

Mrs. Frances Trollope—DOMESTIC MANNERS OF
THE AMERICANS
with an introduction and notes by Donald Smalley

These are BORZOI BOOKS, *published in New York by* ALFRED A. KNOPF

An Overland Journey

Horace Greeley

Steel engraving in *Recollections of a Busy Life* (1868)

AFTER A PHOTOGRAPH BY BRADY

AN OVERLAND JOURNEY

FROM

*New York to San Francisco
in the Summer of 1859*

BY

HORACE GREELEY

EDITED, AND WITH NOTES AND AN INTRODUCTION,

BY CHARLES T. DUNCAN

New York · Alfred·A·Knopf · 1964

47160

L. C. catalog card number: 63–18357

THS IS A BORZOI BOOK,
PUBLISHED BY ALFRED A. KNOPF, INC.

FIRST BORZOI EDITION

Contents

I · FIRST LEG

II · KANSAS

CONTENTS

CONTENTS

V · DENVER TO SALT LAKE CITY

VI · UTAH

VII · SALT LAKE TO CALIFORNIA

vii

VIII · CALIFORNIA

IX · EPILOGUE: "MEN AND BRETHREN!"

Illustrations

Editor's Introduction

On May 9, 1859, a most remarkable man left New York City on a most remarkable journey—alone, without fanfare, and as casually as if he were taking the train to Albany on business.

It was Horace Greeley, editor of the New York *Tribune*, setting out on what was to become one of the most famous trips in the annals of journalism, a profession noted for the travels of its practitioners. Carpetbag and umbrella in hand, and clad, we can assume, in the white hat and white duster that had already become his trademark, Mr. Greeley was off to see for himself the vast, fabled, and largely unexplored American West. He was California-bound.

It is difficult to imagine modern counterparts of the man, the journey, and the circumstances. In the first place, there is no one in American journalism today who comes even close to being the like of Horace Greeley. If there were such a man, it would be hard to conjure up a trip for him to undertake that could be compared to Greeley's in arduousness, uncertainty, hazards, and length of time required to reach his destination, while utilizing the best, most modern means of transportation that the day affords. And if the man could be found and the journey laid out, it cannot be imagined that he could embark upon it without considerable public notice and attention, genuine or contrived.

To be sure, Horace Greeley did not depart in secret, nor were his readers unaware of his plans. In fact, he would have welcomed some company. Recounting the journey many years later, he recalled how he long had been resolved to make it, but he had found no opportunity before 1859. Then, jocularly but with what seems a note of wistfulness, he says: "I then hoped, rather than confidently expected, that, on publicly announcing my intention, some friend might offer to bear me company on this journey; but my hope was not realized. One friend did propose to go; but his wife's veto overruled his not very stubborn resolve. I started alone, on the 9th of May . . ."[1]

It was more than natural curiosity and restlessness—he was richly endowed with both—that prompted the country's most prominent, most influential newspaper editor to leave his desk, not to mention his family, for nearly five months of arduous, uncomfortable travel. An enthusiastic champion of westward expansion and western development, Greeley early saw a railroad to the Pacific as "a National necessity" and he burned to have a look at the terrain such a road would have to cross. By his own testimony, he had been advocating a transcontinental railroad for at least ten years.

"From the hour when, late in 1848, the discovery of rich gold placers in California had incited a vast and eager migration thither, insuring the rapid growth of energetic and thrifty settlements of our countrymen on that remote and previously unattractive, thinly peopled coast, the construction of a great International Railway from the Missouri to the Pacific seemed to me to be imperative and inevitable. I could not deem it practicable to retain permanently under one government communities of many millions of intelligent, aspiring, imperious people, separated by fifteen hundred miles of desert, traversed by two great mountain-chains, besides innumerable clusters, spurs and isolated summits,

[1] Horace Greeley: *Recollections of a Busy Life* (New York: J.B. Ford and Company; 1868), p. 360.

and compelling a resort, for comparatively easy, cheap and speedy transit, to a circuit of many thousands of miles. A Pacific Railroad was thus accepted by me at a very early day as a National necessity, alike in its political and its commercial aspects; and, while others were scoffingly likening it to a tunnel under the Atlantic or a bridge to the moon, I was pondering the probabilities and means of its early construction. I resolved to make a journey of observation across the continent, with reference to the natural obstacles presented to, and facilities afforded for, its construction; but no opportunity for executing this purpose was afforded me prior to the year 1859."[2]

A natural question would be: Why didn't Greeley send a good reporter from his paper? Since nowhere does he mention such a possibility, the chances are the thought never entered his head. It was entirely in character for him to go himself. ". . . the man was everywhere," says one of his biographers. "The present-day editor seldom makes a public appearance . . . Greeley covered all outdoors. He missed few public occasions, spoke much, lectured more, took part in conventions, either as a delegate or reporter, conferred constantly with the great and near great, led in party counsels, and went to church . . . Besides his remarkable ability as a writer of editorials, Greeley was a first-class reporter."[3]

Biographer Don Seitz's vivid description of Greeley's person might well apply to the great editor as he stood that May evening in the Erie Station, waiting to board the train—unless, as seems more likely—he came rushing up at the last minute and clambered aboard as the train was about to pull away.

". . . No stranger looking figure appeared among the noted

[2] *Ibid.*
[3] Don C. Seitz; *Horace Greeley* (Indianapolis: Bobbs-Merrill; 1926), pp. 3 and 8.

men of his day," Seitz begins. "He was rather tall in stature, five feet ten and a half, with a frame badly set and a large queer-shaped head. It was round as a ball. The forehead bulged, betokening brain power behind it, while on the edge of the dome the blue eyes gazed unblinking at mankind. The eyes had no sparkle; indeed were mild and pale. The complexion was white—so white as to be startling, though there was nothing unhealthy in the pallor. This whiteness was set off by a crown of thin silky hair, so light as to suggest the albino, which in middle life came to extend around the face and under the chin, framing the baby countenance . . . He had no graces. His voice was high and shrill . . .

"His dress, if dishevelled, was scrupulously neat and clean. His linen was of the choicest and always fresh from the laundry. He liked linen clothes, and in the summer wore a fresh suit daily, covered with a long 'duster.'

"Men of that day wore boots . . . formidable affairs with leather tops reaching to the knees. It was somewhat difficult to adjust the trouser legs smoothly over these leather cylinders and coax them down to the bridge of the feet. Greeley seldom tried thus to perfect his toilet, with the result that one leg or the other of the trousers was usually snagged somewhere on a boot-top. This became a fixture in his costume and, once he became famous, was eagerly seized upon by the cartoonists to the end of exaggerating his eccentricities.

"The blue eyes were weak and had early to take to spectacles . . . These glasses gave him an owl-like aspect, much appreciated by the artists. His collar sat around his rather slender neck like the edge of a bowl, and over it the silken whiskers flowed. A string necktie, that worked easily round toward one ear or the other, usually completed his adornment. For headgear he liked a broad-brimmed hat of straw or felt, usually white. Indeed, white was his favorite garb, it would appear, so that his picture is always pale in toto . . . His pet public topper was a tall white hat, built on the model of the ancient beaver, but of plain felt. This became his trademark.

"He usually carried a fat umbrella that bulged a good deal, due to the fact that its ribs were whalebone . . . It will be seen that this combination of hat, spectacles, necktie, boots and umbrella made a figure not to be easily overlooked."[4]

At forty-eight Horace Greeley was in full stride. As the outspoken editor of America's most widely read newspaper, he was known throughout the country and would be as likely to be recognized on the Kansas prairie as in New York City. Albert D. Richardson, an able young reporter from Boston who was by chance a fellow passenger on Greeley's stage-coach westward out of Manhattan, Kansas, tells an amusing incident that illustrates Greeley's modesty as well as his fame.

"This afternoon our coach was stopped at a creek-crossing by a mired wagon which blocked the road. Several Ohio emigrants with their weary cattle were endeavoring to extricate it. Mr. G. assisted them in their efforts to lift the wheels out from the Slough of Despond. While they paused one inquired of the stranger his business. He replied that he was connected with a New York daily journal.

" 'What journal?'

" *'The Tribune.'*

" 'Ah! That's old Greeley's paper, isn't it?'

" 'Yes sir.'

"Just then another of the party who had been absent, returned and recognizing the ablest editor and most influential American of our generation laboring at the wheel, said to his comrades:

" 'Gentlemen, this is Mr. Greeley of New York.'

[4] *Ibid.*, pp. 1–4.

"The curious interrogator was struck dumb with amazement and chagrin."[5]

Mr. Greeley was widely traveled in the United States and had made two lengthy and well-publicized voyages to Europe. He had served a short term in Congress, where he had created more uproar in three months than most Congressmen do in thirty years. He was a noted and popular lecturer and was, at this time, the author of three books. Influential in politics, he had played a prominent part in the founding of the Republican Party three years earlier and was soon to have a key role in the most fateful political event in the country's history, the nomination of Abraham Lincoln for the Presidency.

At forty-eight, Horace Greeley had known more struggle, poverty, disappointment, and sorrow than, mercifully, are the lot of most men in a long lifetime. His marriage, in 1836, while not a failure, had certainly not brought him happiness and contentment. Moreover, it had been deeply scarred by tragedy. Horace and Mary Greeley's first two children died soon after birth, a boy in 1838, a girl in 1842. In between there were two miscarriages. Then came Arthur Young Greeley, their third child, a beautiful boy who grew to be the darling of their hearts, pampered by his father, badly overprotected by his mother. "Pickie" died in 1849, at the age of five, of cholera. The letter written by the heartbroken Greeley to Margaret Fuller, his dear friend and at the time a *Tribune* correspondent in Italy, is a poignant and moving lament.

Meantime, to continue the dismal recital, in the last year of Pickie's brief life a second daughter had been born, only to die at the age of six months. A few years after Arthur's

[5] Albert D. Richardson: *Beyond the Mississippi* (Hartford, Connecticut; American Publishing Company; 1867), p. 169. Richardson later joined the *Tribune* staff and became one of Greeley's most valued reporters during the Civil War.

death, another son was born. Ralph was a joy and solace to his father, but at six he died of croup, and again Horace Greeley was crushed under almost intolerable grief.

Of Horace and Mary's seven children (not counting those stillborn), only two—daughters Ida and Gabrielle—lived to survive their parents.

There was yet one more heavy blow in store for Greeley. He longed for the return to America of his beloved—platonically, by the most reliable accounts—Margaret Fuller, the brilliant, eccentric feminist and intellectual, who had been a dear friend to Mary as well as to Horace. Margaret had married an impecunious Italian nobleman while abroad and had borne a son by him. On July 16, 1850, just a year and five days after the death of Pickie, whom Margaret also adored, the entire d'Ossoli family perished when the ship bringing them to New York went hard aground on Fire Island in a fog and broke up. Again Horace Greeley drank from the bitter cup.

All this sorrow was behind him, however, by the spring of 1859 when he set forth on his journey. It would have been characteristic of him to approach it with zestful anticipation.

Greeley's biographers are not uniform in the attention they devote to his cross-country adventure nor in the significance they attach to it, but they are as one in giving as the principal motivation his great interest in the dream of a railroad to the Pacific Ocean.

Ingersoll says: "... A railroad to the Pacific had been early advocated by him as a national necessity ... He left home on the 9th of May and reached New York on his return near the close of September—a period of his busy life of notable interest, and of great usefulness to his country then and afterwards."[6]

[6] L. D. Ingersoll: *The Life of Horace Greeley* (Chicago: Union Publishing Co.; 1873), p. 335.

"It was now time for another Greeley pilgrimage to distant places," writes Stoddard. ". . . Greeley determined to find out for himself if there was a West—a Pacific coast West—and what the treasure house of limitless gold really looked like. It was a lure he could not resist. Besides, he had been one of the earliest advocates of building the Union Pacific Railroad. He now wanted to cross the deserts, mountains and rivers over which it would pass, and thus know their difficulties. Pessimists were saying that 'constructing a railroad across fourteen hundred miles of such deserts and mountains would be like building a bridge to the moon or tunneling under an ocean.' Greeley had more faith. So this fifty-year-old newspaper chieftain [he was actually forty-eight at the time] hazarded the discomforts and dangers of a stagecoach journey to the coast. 'I want to learn what I can of that country with my own eyes,' he explained, 'and to study men in their cabins and at their work instead of reading about them in books.'

"If any traveler to the 'Gold Coast' during the 1850 decade wrote of his experiences with more human interest than did Greeley in letters to the *Tribune* and in his book *An Overland Journey*, the story has yet to be read by this author."[7]

William Harlan Hale tends to subordinate the interest in the railroad to Greeley's lifelong advocacy of westward expansion, although of course the two were inseparable and complementary. And Hale saw other, deeper, more intangible reasons. ". . . Greeley had been busy promoting emigration to the West ever since *New Yorker* days in the 1830's," says Hale. "Now, in 1859, he decided it was time that he travel all the way out across the country and see the future for himself. He wanted to look over and report on possible west-

[7] Henry Luther Stoddard: *Horace Greeley, Printer, Editor, Crusader* (New York: G. P. Putnam's Sons; 1946), p. 187.

ern railroad routes, on the new mining towns, on life in the faraway oasis of Utah, on the growing wonders of California. He wanted to get away for awhile from the political turmoil. He may have thought it would be a good thing to get his readers' minds off it too. The West was America's greatest adventure. It might also prove now to be its place of self-renewal and salvation."[8]

Seitz says very little about the overland journey itself, nothing whatever about the circumstances of its undertaking. Of the slightly more than four pages devoted to the California trip, Seitz fills three of them with Artemus Ward's windy version of Greeley's wild "Ride to Placerville" in the swaying, jolting stagecoach of the immortal Hank Monk. With that he abruptly closes the subject, observing only that "Greeley based many letters on [the overland journey], coming out strongly for the completion of the cross-continent railroad. Unfortunately, whatever pleasure there might have been in the trip was soon taken away by the sudden crisis of events in the South."[9]

It is Parton, Greeley's contemporary, great admirer, and first biographer, who, by availing himself of the editor's own announcement in the *Tribune*, gives the most intimate, least pretentious version of how Greeley came to make the trip just then. "In the summer of 1859 Mr. Greeley made his celebrated journey across the Plains to California, the particulars of which, according to his custom, he related to his readers. The manner in which he announced his purpose," observes Parton, "was characteristic:

'About the 1st of October next we are to have a State election; then a city contest; then the organization and long session of a new Congress; then a Presidential

[8] William Harlan Hale: *Horace Greeley, Voice of the People* (New York: Harper and Brothers; 1950), p. 196.
[9] Seitz: op. cit., p. 306.

xix

struggle; then Congress again, which brings us to the forming of a new national administration and the summer of 1861. If, therefore, I am to have any respite from editorial labor for the next two years I must take it now.' "[1]

In short, Greeley saw a break in the heavy political weather ahead and decided he'd better go while the going was good. Astute journalist that he was, he may well have also sensed the imminence of events far more significant than routine elections in the years immediately ahead.[2]

The letters or dispatches that Greeley sent back to the *Tribune* were published the following year by C. M. Saxton, Barker & Co., New York, under the title, *An Overland Journey from New York to San Francisco in the Summer of 1859*. There were thirty-two letters, written en route, plus a capstone article arguing the merits of the railroad to the Pacific, written after his return to New York. The dispatches are numbered in Roman numerals I through XXXIV in the Saxton volume, but there are only thirty-three of them, including the office-written finale. The discrepancy arises from the erroneous numbering of the letter entitled "Two Hours with Brigham Young." Although actually the twentieth chapter, it is numbered XXI, and the erroneous numbering is continued throughout the remainder of the book.

The main body of Greeley's *Overland Journey* (after the first letter, which sets the stage) divides readily into seven main parts:

---

[1] James Parton: *The Life of Horace Greeley* (Boston: Fields, Osgood, & Co.; 1869), p. 451.

[2] Without much evidence in Greeley's own writing to support it, some writers include his interest in the Colorado gold rush among the reasons for the trip. "Now, in 1859, he intended to see for himself if the gold reports from the Rockies were true or false." Mrs. Elmo Scott Watson: "Horace Greeley, the Man Who Took His Own Advice," *Denver Western Writers Roundup*, Vol. 18, No. 8 (August 1962).

Kansas—four dispatches.
Across the Plains—four dispatches.
Colorado—six dispatches.
Denver to Salt Lake City—four dispatches.
Utah—four dispatches.
Utah to California—two dispatches.
California—seven dispatches.

The final chapter in the book, the discourse on the Pacific railroad, is not part of the narrative proper. It is, however, entirely germane and essential to the whole and, in view of Greeley's purpose, is the most important of the thirty-three pieces.

Horace Greeley had two messages for his readers in his eyewitness reports on the West. One was simple and direct; the other, of broader gauge. The first, of course, and principal message was: let us build a railroad to the Pacific Coast, and the sooner the better. The corollary theme: our American West has a bright future. Greeley saw unlimited promise and opportunity in the farmlands of the Midwest. He satisfied himself that the gold rush to the Rockies was founded on no mirage and correctly predicted the extraction of many millions of dollars in ore. He foresaw growth and prosperity for the Mormon colony in Utah. The potentialities of California—its timber and cattle and gold—nearly swept him off his feet.

The spirit that caused him to say—in effect and many times—"Go West, young man!"[3] is vibrantly alive in this

[3] There are several versions of the origin of this famous dictum. Stoddard says: "Only Harriet Beecher Stowe's immortal *Uncle Tom's Cabin* and Stephen Foster's 'O Susanna!' had greater vogue through the 1850's than Greeley's urgent 'Go west, young man, go west!' It is said that others used the phrase before Greeley did, but if so no one heard it. When Greeley said it the whole country heard, and many thousands acted." According to Hale, the slogan was distilled from this truly Greeleyian line: "If any young man is about to commence in the world,

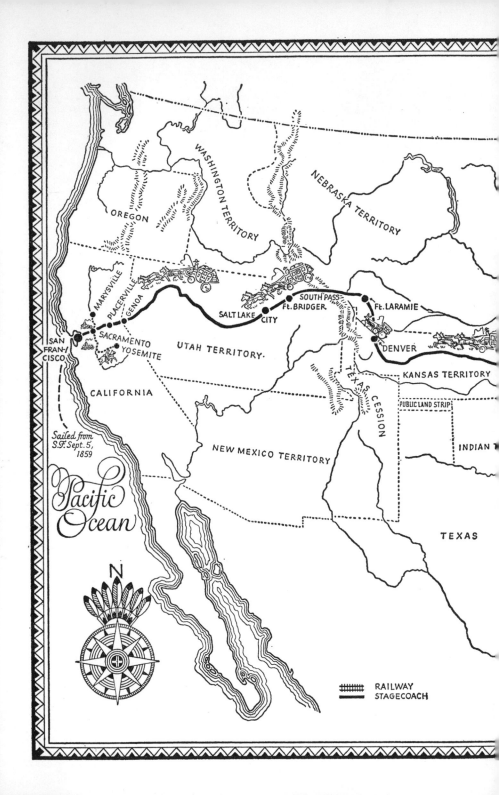

Map of Horace Greeley's Route by RAILROAD and OVERLAND STAGECOACH from New York to San Francisco in the Summer of 1859

0 100 200 300 400
SCALE OF MILES

METZIG

journal. Here is the land of opportunity for men willing to work hard, to be thrifty, and to wring their bread from the soil or by honest trade. These are the cardinal virtues with Greeley—work, save, stay out of debt, and if you can't be a farmer be a tradesman.

He was skeptical of gold-seeking as the road to success. "A little further away," he writes from Atchison, "the tents and wagons of parties of gold-seekers, with faces set for Pike's Peak, dot the prairie; one of them in charge of a gray-head who is surely old enough to know better."[4] Later, at the diggings in Colorado, in the face of abundant evidence that there *was* gold in them thar hills, he remained unimpressed.

"With the gold just wrested from the earth still glittering in my eyes," he wrote from Gregory's Diggings (later Central City) in Colorado, ". . . I adhere to my long-settled conviction that, next to outright and indisputable gambling, the hardest (though sometimes the quickest) way to obtain gold is to mine for it—that a good farmer or mechanic will usually make money faster—and of course immeasurably easier—by sticking to his own business than by deserting it for gold-digging—and that the man who, having failed in some other pursuit, calculates on retrieving his fortunes by gold-mining, makes a mistake which he will be likely to rue to the end of his days."[5]

Greeley never let his enthusiasm for the West get the

---

with little in his circumstances to prepossess him in favor of one section above another, we say to him publicly and privately, Go to the West; there your capacities are sure to be appreciated and your industry and energy rewarded." A third version has it that Greeley said: "Go West," all right, but what he had in mind was western Pennsylvania." Bartlett's *Familiar Quotations* gives as the source an article by John Babsone Lane Soule in the Terre Haute, Indiana, *Express* in 1851. According to Bartlett's, Greeley reprinted Soule's article, with due credit.

[4] Below, p. 14.
[5] Ibid., pp. 105–6.

better of his habit of telling the truth as he saw it, however. Where the country appeared to him as useless wasteland, he said so with unmistakable directness. He had a poor opinion of the plains between the Kansas outposts and the mountains, especially of that part he defines as "the three hundred miles or so that separate the present buffalo range from the creeks that carry snow water to the Platte and the pines that herald our approach to the Rocky Mountains." His merciless description of it (No. 12. "The Plains—the Mountains") leaves nothing to be salvaged.

Later he gained an even lower opinion, if possible, of the baleful desert reaches of Utah and Nevada, reserving the most withering of his powers of execration for the Humboldt River, "the meanest river of its length on earth." His description of it is one of the most vivid passages of the entire journal: ". . . Its water, for at least the lower half of its course, is about the most detestable I ever tasted. I mainly chose to suffer thirst rather than drink it. Though three hundred and fifty miles in length, it is never more than a decent millstream . . . its narrow bottom produces grass; but so course in structure, and so alkaline by impregnation, that no sensible man would let his stock eat it, if there were any alternative. Here, however, there is none. Cattle must eat this, or die—many of them eat it, and die. I thought I had seen barrenness before —on the upper course of the Republican, on the North Platte, Green River, etc.—but . . . here, on the Humboldt, famine sits enthroned, and waves his scepter over a dominion made expressly for him . . . the sagebrush and greasewood, which cover the high, parched plain on either side of the river's bottom, seem thinly set, with broad spaces of naked, shining, glaring, blinding clay between them; the hills beyond, which bound the prospect, seem even more naked. Not a tree, and hardly a shrub, anywhere relieves their sterility . . . the Humboldt may continue for years to be traveled; but I am sure no one ever left it without a sense of relief and thankfulness."[6]

A lesser man might well have glossed over the unprepossessing features of the West which Greeley described in such detail and with such candor, and have been forgiven for it in his zeal to win popular support for the railroad.

Oddly enough, he says relatively little about the railroad in the letters he sent back to the *Tribune*. To be sure, the final chapter, written after his return to New York, makes a powerful and persuasive case for the building of the road, but, either by design or because he was too engrossed with the sights and events of the journey, he did virtually no tub-thumping for his great pet idea in the dispatches themselves.

If the rail project were neglected, few other topics were. A partial list suggests the encyclopedic range of Greeley's interests. Foremost is agriculture, a subject from which his mind seemingly never strayed far. Mining and mineralogy receive generous attention. The flora and fauna of the regions through which he passed are noted in detail and frequently, as in the description of prairie dogs, owls, and rattlesnakes, with whimsical humor. Other subjects include Indian life; the manners and morals of the miners, gamblers, settlers, and others; Mormonism, politics, the army, geography, geology, stagecoaches, food and clothing, literature, history, and much that comes under the heading of plain sightseeing. His description of the Yosemite Valley, for instance, is inspired writing.

The most conspicuous absence from the pages of *Overland Journey*, with the exception of the transcontinental railroad itself, is people—individual persons, that is. Passionately humanistic though he was, Greeley was more interested in ideas and in people collectively than in individuals. Relatively few persons are mentioned by name in the entire account. He was with other people at all times while on the

[6] Ibid., pp. 230–1.

road, but seldom does he refer, other than vaguely, to his traveling companions except as "we" or "the passengers." Not a single name is mentioned nor a single person referred to individually in that entire first leg of the journey, a full week of travel. In eastern Kansas, he and other travelers were forced to spend the night at the village of Stanton, having been prevented by darkness and high water from reaching Osawatomie, and there they crowded into the tavern and "all were snugly bestowed except another editor and myself, who accepted the kindly proffered hospitality of a Republican farmer, and were capitally entertained at his house, half a mile distant." The fellow editor is not identified and is not mentioned again.

Greeley was in the company of two younger journalists during part of his travels, but he scarcely mentions them and never fully identifies them. These two were A. D. Richardson, then of the Boston *Journal*, and Henry Villard, of the Cincinnati *Commercial*. He and Richardson fell in together at Manhattan, Kansas, where Greeley boarded the Denver-bound stagecoach in which Richardson had been, to that point, the sole passenger.[7] Greeley met Villard in Denver, where the young German-born reporter introduced himself to the great editor. The three of them subsequently made their memorable trek to Gregory's Diggings, the raw mining camp in the mountains to the west. Richardson and Villard both wrote about their experiences with Horace Greeley, recounting in some detail what he said and did, but Greeley refers only once to "Mr. Villard, of Cincinnati," and mentions a "Mr. Kershaw, of New York." Richardson is referred to earlier, but not by name.

It is not likely that Greeley was unaware of these men or that he disdained to accord them a place in his dispatches. In fact, it can be inferred that he was very much aware of them and that he was well impressed by both, for within

[7] Richardson: op. cit., p. 161.

less than five years Richardson and Villard were top-flight Civil War reporters for the New York *Tribune*.

Considering its historical interest, its influence on the completion of the railroad,[8] its contemporary value as a document of economic, political, and social significance (it was one of the first reports on the Colorado gold diggings and unquestionably the most authoritative), the *Overland Journey* is a journalistic achievement of great magnitude.

Greeley was a brilliant reporter. His pale blue eyes missed little, and although he held strong opinions on nearly every subject and was seldom diffident about expressing those opinions, he was able to report factually and dispassionately when the occasion called for the giving of straightforward information. The pungency of his style and the forcefulness of his views enrich the solid factualness of his on-the-road dispatches, all thirty-two of which are crammed with pertinent and objective observations about the country, the economy, and the inhabitants.

Had the dispatches been written under optimum conditions, they would still have been first-rate reporting. Produced as they were—scribbled on the run and without benefit of maps or other reference works, certainly with little opportunity for reflection and polishing, and frequently under extremely trying circumstances—they represent journalism at a high level of professional competence.[9]

Purely from the standpoint of quantitative output, the dispatches constitute a formidable accomplishment. They range in length from approximately 1,800 to nearly 5,500

[8] "Had Mr. Greeley not visited California, the Pacific Railroad would have been built; not, indeed, so soon as it was . . . He hastened its construction by many years. This is the praise to which he is entitled in this regard; no more, no less." Ingersoll: op. cit., p. 335.

[9] Since the dispatches were handwritten and since Greeley's handwriting, at best, was notoriously undecipherable, one's sympathy for Greeley as he labored under adverse conditions must, in decency, extend also to the compositors back in the *Tribune* plant who had to transmute the frightful scrawl into clean, neat type. A note in A. D. Richardson's

words each, amounting to a total of roughly 120,000 words. The first was dated May 15, 1859, from Atchison, Kansas; the last, September 9, from San Francisco. Thus Greeley wrote thirty-two dispatches, averaging 3,750 words in length, over a period of 116 days, or, on the average, one every three and a half days.

They were all handwritten of course, often under miserable conditions. He wrote in wind-whipped tents and drafty cabins; he wrote in cold, in heat, in dust, and in rain; he wrote when he was bone-weary and when in severe pain from injuries received in mishaps en route.

But it is the inimitable Greeley style that leaves the lasting impression. "He learned to write as he talked: in brisk, astringent phrases, without decoration and without ceremony," observes Hale. Even E. L. Godkin, erudite editor of the *Nation* and no admirer of Greeley, paid tribute to his self-educated contemporary's writing ability. ". . . [Greeley] has an English style which, for vigor, terseness and simplicity has never been surpassed, except, perhaps by Cobbett."[1]

Let a few examples, plucked readily from the *Overland Journey*, bear witness to his power of expression.

HORACE GREELEY ON THE SUBJECT OF SLEEPING CARS:

"Coming up the Erie Road, I tried a sleeping-car for the third time, and not very successfully. We all retired at ten

---

Beyond the Mississippi suggests that Greeley's penmanship was a topic of common talk among his contemporaries. "Stopped for the night at Station Nine, consisting of two tents. In the evening wrote newspaper letters in the coach by a lantern. As the air was damp and chill with rain and the vehicle shaken with wind, I fancy the *Tribune* printers will find Mr. Greeley's manuscript even less legible than usual." Greeley's letter from Station 9 (May 28) was a sprightly one nevertheless. It contains one of the most famous passages of the entire journal, his humorous logging of his descent of "the ladder of artificial life" as he proceeded westward (see Dispatch No. 6). In it appears one of his few references to Richardson, who goes nameless as usual.

[1] Hale: op. cit., p. 85.

Facsimile of Greeley's handwriting
"A Specimen of Editorial Penmanship"
for a *Tribune* editorial,
from Albert D. Richardson's *Beyond the Mississippi* (1867)

o'clock, with a fair allowance of open windows and virtuous resolutions; but the rain poured, the night was chill and damp, and soon every orifice for the admission of external air, save the two or three humbug ventilators overhead, was shut, and a mephitic atmosphere produced . . . After gasping a while like a netted fish on a hot sandbank, I rose to enter my solemn protest against all sleeping-cars not provided with abundant and indefeasible means of ventilation. . ."

GREELEY ON THE MISSOURI RIVER:

". . . Its muddiness is beyond all description; its color and consistency are those of thick milk porridge; you could not discern an egg in a glass of it . . . With its deep, rapid, boiling, eddying current, its drifting logs and trees, often torn from its banks by its floods, and sometimes planted afresh in its bed, so that the tops rise angularly to a point just below or just above the surface of the water, forming the sawyer or snag so justly dreaded by steamboats, the Missouri stands alone among the rivers of the earth, unless China can show its fellow."

GREELEY ON SHIFTLESS KANSANS:

"But an unpleasant truth must be stated: There are too many idle, shiftless people in Kansas. I speak not here of lawyers, gentlemen speculators, and other non-producers, who are in excess here as elsewhere; I allude directly to those who call themselves settlers, and who would be farmers if they were anything. To see a man squatted on a quarter-section in a cabin which would make a fair hog-pen, but is unfit for a human habitation, and there living from hand to mouth by a little of this and a little of that, with hardly an acre of prairie broken (sometimes without a fence up), with no garden, no fruit trees, 'no nothing'—waiting for someone to come along and buy out his 'claim' and let him move on to repeat the operation somewhere else—this is enough to give a cheerful man the horrors."

GREELEY ON INDIANS:

". . . If, then, the hope of Indian renovation rested mainly on the men, it would be slender enough . . . Squalid and conceited, proud and worthless, lazy and lousy, they will strut out or drink out their miserable existence, and at length afford the world a sensible relief by dying out of it.

"But it is otherwise with the women. Degraded and filthy as they are . . . they bear the germ of renovation of their race, in that they are neither too proud nor too indolent to labor."

That such lean, precise, fast-paced, and graphic prose should flow from the pen of a man whose formal education encompassed only a few years of the excessively brief terms common to the country schools of his boyhood days (he started school two months before his *third* birthday!) is all the more remarkable by reason of its contrast to the elegant and affected verbosity generally in vogue at that time.

Horace Greeley's *Overland Journey* is, above all, a travel book, and a magnificent travel book at that. But it is also a book with a definite purpose and a message. Greeley was incapable of writing anything without a message—often moralistic; usually constructive, positive and optimistic, if dogmatic; frequently exhortative; always vigorous.

When the quality and the quantity of his work are considered, not forgetting the conditions under which these dispatches were written, we perceive in Horace Greeley's *Overland Journey* a journalistic *tour de force* that bears the unmistakable mark of a master's hand.

CHARLES T. DUNCAN

xxxii

CHRONOLOGY

Highlights in the Life of Horace Greeley

February 3, 1811   Born, Amherst, N.H.

Spring of 1826   Apprenticed to Amos Bliss, owner of the *Northern Spectator*, East Poultney, N.H.

1830   *Northern Spectator* suspended publication.

August 17, 1831   Arrived in New York City, seeking work as a printer. Ten dollars to his name.

January 1, 1833   Founded (with Francis V. Story) *The Morning Post*, said to have been the first penny paper; lasted less than a month.

March 22, 1834   Founded (with Jonas Winchester, his new partner) *The New Yorker*, a weekly devoted to literature, news summary, political commentary.

July 5, 1836   Married to Mary Y. Cheney of Cornwall, Conn., in Warrenton, N.C.

April 10, 1841	Founded the New York *Tribune*, daily newspaper, one cent a copy. "The Tribune . . . will labour to advance the interests of the People, and to promote their Moral, Social and Political well-being."
July 31, 1841	Formed partnership with Thomas McElrath, well-established printer and lawyer, under the firm name of Greeley & McElrath. This gave the *Tribune* much-needed financial support.
September, 1841	Founded the *Weekly Tribune*. This was a merger of *The New Yorker* and *The Log Cabin*, the latter a weekly campaign paper founded by Greeley in 1840 to support the candidacy of William Henry Harrison.
January 3, 1843	Delivered his first public lecture, New York Lyceum. Subject, "Human Life."
December 1848– March 1849	Served as U.S. Representative to Congress (30th) from New York City. Highlight of his brief, stormy career as a Congressman was his exposé of abuses of mileage expense money by his colleagues.
July 12, 1849	Death of Arthur Young Greeley, his beloved son "Pickie," at age 5, of cholera. (Only two of the Greeleys' seven children survived infancy or childhood, daughters Ida and Gabrielle.)
July 16, 1850	Death of his great friend, Margaret Fuller.

April 16–August Traveled in Europe. Attended the Great
6, 1851   Exhibition in London; visited Paris, Lyons,
                 Rome, Sardinia, Venice, Switzerland, Ger-
                 many, Belgium, Scotland, and Ireland.

Spring and sum- Second visit to Europe. This trip was dis-
mer, 1855   tinguished by Horace Greeley's celebrated
                 incarceration in a French prison. A French
                 exhibitor who claimed he had lost money
                 at the New York Crystal Palace, of which
                 Greeley was one of the directors, brought
                 an action which resulted in Greeley's
                 spending two days in Clichy prison in Paris
                 before the matter could be straightened out.

July 1856   Took part in the founding of the Republi-
                 can Party. Supported its first Presidential
                 candidate, John C. Frémont, who was de-
                 feated by James Buchanan.

May–September,   Overland journey to California. By rail to
1859   Missouri, thence by stagecoach, via Den-
                 ver, Ft. Laramie, Salt Lake City, Hum-
                 boldt River, and Carson Valley, to Sacra-
                 mento. Home by steamship via Isthmus of
                 Panama.

May 1860   Attended Republican national convention
                 in Chicago as delegate representing Oregon;
                 was instrumental in bringing about the
                 nomination of Abraham Lincoln.

1861   Unsuccessful candidate for United States
                 Senator from New York.

July 1863   *Tribune* building attacked by mob during infamous New York City draft riots. Greeley was in great personal danger.

July 1864   Unsuccessful attempt to negotiate a peace, with President Lincoln's approval, with Confederate representatives at a meeting in Canada.

May 13, 1867   Was one of several distinguished Northern men to sign bond for Jefferson Davis, who had been a federal prisoner since his capture shortly after the end of the Civil War. For this act of magnanimity Greeley was applauded in the South, where his name had long been anathema, and vilified in the North.

1871   Toured the South, including Texas.

May and June, 1872   Nominated for President of the United States, first by the Liberal Republican Party, later by the Democratic convention. His opponent, President Ulysses S. Grant, whom Greeley had originally supported.

October 30, 1872   Death of Mary Greeley, his wife.

November 6, 1872   Defeated by Grant, who carried 31 states to 6 for Greeley, in the worst defeat ever suffered by a Presidential candidate up to that time. The popular vote was 3,597,070 for Grant to 2,834,079 for Greeley.

November 29, 1872

Died at age 61, exhausted and broken from strain of campaign, Mary's death, and his own defeat. Attended by daughters Ida and Gabrielle. Despite his wishes for a simple funeral, it was a day of public mourning in New York City. Huge crowds thronged the streets. The funeral was attended by scores of dignitaries, including President Grant.

Horace Greeley's Published Works

AN

OVERLAND JOURNEY,

FROM

NEW YORK TO SAN FRANCISCO,

IN

THE SUMMER OF 1859.

BY

HORACE GREELEY.

NEW YORK:

C. M. SAXTON, BARKER & CO.

SAN FRANCISCO: H. H. BANCROFT & CO.

1860.

[Facsimile of title page of 1860 edition]

Preface

The following letters, as is generally known, were written to THE NEW YORK TRIBUNE during a journey through Kansas, Utah, and California, last summer. No one can be more conscious than the writer that they present the slightest possible claims to literary merit or enduring interest. Their place is among the thousand ephemeral productions of the press on which the reading public, if good-natured, bestows a kindly glance, then charitably forgets them. Ten years hence, hardly a hundred persons will be able, without sustained effort, to recollect that these letters were ever printed. Hurriedly written, mainly in wagons or under the rudest tents, while closely surrounded by the (very limited) appliances and processes of pioneer meal-getting, far from books of reference, and often in the absence of even the commonest map, they deal with surfaces only, and these under circumstances which preclude the idea of completeness of information or uniform accuracy of statement. The value of such a work, if value it have, must be sought in unstudied simplicity of narration, in the freshness of its observations, and in the truth of its averments as transcripts of actual experiences and current impressions.

By consulting and studying the reports of eminent official explorers and pioneers, from Lewis and Clark to Frémont and Lander, who have traversed the Plains, the Rocky Mountains, and the Great Basin, a far more complete and reliable book might have been made, but one extending to several volumes, and of which the public does not seem to stand in conscious, urgent need. That herewith submitted, though of far humbler pretensions, has at least the merit of owing little or nothing to any other.

If any excuse for printing these letters were wanted, it might be found in the fact that much of the ground passed over by the writer was absolutely new—that is, it had never before been traversed and described. The route up Solomon's Fork and the upper portion of the Republican, from the forks of the Kansas to Cherry Creek; that from Denver to the gold diggings in the Rocky Mountains, near Ralston's Fork of Clear Creek; the trail from Denver to Laramie, along the eastern base of the Rocky Mountains; and that from Salt Lake southwestwardly through central Utah to Pleasant Valley, and thence northwestwardly to the Humboldt at Gravelly Ford, are believed to stand in this category. But another reason for printing these hasty sketches is found in the fact that very great and rapid changes in most of the region lying directly between Missouri and California are inevitable. The Leavenworth Express route, through the heart of what in June is the buffalo region, which was hardly four weeks old when I traveled it, was soon after abandoned, and has reverted to the domain of the wolf and the savage, while the rude beginning of a settlement I found, scarcely three weeks old, at Gregory's Diggings has since been Mountain City, with its municipality, its newspaper, and its thousands of inhabitants, and is now in its decline, having attained the ripe age of nearly half a year. Captain Simpson has, since July, completed his exploration of a military and mail route through Central Utah, whereby more than a hundred miles of that I traveled are saved and the detested Humboldt wholly avoided; and Carson Valley, under the impetus of rich mineral discoveries, is rapidly increasing in population and consequence, and about to stand forth, the nucleus of the embryo Territory of Nevada. Whoever visits California a few years hence, will doubtless find it greatly changed from the California so hastily run over but faithfully described by me in August, 1859. Should, then, a few copies of this book, lost in the dustiest recess of some all-embracing, indiscriminate library, evade the trunk-makers to the close of the next decade, the antiquary of 1870 may derive gratification if not instruction from a contrast of the populous, enterprising, and thrifty Central North America of his day, with that same region overrun and roughly depicted by me in the summer of 1859. Should such prove the fact, I commend my hasty letters to his generous indulgence.

H. G.

New York, Nov. 1, 1859

An Overland Journey

A KEY TO THE NOTES IN THIS EDITION

Footnotes by Horace Greeley in the original edition
are indicated by an asterisk (*).

Footnotes by the editor are numbered.

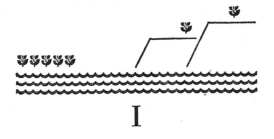

I

FIRST LEG

Dispatch 1

Greeley's first letter back to the Tribune *clearly shows where his interests lay—agriculture, weather, nature (he was ever the farmer at heart), economic development, politics, and morality. These are the dominant themes throughout the journal, and he wasted no time in warming up.*

The trip from New York to Kansas lasted a week. Across Missouri the roadbed was so spongy after the spring's heavy rains that the rails rose and fell, first on one side, then the other. The train chuffed the 206 miles from Hannibal to St. Joseph in twelve hours, an average of seventeen miles an hour.

Setting foot in Kansas for the first time, Greeley immediately picked up the scent of politics wafting across the prai-

3

ries, and he was off on a round of speech-making at dawn the next day.

1

FROM NEW YORK TO KANSAS

Atchison, Kansas, May 15, 1859

I left New York by Erie Railroad on Monday evening, 9th inst., just as our fortnight of bright, hot, planting weather was closing. Two hours later, the gathered clouds burst upon us in a rain which continued through the night, though the city was not refreshed by it till some hours later. We had glimpses of sunshine as we skirted the southern shore of Lake Erie on Wednesday, and some more after a heavy shower at Chicago on Thursday; beside these, cloudy skies, easterly winds and occasional rain, have been my portion since I bade adieu to the hot, dusty streets of New York. But it is breaking away as I write, and I hope to see Kansas, for the first time, under skies which image her sunny future rather than her stormy past.

Coming up the Erie Road, I tried a sleeping-car for the third time, and not very successfully. We all retired at ten o'clock, with a fair allowance of open windows and virtuous resolutions; but the rain poured, the night was chill and damp, and soon every orifice for the admission of external air, save the two or three humbug ventilators overhead, was shut, and a mephitic atmosphere produced, in which the soul of John G. Saxe[1] might have disported and fancied it Elysium. After gasping a while, like a netted fish on a hot

[1] John Godfrey Saxe (1816-87) was a Vermont (and later New York) poet-humorist in vogue at the time. Saxe was also a lawyer and a Democrat, neither of which distinctions would have recommended him to the *Tribune* editor.

sandbank, I rose to enter my solemn protest against all sleep-ing-cars not provided with abundant and indefeasible means of ventilation. I tried one, two nights later, on the Michigan Southern Road, which served much better, though still far from perfect. It is very true that no arrangement can secure a healthy circulation of air by night in any passenger-car, while the popular ignorance is so dense that the great ma-jority imagine any atmosphere healthful which is neither too cold nor too hot, and rather laugh at the wit than pity the blindness of Saxe in holding up to ridicule a woman who knows (and does) better than to sit all night in a close car, with thirty or forty other human beings, all breathing an atmosphere which they, in twenty minutes, render absolutely poisonous; but the builders of cars have no right to be igno-rant of the laws of life with which they tamper; and two or three presentments by Grand Juries of the makers of un-ventilated cars, especially sleeping-cars, as guilty of man-slaughter, would exert a most salutary influence. I commend this public duty to the immediate consideration of jurors and prosecutors.

Stopping at Hornellsville, at seven next morning, I took the train for Buffalo thence at noon, and halted at Castile, to fulfill an engagement to speak at Pike, formerly in Alle-gany, now in Wyoming County.

I left Pike for Castile at five on Wednesday morning; took the cars to Buffalo at half past seven; was in ample season for the Lake Shore train at ten; ran into Cleveland a little after five; left at six for Toledo, where we changed cars be-tween ten and eleven, and were in Chicago at seven next morning as aforesaid. Along the south shore of Lake Erie, as in our own state, it was plain that the area plowed on or before the 11th of May was greater this year than ever be-fore. And well it might be, for the country was hardly ever so bare of food for man and beast as in this same May of

5

1859. Flour is higher and wheat and corn scarcely lower in Chicago than in New York or Liverpool; oats nearly the same. Thousands of cattle, throughout the Prairie States, have died of starvation this spring, though prairie hay might almost anywhere have been put up last fall at a cost of less than two dollars per ton; Minnesota, with, perhaps, the best soil for winter wheat in America, is buying flour in Chicago by the thousand barrels; and I hear from different sections of this great granary of nations—from Illinois, from Iowa, from Missouri—of whole neighborhoods destitute alike of bread and of the wherewithal to buy it. Unpropitious as last season was, it does not fully explain this scarcity, especially of fodder. I trust the like will never occur to need explanation again.

Coming down through Illinois from Chicago southwestwardly to Quincy (268 miles), it was gratifying to see how general are the effort and obvious resolve to look starvation out of countenance this year. Though the breadth of winter wheat was but moderate, owing to the incessant rains of last autumn, it is plain that the farmers began to plow and sow as early as possible this spring, putting in, first, spring wheat, then oats, latterly corn, and they mean to keep putting in corn and oats for a month yet. If Illnois and Iowa do not grow for more grain this year than ever before, it will hardly be the fault of the cultivators, for they are bent on doing their utmost. Considering their bad fortune last year, this resolute industry does them credit; but they are generally in debt, out of money and almost out of credit, and are making a final stand against the sheriff. I heartily wish them a good deliverance.

And, despite the hard times, Illinois is growing. There are new blocks in her cities, new dwellings in her every village, new breakings on this or that edge of almost every prairie. The short, young grass is being cropped by large

6

herds of cattle, whose improved appearance within the last
fortnight is said by those who have observed them from day
to day to be beyond credence on any testimony but that of
eyesight. Here, every horse or ox that can pull is hitched to
a plow or harrow whenever darkness or rain does not forbid;
and, by plowing the dryest ridges first and seeding them,
then taking the next dryest and serving them just so, nearly
every cultivator can keep putting in seed at least four days
per week from March till June. Many will plant corn this
year till the middle of June, and even later, unless compelled sooner to desist in order to commence cultivating that
first planted. Then cultivating will require every hour till
harvesting begins; and this (including haying) will last
till it is full time to plow for winter wheat. No busier season
was ever seen than this is to be; from the Hudson to the
Mississippi, you see four horses or oxen at work to one in
pasture; and there are thousands of farmers who would plant
or sow a quarter more, if they had grain to feed their teams,
than they will now be able to do. There are few traveling in the cars, few idling about stores or taverns, but many
in the fields. May a bounteous Heaven smile on their labors!

Illinois is just beginning to be cultivated. I presume she
has no railroad along which half the land within a mile has
ever been touched by a plow. Back from the roads, there
is of course still less cultivation; probably less than a tenth
of her soil has ever yet been broken. Possibly one-fourth of
her spontaneous product of grass may now be eaten by animals that contribute to the sustenance or comfort of man,
though I think one-sixth would be nearer the mark. She has
far more coal than Great Britain—I believe more than any
other state—but has hardly yet begun to mine it. Her timber
is not so excellent; she lacks pine and all the evergreens, but
she is bountifully and cheaply supplied with these from
Michigan and Wisconsin. Boards are sent through her canal

7

from Chicago to the Illinois, and thence around by St. Louis and up the Missouri to build houses in Kansas and Nebraska. Her timber, such as it is, palpably increases from year to year, and will increase still more rapidly as roads and plowing check the sweep of prairie fires. If her prairies were more rolling, they would be dryer and could be worked earlier; but then they would wash more, and probably have less depth and richness of soil. Doubtless, the child is born who will see her a state of ten millions of people, one million of them inhabiting her commercial emporium.[2]

I stopped overnight at Quincy, and took the steamboat *Pike* at half past seven next morning for Hannibal, twenty miles below. I had repeatedly crossed the Mississippi, but this was my first passage on it. The river is very high, so that its banks are submerged, and the water flows under the trees which line either shore. Islets covered with trees and shrubbery abound; the bluffs recede some miles on either hand, and are softened to the view by the deep green of the young foliage; hardly a clearing breaks the uniformity of the almost tropical prospect, though here and there a miserable little hut in the last stages of decay tells where a chopper of steamboat wood held on until whiskey or the ague took him off. In flood, as it is, the river is turbid, not muddy, and pursues its course with a deliberation and gravity befitting the majestic Father of Waters, to whom, with head bare and reverent spirit, I wave a respectful adieu.

For our good boat has reached Hannibal, the first point below Quincy at which the Missouri bluff approaches the river, and whence the valley of a streamlet makes up through the hills to the broad, level prairie. Hannibal is pleasantly

---

[2] Greeley overestimated Illinois's rate of growth and underestimated Chicago's. Chicago passed the million mark in 1890, by which time a child born in 1859 would have been thirty-one years old. The state's population did not exceed 10,000,000 until 1960.

situated on the intervale[3] of the creek and up the side of the bluff, so as to be entirely commanded by a steamboat passing up the river. It is a bustling, growing village of some four thousand inhabitants, which the new Hannibal and St. Joseph Railroad has suddenly raised from local to general importance. Like most villages on the great Western rivers, it has no wharf, and the river is now threatening to eat away a part of the bank on which railroad and steamboat freight is heaped in wild disorder. Its new consequence must soon work a change. I look for a wharf and a great storehouse when I next land or embark here.

The *Pike* rounded to, and sent us ashore; the train backed down to within forty feet of her; the passengers got aboard the cars and were followed by their baggage, and in half an hour we were steaming up through the woody ravine to emerge on one of the largest prairies in northern Missouri. Across this—or, rather, along it—we took our course westward, almost as the crow flies, to St. Joseph on the Missouri, two hundred and six miles distant, which we reached in a little more than twelve hours, or at half past ten last evening. The road was completed in hot haste last winter, in order to profit by the Pike's Peak migration this spring; no gravel is found on its line, unless in the immediate vicinity of the Mississippi; and it was raining pitilessly for the second day nearly throughout, so that the roadbed was a causeway of mortar or ooze, into which the passing trains pressed the ties, first on one side, then on the other, making the track as bad as track could well be. A year hence, it must be better, even with the frost just coming out of the ground; after a dry week, it will probably be quite fair; but yesterday it afforded more exercise to the mile than any other rail-

[3] This is a favorite word with Greeley and appears often in his journal. An intervale is a tract of low ground between hills or along the banks of a stream.

road I ever traveled. About one-third of the way from Hannibal, it is intersected by the North Missouri Railroad from St. Louis, which city is about one hundred miles further from St. Joseph than Hannibal is, the train from St. Louis starting at 5 A.M. to connect with ours which ought to have left Hannibal at half past nine. Each road is completed, so that St. Louis as well as Hannibal is within a day's ride by rail of St. Joseph, which faces Kansas almost up to the Nebraka line.

Though the day was dreary, I noted with deep interest the country through which we passed, which disappointed me in these respects:

1. The land is better than I had supposed.

2. It is of more uniform grade—hardly anything worth calling a hill being seen after rising the bluff from the Mississippi till we come in sight of the bluffs which enclose the Missouri.

3. There is more prairie and less timber than I had expected.

4. There are infinitely less population and improvement.

Of course, this road was run so as to avoid the more settled districts, and thus to secure a larger allotment of the public lands whereof the alternate sections for a width of five or six miles were granted to the state in aid of its construction; but I had not believed it possible to run a railroad through northern Missouri so as to strike so few settlements. Palmyra, near the Mississippi, and Chillicothe, a hundred miles further west, are county seats and villages of perhaps two hundred dwellings each; beside these, there is no village of any size, unless it be one of those we passed in rain and darkness as we neared the Missouri. For some fifty miles after passing Palmyra, we traversed a level prairie, admirably grassed, but scarely broken, save where the needs of the railroad had called up two to half a dozen petty buildings. Yet, for most of the way, timber was in sight on one side or on both, often within a mile; and the soil, though but a thin, black mold resting on a heavy clay, therefore not so well adapted to grain as prairie soils are apt to be, is admirably fitted for stock-growing. It seems incredible that such land, in a state forty years old, could have remained unsettled till now. We traversed other prairies, five to twenty miles long, separated by the richest intervales skirting Grand River and sundry smaller streams, well timbered with elm, hickory, etc. Interposed between the prairies are miles on miles of gently rolling ridges, thinly covered with white oak, and forming "oak openings" or "timbered openings," while a thick growth of young wood, now that the annual fires are somewhat checked by roads and cultivation, is coming forward under the full-grown oaks, the whole forming one of the most beautiful and inviting regions I ever passed over. They tell me that the rolling prairies near St. Joseph, to which we passed after dark, are richer and finer than those I saw; but they surely need not be. With such soil and timber, the Mississippi on one side, the Missouri on the other, and a railroad connecting them, it must be that northern Missouri is destined to increase its population speedily and rapidly. I am sure beef can be made there at less cost per pound than in any other locality I ever visited.

St. Joseph is a busy, growing town of some ten thousand inhabitants. It is beautifully situated on a bend of the Missouri, partly on its intervale (which the river is gouging out and carrying away), and partly on the southward slope of the bluff, which rises directly from the river bank, at the north end of the town. Other towns on the Missouri may have a grander future; I doubt than any has a finer location. The river bank must be piled or docked, or in some way fortified against the boiling current which sets against the town site with fearful power and effect.

I believe this is further west than any other point reached

by a railroad connecting eastward with the Atlantic ports. At all events, the travel and part of the trade of the vast wilderness watered by the Upper Missouri and its tributaries, seem to center here. At the City Hotel, where I stopped, some of the guests were of, and from Salt Lake; one, an Indian trader from the headwaters of the Columbia, who came down the Yellow Stone from the Rocky Mountains last fall in a canoe, and is now returning. Army officers and sutlers for the forts far up the Missouri and its tributaries are constantly arriving and departing. I may never see St. Joseph again, but she will long be to me a pleasant recollection. Elwood, in Kansas, opposite, is a small place, which must grow with the country behind her.[4] The mighty, boiling flood, which is tearing away the soil of the St. Joseph, is piling up new bars and banks in front of, and just below Elwood, rendering approach to her wharf (if wharf she has or should have) difficult for river steamboats, and thus shutting her out from the upriver trade.

I took passage from St. Joseph for this place at eight this morning on the good steamer *Platte Valley*, Captain Coursey, and defied the chill east wind, and damp, cold atmosphere, to take my first lesson in Missouri navigation. The distance by water is some forty miles, by land considerably less, the river being here, as everywhere, crooked and capricious. I regretted to note that it tends, if unchecked, to grow worse and worse, the swift current rapidly forming a bank below every projecting point, and thus setting the stream with ever increasing force against the yielding, crumbling mold or silt of the intervale which forms the opposite shore, which is thus rapidly undermined and falls in, to be mingled with and borne away by the resistless flood. The banks are almost always nearly perpendicular, and are seldom more than two or three feet above the surface of the water at its present

[4] Elwood, Kansas, had a population of 1,191 in the 1960 census.

high stage, so that the work of devastation is constantly going on. The river is at once deep, swift, and generally narrow— hardly so wide in the average as the Hudson below Albany, though carrying the water of thirty Hudsons. It cannot be half a mile wide opposite this city. Its muddiness is beyond all description; its color and consistency are those of thick milk porridge; you could not discern an egg in a glass of it. A fly floating in a teacup of this dubious fluid an eighth of an inch below the surface would be quite invisible. With its usually bold bluffs, two or three hundred feet high, now opposing a rocky barrier to its sweep, now receding to a distance of two or three miles, giving place to an intervale, many feet deep, of the richest mold, usually covered by a thrifty growth of elm, cottonwood, etc., its deep, rapid, boil- ing, eddying current, its drifting logs and trees, often torn from its banks by its floods, and sometimes planted afresh in its bed, so that the tops rise angularly to a point just below or just above the surface of the water, forming the sawyer or snag so justly dreaded by steamboats, the Missouri stands alone among the rivers of the earth, unless China can show its fellow.

I have not yet learned to like it.

Atchison gives me my first foothold on Kansas. It was long a border-ruffian nest, but has shared the fortunes of many such in being mainly bought out by free-state men, whose growth has been quite rapid; of its four or five hundred dwellings, I think, two-thirds have been built within that period. The Missouri at this point runs further to the west than elsewhere in Kansas; its citizens tell me that the great roads westward to Utah, etc., from St. Joseph on the north and from Leavenworth on the south, pass within a few miles of Atchison when thrice as far from their respective starting points. Hence the Salt Lake mail, though made up at St. Joseph, is brought hither by steamboat and starts overland

13

from this place; hence many trains are made up here for Laramie, Green River, Fort Hall, Utah, and I hear even for Santa Fé. I have seen several twelve-ox teams, drawing heavily loaded wagons, start for Salt Lake, etc., today; there are others camped just outside the corporate limits, which have just come in; while a large number of wagons form a corral some two miles westward. A little further away, the tents and wagons of parties of gold-seekers, with faces set for Pike's Peak, dot the prairie; one of them in charge of a gray-head who is surely old enough to know better. Teamsters from Salt Lake, and teamsters about to start, lounge on every corner; I went out three or four miles on the high prairie this afternoon, and the furthest thing I could see was the white canvas of a moving train. I have long been looking for the West, and here it is at last.

But I must break off somewhere to prepare for an early start for Leavenworth and Lawrence tomorrow, in order to reach Osawatomie next day in season to attend the Republican Convention which is to assemble at that place on Wednesday, the eighteenth.

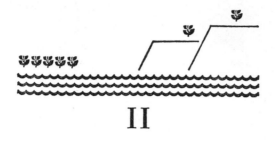

II

KANSAS

Dispatches 2 through 5

Greeley spent ten days slogging about rain-soaked eastern Kansas. Nearly everywhere he stopped, he spoke in the Republican cause, sometimes impromptu. Considering the sparseness of the population, he drew large crowds.

These four dispatches reveal many facets of the great editor's character: the passion of his antislavery feelings, his opposition to a standing army, his compassion for dumb animals, his contempt for idleness and his admiration for industry, and always his fervent advocacy of good agricultural practices and conservation of natural resources.

2

NOTES ON KANSAS

Lawrence, Kansas, May 20, 1859

It resumed raining in Kansas, after a few dry days, on Thursday, the 12th inst., and rained "off and on" till Saturday night. Sunday, the 15th, was cloudy and chilly, but without rain, until evening, when thundershowers came up from every side, and kept flashing, rumbling, and pouring nearly throughout the night. Kansas brags on its thunder and lightning; and the boast is well founded. I never before observed a display of celestial pyrotechny so protracted, incessant and vivid as that of last Sunday night. The country, already saturated with water, was fairly drenched by this deluge, which rendered many streams ordinarily insignificant either dangerous or for a season impassable.

At 6 A. M. on Monday morning, four of us left Atchison in a two-horse wagon, intent on reaching Osawatomie (some eighty miles rather east of south—one hundred by any practicable route) next evening. The sky was still threatening; we knew that the streams were swelled beyond reason; but our pilot was a most experienced pioneer, who had forded, been ferried over or swam every stream in eastern Kansas, and was confident of his ability to go through by some route or other. So we went ahead in a southerly direction, across swells of prairie rather steep-sided for Kansas, and through ravines in which what were usually rills were swelled into torrents. From the high level of the prairies, little but a broad sweep of grass on every side was visible; but soon we were descending into a new ravine, and now belts and spurs of timber were seen, generally widening as they tend toward the Missouri. I noted that these woody spurs, composed

16

mainly of black oak and cottonwood (the latter a very poor but quick-growing timber, ranging somewhere between poplar and basswood), began to spread on every side wherever the annual fires were repelled from the adjacent prairie, whether by the interposition of a road or otherwise, and that the young trees that thus spring up along the sides of the ravines and run out into the level prairie, are quite often hickory, white ash, etc., even where none such are visible among the adjacent timber. I was fully convinced that wood becomes more abundant with the progress of settlement and cultivation. Of course, there is timber enough today in the territory, but the better portion of it is too generally confined to the intervales of the larger streams, too far for their comfort from most settlers on the prairies. Could prairie fires be wholly arrested, the increase of timber would overbalance tenfold the annual use and waste; and the quality improves even faster than the quantity. This is real progress. For, though there is quite enough in Kansas, and a pretty good variety of all species except the evergreens, which are lamentably deficient, there are points at which there is none within several miles—the little that formerly ran up the small ravines which here cut in upon the great high prairies being soon exhausted by use for building, fuel, and fencing, and requiring years for its reproduction.

Twelve or fifteen miles south of Atchison, we struck the great California trail from Leavenworth, and thence followed it east by south into that city, some fifteen to eighteen miles. I should have liked Gerrit Smith as one of our party, that I might show him the practical working of his theory that government has no other legitimate business than to keep one man's fingers off another man's throat and out of any pocket but his own. The great California trail, like the Santa Fé and all other primitive roads through this prairie country, keeps along the highest "divides" or prairie swells, avoiding the miry "bottoms" of the streams and (so far as possible) the ravines which the water falling on the high prairie has cut down to them, of course winding considerably, but making the best and most serviceable natural road that can be, and one that in dry weather is excellent, and in wet as good as possible. But each settler along this trail, in the absence of any legal establishment of the trail as a highway, is at liberty to run his fences right across it as the line of his land runs, and so crowd it off the high "divides" into all manner of angles and zigzags, across this ravine and into that slough, until the trail is fast becoming the very worst road in all Kansas. I have had a pretty full experience of bad roads during this week; but the very worst and miriest was that portion of the California trail (and United States military road from Fort Leavenworth west to other forts) which works its sinuous way through the region generally settled by thrifty farmers, lying directly west of Leavenworth. And the worst hill for teams I have seen in Kansas is traversed by this road within five miles of Leavenworth, between the fort and the rich but miry valley of Salt Creek on the west. This road, unless it can be restored, will soon have to be abandoned, and thence Leavenworth must suffer.

As we neared the California trail, the white coverings of the many emigrant and transport wagons dotted the landscape, giving the trail the appearance of a river running through great meadows, with many ships sailing on its bosom. Most of the independent wagoners were still encamped by the wayside, unable or unwilling to brave the deep mud; their cattle feeding on the broad prairie; the emigrants cooking or sitting beside the wagons; women sometimes washing, and all trying to dry their clothing, drenched and soaked by the pouring rain of the past night. One great wagon train was still in corral with its cattle feeding and men lounging about; the others might better have been, as it was clearly impossible to make their lean, wild-looking oxen (mainly of the long-horned stripe, which indicates Texas as their native land, and which had probably first felt the yoke within the past week) draw them up the slightest ascent through that deep, slippery mire. A great deal of yelling, beating, swearing, was being expended to little purpose, as I presume each train corraled for the ensuing night within a mile of the point it left in the morning. These contractors' wagons are very large and strong, each carrying a couple of good extra axles lashed under its body, to be used in case an old one gives way under a heavy jerk; the drivers are as rough and wild-looking as their teams, though not quite so awkward at their business; but to keep six yoke of such oxen in line in the road, and all pulling on the load, is beyond human skill. It is a sore trial to patience, that first start of these trains on their long journey—to Utah, Fort Hall, Green River, and some of these to New Mexico, though this is not the Santa Fé trail. The loads are generally fifty hundred weight; the wagons must weigh at least fifteen hundred each; and, though this would seem moderate for twelve oxen, it must be remembered that they are at this season poor and at first unbroken, and that the road is in spots a very bad one. A train consists of ten to thirty wagons; each train has its reliable and experienced master or director; and when a team is stalled, another is unhitched from its own wagon and sent to the aid of the one in trouble. The rate of progress is necessarily snail-like; these trains will do very well if they make twenty miles the first week, considering the weather. But then the feeding of the teams (like the lodging of the men) costs nothing, as they live on the broad prairie, and though they will often be fearfully hungry or dry in traversing grassless tracts on their route, they are said generally to gain in flesh (for which there is ample room) during a journey of three or four months. Of course,

19

they improve in docility and effectiveness, being at first so wild that, in order to be yoked, they have to be driven into the corral (formed, as I may have explained, by the wagons closely ranged in a hollow square, the tongue of each being run under its next neighbor, for defense against Indians or other prowlers). Very few wagons or cattle ever come back; the freighting is all one way; and both wagons and cattle are usually sold at or near their point of destination for whatever they will fetch—to be taken to California or disposed of as they best may.

We drove into Leavenworth City about 11 A. M., and found that the delegates from this county had generally given up the idea of reaching Osawatomie, judging that the Convention would have to be adjourned or postponed on account of the swollen and impassable streams. Stranger Creek barred all egress by way of Lawrence, which we had intended to make our resting place for the night; a creek nine miles south of Leavenworth had turned back the stage running in that direction; in fact, no stage made its way out of Leavenworth that day in any direction which was not forced to return, baffled by the high water. So at 3 P. M. we shipped our horses and wagons on board the steamboat *D. A. January*, and dropped down the Missouri some fifty miles, past the bleaching bones of several dead cities (not including Quindaro, which insists that it is still alive) to Wyandotte, in the lower corner of Kansas, with Kansas City, Missouri, three miles off, in plain sight across the mouth of the Kansas or Kaw River. Wyandotte, though hemmed in and impeded, like Quindaro, by an Indian reserve back of it, is alive, and is becoming, what it ought fully to be, the outlet and inlet between Southern Kansas and the Missouri River. It has a beautiful location, and decided natural advantages over Kansas City, which, with other border-ruffian strongholds south of it, has hitherto engrossed too much of the travel and trade of Kansas. We halted at Wyandotte over night, had an impromptu Republican gathering and some offhand talk in the evening, and set forth at six next morning for Osawatomie (forty-six miles a little west of south by a beeline, but over fifty by any practicable route), which we were desirous of reaching before night, as the Convention was to be held next day.

Our route led southwest over rolling woodland through the Wyandotte Reserve, descending into the bottom of the Kansas or Kaw River—said bottom being from one to two miles wide, and very heavily timbered with elm, yellow oak, black walnut, hickory, cottonwood, sycamore, basswood, etc. Nearly all the rivers and larger creeks of Kansas run through similar bottoms or intervales, from half a mile to three miles wide, and timbered much like this. These intervales are composed of a dark, rich mold, oftener over than under three feet in depth, but they are so level that they could hardly be cultivated without drainage, even were it advisable to strip them by wholesale of timber, as it decidedly is not. The houses and barns that shall yet thickly dot the adjacent prairies are now mainly growing in these bottoms, and should stand there as trees till they are wanted. When cleared and drained—and in some places the rotting out of the stumps, and thorough plowing thereafter will go far toward effecting the drainage required—they will yield bounteous crops of almost anything that does not dread frost. Though it seems hardly possible that their soil should be richer than that of the prairies, it is deeper, and probably contains a more varied and choice admixture of the elements of vegetation. But the Kansas or Kaw bottom was not only soaked but covered with water—for it had rained here smartly only the preceding morning after it ceased at Atchison, and the road across the bottom was for the time an all but impassable morass. I trust the citizens of Wyandotte will not long leave it thus.

We crossed the Kaw on a fair wooden toll bridge, one

thousand two hundred feet long, just erected—or, rather, not quite completed. In default of a tollhouse or gatekeeper, a man at work on the bridge in his shirtsleeves, took the toll. I believe no other bridge across the Kaw is now standing, though there has been one at Topeka, fifty miles up, and perhaps at other points. Bridges are sorely needed throughout Kansas, not only because the streams are addicted to rapid and vast augmentations from thaws or rains, but because their banks are almost perpendicular, and often miry toward the bottom, while the streams are nearly as deep at either shore as in the middle, making the attempt to ford difficult, even when it is not dangerous.

The Kaw was, of course, nearly full (all the rivers of Kansas have low banks), and was running very swiftly; still, it seems of moderate size, for a river which leads about six hundred miles westward of its mouth; but all the rivers of this region, the Missouri included, seem small, considering the area drained by them. The facts that they run rapidly, are apt to be deep, and that their depth is nearly uniform from side to side, account in part for this appearance.

Half an hour after crossing the Kaw, we emerged from the road and the reserve upon the high prairie, the clouds of the morning broke away, and the day was henceforth perfect. The young grass of the prairie, refreshed by the heavy rains, appeared in its freshest, tenderest green; the delicate early flowers were abundant, yet not so numerous as to pall by satiety the pleasure of looking at them, and the panorama presented was magnificent. Passing Shawnee, a prairie village of twenty or thirty houses, with a large hotel, our road bore more directly south, and soon brought us in sight of the great Santa Fé trail, with its white-topped emigrant wagons, and three great contract trains, one of them still in corral, the others with six pair of mules to each wagon, attempting to make progress toward New Mexico—attempting it, for the most part, in vain. The mules were small, and new to work—to *this* work, at all events—and drew badly; while the wheels cut so deeply into the yielding paste beneath them that little or no advance was made. I presume they all corraled for the night within two miles of the places where we saw them.

Crossing the trail almost at right angles, we left the smart village of Olathe (county seat of Johnson county) a mile or so to the west, and struck off nearly due south, over high prairies sloped as gently and grassed as richly as could be desired, with timber visible along the watercourses on either hand. Yet there was little or no settlement below Olathe—for the next twenty miles that we traveled there was hardly an improvement to each four square miles of the country in sight. And yet, if the Garden of Eden exceeded this land in beauty or fertility, I pity Adam for having to leave it. The earth was thoroughly sodden with rain, so that temporary springs were bursting out on almost every acre, while the watercourses, including those usually dry, ran heavy streams, each of them requiring skill in the charioteer and good conduct on the part of the horses to pass them without balk or break. We must have crossed over a hundred of these "runs" in the course of this day's travel, each of them with a trying jerk on the carriage, and generally with a spring on the part of the horses. These waterways have generally a limestone bottom not far below the surface of their bed; but their banks are apt to be steep, and are continually growing more so by reason of the water washing away the earth which has been denuded of grass and worked loose by hoofs and wheels. Traveling by jerks like this is not so pleasant as over a macadamized road, yet our day was a bright and pleasant one.

Thirty miles of progress, twenty of them over prairie, brought us to Spring Hill, a hamlet of five or six dwellings, including a store, but no tavern. Our horses needed food and rest—for the wagon, with its four inmates, was a heavy drag over such going—so we stopped and tried to find refreshment, but with limited success. There was no grain to be had, save a homoeopathic dose sold us for a quarter by a passing wagoner, and thankfully received; we gave this to our steeds, regaled ourselves on crackers and herring, and pushed on.

Our direct route led due south to Paoli, county seat of Lykins; but persons we met here assured us that there was no crossing Bull Creek on this road, and that we must bear away to the west through Marysville (a village of perhaps a dozen houses, including a store and a tavern), so as to cross at Rock Ford, three miles beyond, which opened the only chance of getting over. We did so, and crossed in safety, with the usual jokes when we were fairly over; but I confess that the wide, impetuous stream, so impenetrable to the eye, and so far above its average level, wore a vicious look to me when we approached and plunged into it. Its bottom is here hardly half a mile wide, but is capitally wooded with hickory, oak, black walnut, etc. Emerging from it, we rode over twelve miles more of high, gently rolling prairie, with wood in the ravines on either side, which brought us to the village of Stanton (of twenty or thirty houses, including two stores and a tavern) which we reached before sunset, having traveled at least fifty miles since we started in the morning. Night and the Marais des Cygnes here brought us to a halt—the creek being at this time impassable—and we had to forego our determination to reach Osawatomie before sleeping. So we halted at the little tavern, where we found five or six others bound to Osawatomie, like ourselves, at least one of whom had swam three creeks since the morning. Fifteen or twenty others drove up during the evening; we had supper, a neighborhood meeting and

a Republican talk at the schoolhouse, and adjourned to fill
all the beds and floors of the tavern as full as they could hold.
The kind, active, efficient landlady did her best, which was
good enough; and all were snugly bestowed except another
editor[1] and myself, who accepted the kindly proffered hospitality of a Republican farmer, and were capitally entertained at his house, half a mile distant.

As night fell, the lightning had begun to gleam and flash
nearly around the horizon; by ten o'clock, the thunder rolled;
at twelve, a high gale could be heard sweeping over the
prairies some moments before it struck us. The lightning
blazed almost incessantly for hours; yet the rainfall at Stanton was very slight. But there were heavy showers at Marysville, at Paoli, and almost everywhere else around us, still
further raising the streams, so that many who had come
part way were unable to reach Osawatomie next day.

We were early on the bank (a mile from Stanton) of the
Marais des Cygnes, which was running heavy driftwood,
and otherwise misbehaving itself. It had buried up the ferry
rope, without whose aid the boat could not be propelled
across its sweeping current; one of the trees to which that
rope was attached was now nearly in the middle of the
stream; and there had been no crossing for a day or two.
But a new rope had been procured and somehow stretched
across the stream, whereby we were taken across in our turn,
after waiting somewhat over an hour. A mile or so of well-
timbered and too-well-watered bottom brought us again to
prairie, over which we drove rapidly into Osawatomie, which
we reached before 10 A. M.

Osawatomie is a village of at most one hundred and fifty
houses, situated in the forks of the Marais des Cygnes and

---

[1] Greeley gives no clue as to this editor's identity. Throughout the
journal he is very casual about naming and identifying his traveling
companions.

Potawatomie, a somewhat smaller creek, which comes in from the southwest. The location is a pleasant and favorable but not a commanding one; the surrounding country is more considerably cultivated than any I had passed south of the Kaw. The two creeks supply abundant and good timber; an excellent steam sawmill has taken the place of that which the border ruffians burned; a flouring mill, tannery, brewery and a large hotel are being erected or completed. I presume there is a larger town somewhere in what is known as Southern Kansas, though I do not know which it is.

But Osawatomie has a higher interest than any other spot in Kansas, except possibly Lawrence, because of her honorable eminence in the struggle which has secured Kansas to free labor. She was long the only settlement near the Missouri border which was avowedly, decidedly free-state; the only free-state village that could be reached by a night's march from Missouri. To be known as a free-state man at Topeka, Waubonsee, Emporia, or any other post well inland, involved struggles and sacrifices; to be one at Osawatomie, was to live in nightly and well-grounded apprehension of robbery, arson and murder. The pro-slavery settlements in the neighborhood were strong and malignant; and they had only to draw upon Missouri at sight for any amount of force, and the draft would be honored. Yet to surrender this outpost was virtually to give up all Kansas south of the Marais des Cygnes; and, though its maintenance was sure to cost property and blood, it was not surrendered, for OLD JOHN BROWN was among its early settlers. Twice was it sacked and laid in ashes, once after a desperate fight of two hours, in which Old Brown with forty of his neighbors held at bay four hundred well-armed Missourians, who had the advantage of a cannon. So fearfully outnumbered, Old Brown, after seeing his son and several of his neighbors shot dead by his side, and after killing at least as many Missourians as there were of his own party altogether, was gradually driven back through the open timber north of the village, and across the Marais des Cygnes, the ruffians not venturing to pursue their victory, though they had attacked from the west, and so were driving the free-state men toward Missouri.

The women and children had meantime fled to the woods on the south; the village was burned after being robbed, the only iron safe therein having been blown open by firing a cannon into its side; and so plundered of some silverware and a considerable sum in money, Osawatomie was thus a second time "wiped out." But it has risen again from its ashes, and is once more the home of an undaunted, freedom-loving people, who are striving to forget their bereavements and sacrifices in view of the rich fruits they have borne to liberty and human good. They have gathered the dust of their martyred dead into a common grave on a prairie knoll just west of their village, and propose to erect there a monument which shall teach their children and grandchildren to love and cherish the cause for which those heroes joyfully laid down their lives. I beg leave to suggest an enlargement of the scope of this enterprise—that this monument be reared to *all* the martyrs of freedom in Kansas, and that the name of each be inscribed upon it, and his mortal remains, if his relatives make no objection, be placed beneath the column which shall here be reared as a memorial of the struggle which secured Kansas to free labor, and is destined finally to hasten the expulsion of slavery from Missouri. Should a monument be proposed on this basis, I feel confident that subscriptions in aid of its erection might reasonably be asked of all who prefer freedom to slavery, and would not be asked in vain.

3

MORE NOTES ON KANSAS

Leavenworth, May 23, 1859

The convention at Osawatomie was of course very slow in assembling, and I think not more than half the organized counties were represented at all. Hardly any were present from the southern counties, for whose benefit that place of meeting had been selected. Those who did come got there by swimming many dangerous creeks; but from most localities attendance was a physical impossibility. Ferryboats are scarce in Kansas; bridges, of course, nearly unknown; and the water runs off these rolling prairies so rapidly that a stream which a three-year-old child might ford at night will be running water enough to float a steamboat before morning. Obviously, there can be no ferries maintained on such; and, until bridges can be erected, those whose way lies across them have no further alternative when they are in flood than either to swim or wait. But to swim an angry, turbid, rushing torrent, perhaps a dozen rods across, and running driftwood in a perfectly reckless manner, is a job requiring nerve and skill; so the greater number have simply to stay at home or camp on the bank, and wait until the flood runs out, which it usually will in twelve to thirty-six hours, according to the size of the stream, unless the rain or thaw continues. But it had rained nearly half the time for a week prior and up to the eighteenth, so that few even of those who supposed the convention would be held could reach it. Yet there gathered on the afternoon of that day nearly a thousand of the pioneers, mainly of the immediate neighborhood, to whom, in an interlude of the convention's discussions concerning their organization and platform, I had the satisfaction of setting forth the Republican faith as I understand it, and by whom it was heartily received. It was a labor of love so to speak, but rather a tax to write the speech out, even imperfectly, as I was obliged to do during the next two days in the intervals of riding and speaking, in order that all those people of Kansas who care to do so may consider my notions of Free-State Democracy and Squatter Sovereignty.

The twin courses of Kansas, now that the border ruffians have stopped ravaging her, are land speculation (whereof the manufacture of paper cities and bogus corner lots, though more amusingly absurd, is not half so mischievous as the grasping of whole townships by means of fraudulent pre-emptions and other devices familiar to the craft) and one-horse politicians. Many of these latter were driven into the free-state movement by the enormity of the border-ruffian outrages, by their own terror or indignation, and by the overwhelming force of public sentiment; but, being essentially demagogues, they gravitate irresistibly toward the sham-democracy, in whose embraces the whole tribe will bring up, sooner or later. Their prototype is Mr. H. Miles Moore of this city, who, after having been one of the noisiest and most conspicuous free-state men in 1855-6, after having been driven down the river by the border ruffians, who gave him his choice between leaving Kansas and instant death, and after having been once strung up by the neck by them and choked till nearly dead, is now hard at work trying to put Kansas once more into their hands, and figuring in conventions and on committees with those who didn't quite hang him, as fellow democrats! His case reminds me strongly by contrast of that of the man who observed that, for the first month after marriage, he loved his wife so that he wanted to eat her, while ever since he had wished he had.

The controlling idea of the one-horse politicians is that the Republicans must not let their adversaries have a chance

29

to raise the cry of "nigger" against them—that hence they must be as harsh, and cruel, and tyrannical, toward the unfortunate blacks as possible, in order to prove themselves "the white man's party," or else all the mean, low, ignorant, drunken, brutish whites will go against them from horror of "Negro equality." To which I reply that this sort of cattle are against the Republicans anyhow, and never can be permanently otherwise. They may be driven by circumstances to vote once or twice with us, but the virus of sham-democracy is in their blood, and must come out. That democracy, from long practice and an experience that it pays, can dive deeper, stay under longer, and come up nastier, in this business of Negro-hating, than any other party that ever was or ever can be invented. There is nothing that more strikingly exposes the radical baseness of slaveholding than the fact that its votaries so hate those whom they have long injured, that, beaten in their desperate struggle to force Negroes into Kansas as slaves, they now turn a short corner and insist that, if they cannot come in as slaves, they shall be shut out, and even driven out, altogether.

I apprehend that it will be necessary for the Republicans of Kansas, in view of the inveterate western prejudices of a large portion of her population, to concede, for the present, that the right of suffrage shall be exercised only by white males, or men of European lineage, excluding, on account of their imperfect moral and intellectual developments, Indians, Negroes, and their descendants. Further than this, I would not go, no matter how great the inducement. Leave the Democrats alone in their glory, when they come to propose and support—as they are certain to do—propositions that Negroes shall be expelled and excluded from Kansas, shall be precluded from testifying against a white man, shall be debarred from attending schools frequented by white children, etc., etc. Let any city or district that sees fit, make adequate provision for the education of colored children by themselves; but, in default of this, let the schools be open to all who need their ministrations. Such, I hope, will be the determination of Republicans generally; and, if Kansas has to be lost in consequence, then let her go!

I left Osawatomie on the morning of the nineteenth, in the Lawrence stage, crossing the Marais des Cygnes at Bundy's ferry (where we crossed the day before), and finding the water considerably lower, though still over its regular northern bank, and the access on either side most detestable. Passing Stanton, we kept still west of north into the Ottawa Reserve, so as to leave a mail at Ottawa Jones's, where we struck due north to Prairie City, leaving Peoria City and Ohio City some miles distant on our left, either upon or near the Marais des Cygnes. (It takes three log houses to make a city in Kansas, but they begin *calling* it a city so soon as they have staked out the lots.) I stopped at Prairie City and talked to a Republican gathering of four hundred people, though where on earth so many could have been scared up, within a reasonable ride of this point, one who merely runs over the country could not imagine. True, we had here Prairie City, Baldwin City, and Palmyra in a string, all within three miles; but they could not all have mustered half this audience, and I was forced to conclude that the country is really better peopled than it seems to a mere traveler—that, while the favored roads traverse the high "divides," or middle of the prairies, in order to avoid, so far as possible, the miry bottoms and watercourses, the settlers are nested in the edge of the timber, and down the watercourses, where fencing and fuel are far more accessible.

The country I traversed between Stanton and Prairie City was a little more rolling, and considerably better timbered, than that between Shawnee and Stanton, already described. The oaks often covered considerable tracts of upland, while

31

young timber was visibly spreading on all hands, under cover of the universal hazel bushes of those Kansas uplands which are not burned over every year. Our next post office above Jones's was Hickory Grove, which reminds me that I saw more good hickory this day than in any former day of my life. Some of the oak, also, was very serviceable. These, with the black walnut, are the settler's main reliance for timber, rails included. The elm, cottonwood, sycamore, etc., warp so badly when sawed into boards and seasoned, that very little use can be made of them, though I think I saw a few cottonwood rails. The grass was abundant and superb; the soil generally deep and excellent.

We had another smart thundershower on Friday morning (20th), after which I came from Prairie City to Lawrence, fifteen miles north. My companion was a young pioneer from southern Missouri, reared among slaves and slaveholders, but free-state from the time he could fairly see, who assured me that he knew a large portion of the people of Missouri to condemn and hate slavery, even while they shout and vote in its favor. He came out here in 1855 to be rid of the curse, and had had a pretty fair experience of the struggle, having been with Lane at Bull Creek, when eight hundred Missourians did not venture to attack three hundred and fifty free-state men, but, after being separated by night, beat a retreat across the line, leaving some of their arms and camp equipage behind them. He was also at the somewhat noted Battle of Black Jack, which he described to me substantially as follows:

On the 1st of June, 1856, Henry Clay Pate, at the head of a pro-slavery band, emerging suddenly from the Indian Reserve, which then covered most of the region between this point and the Missouri border, surprised the little settlement of Palmyra, which they sacked without resistance. Next morning, they proposed to extend their operations to

Prairie City, which would probably have shared the same fate, had not Old Brown, lately driven from Osawatomie by an overwhelming force, been camped, with ten of his tried men, in the woods on Black Jack, a little creek four miles eastward. Strengthened by these, Prairie City resolved on resistance, and mustered its sixteen Sharp's rifles, in addition to those of Old Brown's party, and when the ruffians sent in six of their men to sack the place, presuming there would be no resistance, they took four of them prisoners, and chased the other two back to their band, with bullets whistling by their ears. They found the ruffians encamped on the open prairie, but drawn out in line for battle where they stood perfectly still as the free-state men neared them, firing as they neared to get the range of their rifles. As they approached, a small ravine only lay betwixt them, but the two lines could be and were distinctly counted on either side— fifty-four men in rank composing the pro-slavery and twenty-six the free-state party. Soon, two or three of the ruffians went down badly wounded, and one after another of their comrades were seen tailing off, making tracks for Missouri at a 2:40 gait, until barely twenty-two of them remained, when Pate raised a white flag and surrendered at discretion, to just fourteen men standing in the free-state array at that moment. Seven horses, two wagons well laden with the plunder of Palmyra, two drums, and about forty stand of arms, were among the "spoils of victory," and though Colonel Sumner with his United States troops came down on hearing of the affray, liberated the prisoners, and restored what they claimed as their property, the booty taken from Palmyra was left and restored to its rightful owners. Not one free-state man was killed or badly wounded. The wounded Missourians were kindly nursed at Prairie City till they were well enough to travel, when they were recommended to resume that wholesome exercise—a suggestion which

33

they promptly and gladly heeded. Two of those who got away died of their wounds. And, though there were many alarms, and a year of marching, camping, scouting, riding, after that, to the destruction of all industry and progress, Prairie City has seen no organized company of border ruffians at her doors since that 2d day of June, 1856.

The road from that city to Lawrence (fifteen miles) passes over a rolling country, mainly prairie, crosses the great Santa Fé trail, now horribly cut up by many heavy wagons passing in bad weather, then takes over a high "divide" and along a limestone ridge which runs out into the valley of the Wakarusa, and affords a magnificent view of the country for an area of twenty miles in each direction, with the prairie in good part cultivated, gleaming in sunlight on every bend, and the Wakarusa with its belt of timber making its way through them to join the Kaw, with its still larger belt, on the north. Spacious mounds or spurs of limestone covered with soil and grass rise to a height of two or three hundred feet on every side, on one of which, visible for many miles on every side, a flag, when raised, used to give warning of invasion and danger in the troublous days now happily passed away. At the base of one of these spurs, by the side of the Kaw, sits Lawrence, clearly discernible from a distance of ten miles. Descending from the ridge, and passing over a lower prairie two or three miles, we cross the Wakarusa (a moderate creek, hardly twenty yards wide, but very deep and with high, steep banks) on a good toll bridge, traverse its wide, wet bottom, here in good part prairie marsh, and pass over two miles of superb prairie into the renowned citadel of free-state principle, the first-born of northern resolution that Kansas should not be tamely yielded to the slaveholders, and which does not deny its parentage.

Lawrence can only grow with the more thorough development of the surrounding country. Across the Kaw on the north, a large Indian reservation (the Delaware) impedes its progress, while town sites, and very good ones, are so abundant in Kansas that no location but one where navigable water is abandoned for land transportation can be of very much account. I should say Lawrence has now five hundred dwellings and perhaps five thousand inhabitants; and these figures are more likely to be over than under the mark. She has a magnificent hotel (the Eldridge House)—the best, I hear, between the Missouri and the Sacramento—far better, I fear, than its patronage will justify—though it has nearly all that Lawrence can give. She *is* to have a great university, for which a part of the funds are already provided; but I trust it will be located some distance away, so as to give scope for a model farm, and for a perfect development of the education of the brain and the hands together.[1] In our old states, the cost of land is always assigned as a reason for not blending labor with study authoritatively and systematically; here there can be no such excuse. I trust the establishment of the Lawrence University will not be unduly hurried, but that it will be, whenever it does open its doors to students, an institution worthy of its name.

I passed into the town over Mount Oread, a considerable eminence on the southwest, on whose summit the free-state fortress of other days was constructed. It is now dilapidated, but is a place of considerable natural strength as a defensive position, and, in the hands of the grandsons of the men who defended Bunker Hill, would have cost something to whoever might have taken it. As it was, the ruffians, though often in the neighborhood in overwhelming force, and anxious enough for its destruction, never got possession

---

[1] His advice was not followed—not precisely at any rate. The University of Kansas, founded in 1865, has no agricultural college. Kansas's land-grant institution (now Kansas State University) preceded KU by two years, at Manhattan.

of it but once, and then by marching with federal officers at the head and federal writs in their pockets. For one, I regret that even these were suffered to shield them, and thus allow printing presses to be destroyed and houses battered down and burned with impunity.

I did not speak long in Lawrence, for I trust words are not there needed. Her people have had practical illustrations of the great issue which divides the country, and are not likely soon to forget them. Of course, her pioneers will die or become dispersed; new men will come in or rise up to fill their places, and "another king arose who knew not Joseph" will find its parallel in her future. Thus, among her newcomers is the gentleman who led over one thousand armed Missourians from Jackson County in March, 1855, and returned by their votes and revolvers pro-slavery men to represent her in the bogus Legislature of that year. He is, of course, an Old-Line Whig of the Buchanan stripe, and will make a first-rate Free-State Democrat in due season. By and by, when the grogshops, already too numerous in Lawrence, shall have manufactured or attracted thither a sufficient number of ground-tier Democrats, and mortified pride or disappointed ambition shall have wrought its perfect work with quite a number of sometime free-state men, he may be chosen mayor of the city of his young love, and *The Constitution* (or whatever may then be the name of the pro-slavery organ at Washington) may announce with guns and trumpets that "National Democracy has triumphed at last in the great stronghold of Kansas Abolition." But that will not probably happen just yet.

While I was in Lawrence, the little steamboat *Gus Linn*, Captain Beasley, came down the Kaw from Fort Riley, some thirty miles above the fork of the Big Blue, two hundred and thirty-five (I believe) from the mouth of the river, and over one hundred in a beeline. She reached the fort in a little

36

over two days from Kansas City, discharged her cargo, and loaded on her way down with corn, whereof Kansas has a large surplus of last year's growth, after supplying this year's heavy emigration to Pike's Peak. As the territory has little or nothing else to sell, and almost everything to buy, she would like to export her corn if she had any way by which to get it to the Missouri without costing all it will fetch, so that this pioneer passage of a steamboat above Topeka and Manhattan was hailed with general exultation. Her burden is three hundred tons, and she draws when full but thirty inches (when light, scarcely ten), and, in the present stage of water, I presume she might easily go up to the Falls, twenty miles further. Of course, she can only do this to any purpose when the water is very high; but, in the absence of passable roads, the fact that this river can be navigated at all throughout the most thickly peopled portion of Kansas is of some consequence.

I left Lawrence by stage on Saturday morning, crossing the Kaw by a good ferry directly at the city, and rising to a wide and well-timbered bottom on the north. It is probably well for Lawrence ultimately that this timber is in Indian hands, and therefore sure to be preserved for some years, though for the present the reserve is a nuisance to her. Beyond the Kaw bottom stretches beautiful and gently undulating prairie, checkered by belts of timber on the creeks which traverse it, across the reserve and beyond, until we begin to descend the Missouri bluffs to Leavenworth.

Coming to Turkey Creek, the passengers were turned out (as once or twice before), to lighten the coach, which was then driven cautiously through the steep-banked ford, while the passengers severally let themselves down a perpendicular bank by clinging to a tree, and crossed a deep and whirling place above the ford, on the vilest log I ever attempted to walk—twisty, sharp-backed, and every way detestable. One

37

of the passengers refused to risk his life on it, but hired one of the lazy Indians loafing on the further bank to bring over a pony, and let him ride across the ford. At Big Stranger, we changed coaches with the passengers from Leavenworth—who had been waiting our arrival here two hours, and must have been glad to see us—our baggage being first taken across the deep, ugly stream in a skiff, and the passengers next, either coach returning the way it came. We left Lawrence at nearly ten, and arrived here (thirty-five miles) about 6 P.M.

Leavenworth is, of course, much the largest place in Kansas, containing (I judge) one thousand houses and ten thousand inhabitants. The Fort, three miles up the Missouri, is not included in this estimate, though that is a city of itself, with extensive barracks, capacious storehouses, several companies of soldiers, many fine houses for officers, sutlers, etc., and a farm of twelve hundred acres, which Uncle Sam cultivates, I presume, to much the same profit as other gentlemen who have fancy farms and do not oversee them very closely. It is a nice place, that Fort, with many excellent people about it; but I can't help asking what it costs, and who pays, and whether that little bill might not be somewhat docked without prejudice to the public interest. I believe it could. Whenever our people shall have grown wise enough to maintain no standing army whatever but the barest skeleton of one, to be clothed with flesh whenever needed by calling out volunteers, the annual expenditures may be reduced at least one fourth, and we may build a railroad to the Pacific with the savings of three or four years.

But Russell, Majors & Waddell's transportation establishment, between the Fort and the city, is the great feature of Leavenworth. Such acres of wagons! such pyramids of extra axletrees! such herds of oxen! such regiments of drivers and other employees! No one who does not seen can realize how vast a business this is, nor how immense are its outlays as well as its income. I presume this great firm has at this hour two millions of dollars invested in stock, mainly oxen, mules and wagons. (They last year employed six thousand teamsters, and worked forty-five thousand oxen.) Of course, they are capital fellows—so are those at the Fort —but I protest against the doctrine that either army officers or army contractors, or both together, may have power to fasten slavery on a newly organized territory (as has just been done in New Mexico) under the guise of letting *the people* of such territories govern themselves. Yet this is just what "squatter sovereignty," unmodified by a fiery anti-slavery agitation in the free-states, will in practice amount to.

Whether the three great cities of America are to be New York, St. Louis and Leavenworth, as one set of friends seem to think, or New York, St. Louis and Atchison, as another set assure me, I do not pretend to decide. If Atchison had the start that Leavenworth now has, I think she would probably keep it. But not having it, you see, alters the case materially. The Fort is here as a fixed fact; the United States goods are landed at the Fort; so the trains are made up there; and so Leavenworth is Leavenworth, and Atchison (for the present) only Atchison.

I saw a great mule train started from the Fort today, and another will start soon, filled with one hundred and sixty soldiers' wives and babies, on their way to join their husbands in Utah, from whom they have been separated nearly two years. I argue from this fact that Uncle Sam expects to have use for his army in Utah for some time yet.

There has been no rain for three days; the sun is bright and hot; the prairie wind from the west is a gale; the streams are down—all but Big Muddy, which does not give an inch, but rushes by Leavenworth almost bank-full and turbid as ever. The roads which so lately were mud are now blowing dust in clouds; and there is a fair prospect of settled summer weather. I turn my face westward tomorrow.

4

MORE OF KANSAS

Manhattan, May 24, 1859

I left Leavenworth in the Fort Riley stage at 6 A.M. on Tuesday, a day in advance of the Pike's Peak Express, which crosses the U. S. military road at this point, in order to gain time to visit Topeka and Manhattan, and sum up my impressions of Kansas for THE TRIBUNE. Our road from Leavenworth lay over the heavy hill westward (which Leavenworth must soon cut down or it will cut *her* down materially), passing thence through the rich valley of Salt Creek and over a "divide" into that of the Stranger, which we forded at Easton, a village of thirty to fifty houses, famous for border-ruffian outrages and murders in 1856. The bluffs of the Stranger are here one to two hundred feet high, generally timbered with oak, etc., and so covered with limestone boulders that scarcely more than half the ground is visible. These boulders are generally oblong and irregularly flat, making the best of stone wall. I am informed that nine rods of capital wall is regarded as but a fair week's work for a good wall-builder, working by himself. We pass out of the valley just beyond Easton, rising to the slightly rolling prairie; and henceforth for forty miles to Topeka our way lies through a gently heaving sea of grass, with timber generally visible along the watercourses on either side. Occasionally, however, we descend from the crest of the prairie into a barely perceptible hollow, and now nothing but grass and sky are visible, the two meeting at the horizon on every side. I do not like this region quite so well as the more rolling country south of Olathe and Prairie City, across Bull Creek and the Marais des Cygnes; but it is very fertile, fairly wooded, and sufficiently irregular in surface to carry off the water and leave few or no marshes or sloughs except in the road, where the frequent crossing of unbridged watercourses is attended by a jolt and a jerk which render a doze dangerous and scarcely possible. In riding over such roads, all the pleasure must be drank in through the eyes alone.

We stopped for dinner at the crossing of Grasshopper Creek, at the village of Osawkee, once the seat of Jefferson County's public buildings and a land office, both now removed. Grasshopper Falls, I believe, next obtained the coveted distinction of being shire town; but another popular vote removed it thence to Oskaloosa, on the road from Leavenworth to Lecompton, on the north line of the Delaware Reserve, which still covers a good part of Jefferson as well as of Leavenworth and Wyandotte Counties. Osawkee, now probably four years old, is therefore in a state of dilapidation and decay, like a good many Kansas cities which figure largely on the map. Its business having left it, its great hotel was very mysteriously burned, and I presume the insurance on it was duly paid. We dined here at a very modest but comfortable tavern, kept by a kind and worthy Pennsylvania Dutchman, who recognized me from our having met at the Whig National Convention at Harrisburg, nearly twenty years ago. Bearing south of west from Osawkee, we crossed Rock and Muddy Creeks (neither of them more rocky nor muddy than the other), and were obliged by the lack of a bridge (now being repaired) over Halfday Creek, to keep on west to a petty village called Indianola, whence we turned a sharp angle through the magnificently fertile and admirably timbered bottom of the Kaw or Kansas to

41

the Topeka ferry, which we reached a little after sundown, but were delayed by a great contractor's train which had been all day crossing, and was likely to be a good part of the morrow, so that we did not get across and into Topeka till nearly dark. I noticed with sorrow that the oxen which draw these great supply wagons are often treated very cruelly, not merely in respect to the beating and whaling which every human brute delights in bestowing on every live thing over which he domineers, but with regard to food and drink. Here were cattle that had stood in the yoke all that hot, dry day with nothing to eat or drink; and, when they came down to the river mad with thirst, they were all but knocked down for trying to drink. I was assured that oxen are sometimes kept in the yoke, without food or drink, for two days, while making one of these river crossings. There can be no excuse for this. Those which have long to wait ought to be taken off and driven a mile or more if necessary to grass and fed there; at all events, they should be watered at least twice a day. How can a competent train master—to say nothing of humanity—overlook the policy of this?

The river is here wider than at Lawrence or Wyandotte below, is nearly as muddy as the Missouri, and runs with a swift current even to its banks. An attempt had been made during the day to swim across a drove of cattle; but the strong current carried them below the ferry landing on the south, whence the steep bank forbade their getting out, so that they went down the river several miles, and three of them were drowned. The experiment of swimming proved wretched economy, alike in time and money.

Topeka is a village of probably one hundred houses and one thousand inhabitants, situated on the north line of Shawnee County, which has the Sac and Fox Reserve on the south, the Potawatomie on the northwest, and the Delaware at a little distance on the northeast. Along the north bank of the river opposite, a party of half-breeds have a reserve a mile wide by twenty miles long, and I give the good-for-nothing rascals credit for admirable judgment in selecting their land. There is probably not an acre of their tract that could not be made to produce one hundred bushels of shelled corn by the application of less labor than would be required to produce thirty bushels on the average in New York or New England. The soil is a river deposit four to six feet deep; the timber large and choice—oak, elm, bass, black walnut, sycamore, etc., with wild grapevines four to six inches through, and a thick undergrowth of shrubbery and annuals. I begin to comprehend, though I do not excuse, the covetous impatience wherewith Indian reservations are regarded by their white neighbors.

Topeka was one of the strongholds of the free-state cause throughout the dark days of Kansas. Here assembled the first convention chosen by the people to frame a state constitution as a rallying point for defense and mutual protection against the border-ruffian usurpation of 1855; here the free-state legislature, peacefully assembled in 1856 to devise and adopt measures looking to a redress of the unparalleled wrongs and outrages under which Kansas was then writhing, was dispersed by federal bayonets and cannon; here the guns of the U. S. troops were pointed against a mass meeting of the people of Kansas, assembled in the open air to devise and adopt measures for the redress of their intolerable grievances, and that meeting compelled to disperse under penalty of military execution. And here I renew my vows of hostility to that federal standing army until it shall have been disbanded. It is utterly at war with the genius and perilous to the existence of Republican institutions. The regular soldier is of necessity the blind, passive, mechanical instrument of power. If ordered to shoot his own father, he must obey or be shot himself. Twice has the French Republic been crushed by Bonapartean usurpation—crushed by the bayonets of a standing army pointed at the breasts of her faithful

43

legislators. A republic whose citizens are not willing to do their own fighting—all that is necessary and proper—but must have a standing army to do it for them, lies at the mercy of any bold, unscrupulous adventurer who can work his way to the command or the favor of that army. I trust ours is near its end.

After greeting friends and speaking in Topeka, I learned with surprise that the stage for Fort Riley would start at three in the morning, leaving but a narrow margin for sleep. On rising, however, I found that the high wind would not allow us to cross the river yet, and it was nearly six o'clock when we actually started.

We had now enjoyed three dry, bright, warm days, which had turned most of the mire of the roads to a sort of adobe, or sun-burned brick, though enough still remained in sunken holes and brook crossings to remind us of what had been. But the lightning had flashed, and the clouds gathered throughout the night; and, as we drove out through Indianola and took the military road westward, the thunder gave indications of the shower which burst upon us a little before nine o'clock and poured till eleven, turning the brick of the road to mire again. And, though the rain ceased, the day remained sullen and lowering, with transient glimpses of weak sunshine, to the end.

Our route lay for thirty miles through the Potawatomie Reserve, and was no longer encumbered with great army supply trains, as they were either north of us on the California trail to Laramie, or south on the road crossing at Topeka and leading to Fort Union and Santa Fé. A few of the wagons we passed this day may have been heading for Forts Riley and Kearney; while Pike's Peakers, both going out, and returning disheartened, were in considerable numbers. I do not see how those returning could well resist the temptation to halt and make claims, as I hear many have done, generally seeking them in the south part of the territory, where speculation has been less rampant than in the vicinity of the Kaw. With a wagonload of provisions and three or four yoke of oxen, a squatter might, even yet, by the help of a good plow, get in twenty acres of sod corn this season, cut hay for winter, and break a glorious breadth of prairie before hard frost could stop him next fall. Whoever does this judiciously and resolutely will have reason for gratitude to Pike's Peak, even though he never see the color of its gold nor get nearer to it than the Big Blue.

We traveled all day with the timber of the Kaw visible on the south, sometimes quite near us, then one to two or three miles distant. Our road lay for a considerable distance along the bank of what seemed a deserted bed of the river, which has since made a new and deeper channel more to the south. At one point this old bed is so deep that it still retains water, and now figures as a narrow lake. We traversed the prairie, of course, except where it was cut by the creeks coming down from the north to lose themselves in the Kaw. The Soldier, the Red Vermilion, and another Rock Creek, were the principal of these streams. Our road passed St. Mary's (Catholic) Mission, where there is quite an Indian village and a very large improvement, which I guess white men were paid to make. Yet, whether to their credit or otherwise, I believe the truth cannot fairly be disputed, that Catholic Missions have been more successful in establishing a permanent influence over Indians than any others, except, perhaps, those of the Moravians.

At the Red Vermilion—still on the Potawatomie Reserve, but near its western edge—we dined; the landlady a half-breed, the dinner the hardest I ever yet paid half a dollar for. Doubtless, however, my eyes will be opened to an appreciation of cold hog and corn dodger as delicacies, long before they are blessed with a sight of the Sacramento.

A wide, marshy bottom—over which each charioteer seeks an untraversed path, since a rut buries him so much deeper

45

in the mire—lies just west of the Vermilion (which, with two or three other steep-banked streams, we crossed on Indian toll bridges, cheaply built and very profitable to their owners), whence the land rises into rolling sandy ridges, some of them thinly wooded up their sides with white and burr oak. Thence we strike the old-fashioned deep, black prairie again—most inviting to the cultivator, but not so grateful to the traveler, just after a soaking rain—and, passing the stakes and ruinous cabin or so of one or two still-born cities, we reach the Big Blue, which here joins the Kansas from the north. It is nearly as wide as the Kansas or Kaw at Lawrence, but of course neither so swift nor so deep. It is far clearer, even just after a heavy shower, than the Kansas; as is strikingly evinced at and below the junction, where the two streams run for some distance side by side in the same channel without mingling.

The Big Blue rises near the Platte, in what is now Nebraska, but which will be included in Kansas if the Platte is made her northern boundary, as it seems likely to be. Its general course is a little east of south; its length one hundred and fifty miles. I understand that there is a good deal of settlement already along its course and on its tributaries, though I judge from the relative purity of its water that some part of this region must be less fertile than those of Kansas I have seen.

Manhattan is an embryo city of perhaps one hundred houses, of which several were unroofed and three or four utterly destroyed by a tornado on the wild night I passed at Atchinson (15th inst.) So violent was the tempest, that a large signboard was carried across the Blue and thrown down fully half a mile from the spot at which it was taken up; and other heavy articles were swept away which have not since been found. Several families deprived of home and shelter by the hurricane are temporarily lodged in the basement of the new hotel just erected here—a three-story building 55 by 33, with limestone walls and black-walnut finishing—an establishment of which there is urgent need. The embryo city is located on the flat, deep bottom in the forks of the rivers, with a high limestone bluff, affording capital material for building, just behind it. The Kansas comes hither from the southwest, and has Fort Riley and its large military reservation fifteen miles distant on its north bank, with the intended city of Ogden just east and Junction City just west of it, at the forks of the Kansas, whence its more northerly branch is known as the Republican, and its more southerly as the Smoky Hill.

At Junction City is a newspaper—the most westerly, I presume, in Kansas, apart from the Pike's Peak region—founded and kept alive by an army sutler, and of course "Democratic" in its inculcations. In opposition to it, *The Manhattan Express*, is about to be issued here by M. Vivalde, an Italian exile and a devotee of universal liberty, who will of course sustain the Republican cause. I commend him and his journal to the confidence and patronage of all who would like a weekly bulletin from the Far West. I spoke here last evening in the midst of another gathering tempest, which burst in rain as I closed, and it continued to flash and roll all night, with considerable rain, and is cloudy and blowing a gale today. I fear we shall be stopped by high water on the plains.

I had hoped to sum up my impressions of Kansas in this letter, but that would make it too long. Let me close with an incident which is currently reported throughout this region as having recently taken place at a crossing of the Big Blue, known as Marysville (of course not the Marysville of Bull Creek), some sixty miles north of this place:

A party of disheartened gold-seekers, it is said, were returning from the Plains, and came to this ferry, which they insisted on crossing without payment, saying they had no money. The ferryman refused to take them over until paid

47

—(another account says he asked them an exorbitant price) —when they attempted to take his boat and put themselves across—whereupon he drew his revolver, they drawing almost at the same instant. He was of course riddled with balls, and fell dead, but not till he had either killed or severley wounded five of his assailants.

One more illustration of border life: A quarrel recently arose about a "claim"—that fruitful source of frays and lawsuits in new settlements—on one of the creeks a few miles from this place. The stronger party, composed of several who are known here as bad fellows, told the resident he must leave, which he, in fear for his life, consented to do. His wife, however, more resolute, resolved to hold possession, and bade them defiance, turning as she did so to go into the house and bar the door. As she turned, she was fired at and fatally wounded. She died two hours thereafter, having first made a statement of the affair, which was taken down from her dying lips. The adverse party came down at once to the nearest justice and told their story, expecting to clear their leader, who fired the fatal shot; but the justice, after hearing them through, considered that it implicated the whole party (five), and consequently held them to answer to the charge of murder.

5

SUMMING UP ON KANSAS

Manhattan, May 26, 1859

I like Kansas—that is, natural Kansas—better than I had expected to.[1] The soil is richer and deeper; the timber is

[1] In due time Kansas returned the compliment by naming a county and a village after him and another town after his newspaper. Greeley

more generally diffused; the country more rolling, than I had supposed them. There are of course heavy drawbacks in remoteness from the seaboard, heavy charges for bulky goods, low prices for produce, Indian reserves, and the high price of good lumber. For instance, pine boards used in building at this place came from Allegany County, N. Y., and were rafted down some millstream to the Allegheny, thence down the Allegheny to Pittsburgh, and the Ohio to Cairo; were thence taken up the Missouri to St. Louis, the Missouri to Kansas City, and the Kansas to this place, which has but twice or thrice been reached by a steamboat. When here, they were dog cheap at one hundred dollars per thousand superficial feet, or ten cents for every square foot. In the absence of steamboat navigation on the Kansas, they must here be richly worth one hundred and twenty-five dollars per thousand feet. And, while there is pretty good timber here for other purposes, there is little—and that mainly black walnut—that will make good boards. The ready cottonwood along the banks of the streams cuts easily, but warps so when seasoned that it will draw the nails out of the side of a house. Elm is of course equally perverse; and I have seen few indigenous boards that were not either black walnut or oak. But much of the oak is small, short, and gnarly; while the black walnut is likely to be exhausted. I see young ones coming up thickly in some of the river bottoms; but these have much to contend with, and will not at best be large enough to saw for many years. No doubt, the timber of Kansas increases each year, and will increase still faster as roads and improvements are multiplied, limiting the sweep of the prairie fires; but it will always cost more to build a de-

---

County, on the western edge of the state but somewhat south of Greeley's line of travel, was organized in 1888. Its county seat is the city of Tribune, two miles west of which is the village of Horace. Tribune's weekly newspaper is the *Greeley County Republican.*

cent house of wood in the interior of Kansas than in any part of New York or New England—I think twice as much. This is a heavy tax on a new country, where not only houses but barns are a general, primary, and pressing need. I rejoice to see the new timber creeping up the bluffs of the streams; I note with pleasure that much of this is hickory and some of it white ash; I doubt not that there will always be wood enough here for fencing and fuel; but if the Pike's Peak region can send a good lot of pine lumber (even yellow pine) down the Platte and the Arkansas, it will be worth more to Kansas than all her gold.

I consider Kansas well watered—no prairie state better. I do not confine this remark to the present, when everything is flooded, and likely to be more so. I mean that springs, streams, creeks, rivers, are quite universal. For my own private drinking, I should like a supply not so much impregnated with lime; but, for limestone water, this is generally quite good.

And the limestone itself is among the chief blessings of Kansas. I presume it underlies every foot of her soil I have yet traversed, with nearly every square mile that will be comprised within the state of Kansas. You see it cropping out from almost every bluff; it lies thickly strewn in boulders over the surface of every headland or promontory that makes out into the bottoms, low prairies, or ravines; so that if you want to use it, it is always to be drawn (or rolled) downhill. Though not here needed as a fertilizer, it can everywhere be quarried with little labor into building-stone, or burned for use in putting up chimneys and plastering walls. Though somewhat decomposed (I presume, by the action of water upon it through thousands of years), and readily cleaving into blocks of suitable size for house walls, it is said to harden by exposure to the atmosphere, and make a very durable wall. It is the constant though unobserved decomposition of this stone that contributed so largely to the fertility of this soil, and now countervails the enormous waste through the rivers. I presume all the guano imported yearly into our country does not equal in fertilizing value the annual outflow from the Kansas River alone.

I judge that Indian corn can be grown here as cheaply as anywhere on earth. Thousands of acres last year produced their hundred bushels of shelled grain per acre, at a very moderate cost for labor and none at all for manure. An extensive farmer, who grew many thousands of bushels near Leavenworth, assured me that the cost of his corn, cribbed in the ear, was just six cents per bushel of ears, equal to nine cents per bushel of grain—three half-bushels of ears of the great Ohio kind here cultivated making a bushel of grain. Of course, this estimate excludes the cost of land, breaking, and fencing; but, making a fair allowance for these, the net cost of that corn cannot have exceeded twenty cents per bushel. I presume it would now sell in his crib for forty cents, while here in the interior it is worth from twenty-five to thirty-five cents per bushel.

I met at Osawatomie an old Whig and now Republican friend who left New York City (where he had been an industrious mechanic) and settled between Lawrence and Topeka two years ago. He had last year eighty acres in corn, which yielded four thousand bushels, worth to him thirty-five or forty cents per bushel. His clear profit on this corn, above the immediate cost of growing it, can hardly have been less than one thousand dollars. He will grow more this year, with wheat, potatoes, etc.; yet he is one of a class who are popularly supposed incapable of making money by farming. I suspect few lifelong farmers of similar means will have good buildings over their heads and fruit trees and other elements of material comfort around them sooner than my friend.

Wheat and oats did badly last year, owing to the heavy

51

summer rains which rusted and blighted them. Too little of either have been sown for this year's harvest, yet I find both winter and spring wheat looking remarkably well almost everywhere. Oats are scarcely more than out of the ground; yet they, too, promise well, so far as can now be foreseen.

But an unpleasant truth must be stated: There are too many idle, shiftless people in Kansas. I speak not here of lawyers, gentlemen speculators, and other non-producers, who are in excess here as elsewhere; I allude directly to those who call themselves settlers, and who would be farmers if they were anything. To see a man squatted on a quarter-section in a cabin which would make a fair hog-pen, but is unfit for a human habitation, and there living from hand to mouth by a little of this and a little of that, with hardly an acre of prairie broken (sometimes without a fence up), with no garden, no fruit trees, "no nothing"—waiting for someone to come along and buy out his "claim" and let him move on to repeat the operation somewhere else—this is enough to give a cheerful man the horrors. Ask the squatter what he means, and he can give you a hundred good excuses for his miserable condition: he has no breaking-team; he has little or no good rail timber; he has had the "shakes"; his family have been sick; he lost two years and some stock by the border ruffians, etc., etc. But all this don't overbear the facts that, if *he* has no good timber, some of his neighbors have it in abundance, and would be very glad to have him work part of it into rails on shares at a fair rate; and if he has no breaking-team, he can hire out in haying and harvest, and get nearly or quite two acres broken next month for every faithful week's work he chooses to give at that busy season. The poorest man ought thus to be able to get ten acres broken, fenced, and into crop, each year. For poor men gradually hew farms out of heavy timber, where every fenced and cultivated acre has cost twice to thrice the work it does here.

And it is sad to note that hardly half the settlers make any sort of provision for wintering their cattle, even by cutting a stack of prairie hay, when every good day's work will put up a ton of it. If he has a cornfield, the squatter's cattle are welcome to pick at that all winter; if he has none, they must go into the bottoms and browse through as best they can. Hence his calves are miserable affairs; his cows unfit to make butter from till the best of the season is over; his oxen, should he have a pair, must be recruited from their winter's famine just when he most urgently needs their work. And this exposing cattle all winter to these fierce prairie winds is alike inhuman and wasteful. I asked a settler the other day how he *could* do it? "I had no time to make a shelter for them." But had you no Sundays?—did you not have these at your disposal?" "O, yes? I don't work Sundays." "Well, you *should* have worked every one of them, rather than let your cattle shiver in the cold blasts all winter—it would have been a work of humanity and mercy to cut and haul logs, get up a cattle stall, and cover it with prairie hay, which I will warrant to be more religious than anything you did on those Sundays." But the squatter was of a different opinion.

How a man located in a little squalid cabin on one of these rich "claims" can sleep moonlit nights under the average circumstances of his class, passes my comprehension. I should want to work moderately but resolutely, at least fourteen hours of each secular day, until I had made myself comfortable, with a fence around at least eighty acres, a quarter of this partitioned off for my working cattle, a decent, warm shelter to cover them in cold or stormy weather, a tolerable habitation for my family, at least forty acres in crop, and a young orchard growing. For one commencing with next to nothing, I estimate this as the work of five years; after which, he might take things more easily, awaiting the fruit from his orchard and the coming up of his boys

53

to help him. But for the first four or five years, the poor pioneer should work every hour that he does not absolutely need for rest. Every hour's work then will save him many hours in afterlife.

For the farmer who comes in with liberal means, the task is obviously much easier. Let us suppose one to be worth $5,000 the day he lands on the Kansas shore of the Missouri, and see how quickly he can make a farm and a home. He arrives, we will say, in August, when he can see just what the country produces, whether in a state of nature or under cultivation. He buys a quarter-section (which is land enough for any man) in a choice locality, including thirty or forty acres of timbered river or creek bottom, say for $10 per acre, charges $1,000 of the $1,600 thus called for to the account of the pro-slavery democracy, for defeating the free-land bill, and sets to work, with two good hired men. He buys five yoke of oxen for a breaking-team, a span of good wagon horses, a cow in fresh milk, and three heifers which will be cows next spring, puts up a cabin that will just do, and is ready to commence breaking by the 1st of September. As his men break, he follows with the horses, sowing and harrowing in wheat so long as that will answer, but does not stop breaking till the ground is frozen. Now he begins to cut and draw timber for a fitter habitation to which to welcome his family in the spring. Having done this, he gets good mechanics to finish it, while he and his men go to work at fencing, by cutting sawlogs for light, narrow boards, if there be a sawmill convenient; if not, then by cutting for and splitting rails. So soon as the dryest land will answer for it, he begins to put in spring wheat, then oats, then corn, putting up fence whenever the soil is too wet for plowing. Let him not forget to have a few acres seasonably set in fruit trees, some of them dwarfs for early bearing. Thus his money will not have been exhausted by the ensuing fall, when he will have crops coming in and more than a hundred acres of his land broken and subdued for future cultivation. I see no reason why a resolute, good manager should not be comfortable after his first year or two, and henceforth take the world as easily as need be. He who comes in with but $2,000, $1,000 or $500, must of course be much longer in working his way to a position of comfort and independence; but if he will work right ahead, wasting neither days nor dollars, and keeping clear of specu-lation and office-seeking, he can hardly fail to do well.

As to the infernal spirit of land speculation and monopoly, I think no state ever suffered from it more severely than this. The speculators in broadcloth are not one whit more rapa-cious or pernicious than the speculators in rags, while the latter are forty times the more numerous. Land speculation here is about the only business in which a man can embark with no other capital than an easy conscience. For example: I rode up the bluffs back of Atchison, and out three or four miles on the high rolling prairie, so as to have some fifteen to twenty square miles in view at one glance. On all this inviting area, there were perhaps half a dozen poor or mid-dling habitations, while not one acre in each hundred was fenced or broken. My friend informed me that every rood I saw was "pre-empted," and held at thirty up to hundred dollars or more per acre. "Pre-empted!" I exclaimed; how pre-empted? by living or lying?" "Well," he responded, "they live a little and lie a little." I could see abundant evi-dence of the lying, none at all of the living. To obtain a pre-emption, the squatter must swear that he actually re-sides on the quarter-section he applies for, has built a habi-tation and made other improvements there, and wants the land for his own use and that of his family. The squatters who took possession of these lands must every one have committed gross perjury in obtaining pre-emption—and so it is all over the territory, wherever a lot is supposed likely to sell soon for more than the minimum price. I heard of one case in which a squatter carried a martin box onto a quarter-section, and on the strength of that martin box, swore that he had a house there "eighteen by twenty"— he left the officer to presume the feet. So it is all over; the wretched little slab shanty which has sufficed to swear by on one "claim" is now moved off and serves to swear by on another, when the first swearing is done. I am confident there is not at this hour any kind of a house or other sign of improvement on one-fourth of the quarter-sections throughout Kansas which have been secured by pre-emption. The squatter who thus establishes a "claim" sells it out, so soon as practicable, to some speculator, who follows in his wake, getting from $50 to $300 for that which the future bona-fide settler will be required to pay $250 to $1,500 for. Such, in practical operation, is the system designed and ostensibly calculated to shield the poor and industrious settlers from rapacity and extortion; but which, in fact, operates to oppress and plunder the real settler—to pay a premium on perjury—to foster and extend speculation—to demoralize the people, paralyze industry and impoverish the country.

But the fierce, chilly gale has blown away the tempest of last night*—the clouds fly scattered and brassy—it is time to look for the Leavenworth Express, whereof two stages west from this point will bear me beyond the bounds of settlement and civilized life. Adieu to friendly greetings and speakings! Adieu for a time to pen and paper! Adieu to bedrooms and washbowls! Adieu (let me hope) to cold rains and flooded rivers! Hurrah for Pike's Peak!

* There was a heavy snowstorm that night at Denver, and throughout its vicinity.

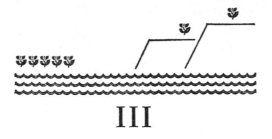

III

ACROSS THE PLAINS

Dispatches 6 through 9

The western journey now begins in earnest. Greeley boarded a stagecoach of the newly-established Leavenworth and Pike's Peak Express Company[1] on May 27. In the eleven days of dusty, jolting travel it took to reach Denver, he became well-initiated into the discomforts and perils of life on the High Plains in the 1850's. He saw Indians by the hundreds, buffaloes by the millions. He was awed by the

[1] The new line had been organized in April, 1859, and was operating two coaches daily, one starting from each end. "The Concord stages of the Pikes Peak Express Company were new, costing $800 apiece, painted red and attached to four fine Kentucky mules, trained to start at a dead run. The stage drivers were well-paid, experienced and fearless. There were 27 stations between Leavenworth and Denver City. The 'through fare' was $100, exclusive of meals." Mrs. Elmo Scott Watson: op. cit.

vastness and emptiness of the land, by the savagery of its weather. He learned the meaning of scarcity of water. Finally, he was the victim of a wreck—the first on the new Pike's Peak Express line—and though he made light of his injuries, they were painful and long-lasting.[2]

As Greeley and his traveling companion (by chance another journalist, A. D. Richardson, of Boston) moved westward, they met many eastbound disillusioned gold-seekers. So numerous were these dejected and impoverished "ex-Pike's Peakers" that at one point Greeley stated flatly: ". . . Pike's Peak is an exploded bubble, which thousands must bitterly rue to the end of their days." The evidence became more contradictory, however, and by the time he reached Denver, his reporter's instinct was completely aroused. "The stories . . . are absolutely bewildering," he wrote. "I have come here to lay my hand on the naked, indisputable facts, and I mean to do it."

His injured leg was so sore he could scarcely walk, but Greeley made arrangements to leave at once for the diggings.

6

ON THE PLAINS

*Station 9, Pike's Peak Express Co.,
Pipe Creek, May 28, 1859*

I was detained at Manhattan nearly a day longer than I had expected to be by high water. Wildcat, five miles west, and Rock Creek, seventeen miles east, were both impassable on Thursday, so that an express wagon from Pike's

---

[2] "For three weeks after our return from the mountains Mr. Greeley lay prostrate with his lame leg. Indeed the injury was so severe, that a year later he still limped." Richardson: op. cit., p. 195. (Mrs. Watson says Greeley limped for the rest of his life.)

Peak was stopped behind the former, while five mail coaches and express wagons faced each other through part of Thursday and all of Thursday night across the latter. Next morning, however, each stream had run out, so that they could be forded, and at one P.M. I took my seat in the Pike's Peak Express, and again moved westward.[1]

Our way was still along the United States military road, crossing Wildcat, now a reasonable stream, and winding for some miles over rugged, thin-soiled limestone hills, then striking down southwestward into the prairie bottom of the Kansas, which is as rich as land need be. A few miles of this brought us to Ogden, a land-office city of thirty or forty houses, some of them well built of stone. Just beyond this begins the Fort Riley Reservation, a beautiful tract of prairie and timber stretching for four or five miles along the northern bank of the Kansas, and including the sad remains of Pawnee City, at which Gov. Reeder summoned the first (bogus) legislature of Kansas to meet—then fifty to one hundred miles westward of anywhere. They obeyed the summons, but forthwith adjoined to Shawnee Mission, a pro-slavery stronghold on the Missouri border. Pawnee City is now of the things that were.

Fort Riley is a position which does credit to the taste of whoever selected it. It is on high, rolling prairie, with the Kansas on the south, the Republican on the west, heavy limestone bluffs on the north, and the best timber in middle or western Kansas all around. The barracks are comfortable, the hospital large and well placed, the officers' quarters

[1] It was here that Greeley joined Albert D. Richardson of the Boston *Journal*, to whom he refers now and then only as "my fellow passenger." Richardson himself is more specific. "Thus far I had been the solitary passenger," he writes. "But at Manhattan Horace Greeley, after a tour through the interior to gratify the clamorous settlers with speeches, joined me for the rest of the journey. His overland trip attracted much attention. A farmer asked me if Horace Greeley had failed in business and was going to Pike's Peak to dig gold!" Richardson: op. cit., p. 161.

spacious and elegant, and the stables most extensive and admirable. I hear that two millions of Uncle Sam's money have been expended in making these snug arrangements, and that the oats largely consumed here have often cost three dollars per bushel. I have seen nothing else at all comparable to this in the way of preparations for passing life agreeably since I left Missouri.

We here crossed by a rope ferry the Republican or northern fork of the Kansas, which, like the Big Blue, twenty-five miles back, seems nearly as large as the Kansas at its mouth, though the Smoky Hill, or southern fork at this point, is said to be the largest of the three. We met at the ferry a number of families, with a large herd of cattle, migrating from southwestern Missouri to California, and crossing here to take the road up the right bank of the Republican to Fort Kearney and so to Laramie. They had exhausted their patience in trying to swim their cattle, and would hardly be able to get them all ferried over till next day. All day, as on preceding days, we had been meeting ox wagons loaded with disheartened Pike's Peakers returning to their homes, but some of them going down into southern Kansas in search of "claims." Most of those we interrogated said they had been out as far as Fort Kearney (some two hundred miles further, I believe), before they were turned back by assurances that Pike's Peak is a humbug.

Across the Republican, between it and the Smoky Hill, is Junction City, as yet the most western village in Kansas, save that another has been started some fifty miles up the Smoky Hill. We stopped here for the night, and I talked Republicanism in the church for an hour or so. Junction has a store, two hotels, and some thirty or forty dwellings, one of which is distinguished for its age, having been erected so long ago as 1858. A patriotic Junctioneer excused his

60

city for not possessing something which I inquired for, but which its rival, Manhattan, was supposed to have; "for," said he, "Manhattan is three years old." As Junction is hardly a year old yet, the relative antiquity of Manhattan, and the responsibilities therein involved, were indisputable. Junction is the center of a fine agricultural region, though timber is not so abundant here as I wish it were. This region is being rapidly shingled with "claims"; I hope it is likewise to be filled with settlers—though that does not always follow. Our landlord (a German) had tried California, then Texas, and now he is trying Kansas, which seems to agree with him.

We started again at six this morning, making a little north of west, and keeping the narrow belts of timber along the Republican and the Smoky Hill respectively in full view for several miles on either side, until the streams diverged so far that we lost them in the boundless sea of grass. A mile or two of progress carried us beyond any road but that traced only this spring for the Pike's Peak Expresses; for ten miles onward, no house, no field, no sign of human agency, this road and a few United States surveyors' stakes excepted, was visible; at length we came to where a wretched cabin and an acre or so of broken and fenced prairie showed what a pioneer had been doing through the last two or three years, and beside it was a tavern—the last, I presume, this side of Pike's Peak. It consisted of a crotched stake which, with the squatter's fence aforesaid, supported a ridgepole, across which some old sailcloth was drawn, hanging down on either side, and forming a cabin some six by eight feet, and perhaps from three to five and a half feet high—large enough to contain two whisky barrels, two decanters, several glasses, three or four cans of pickled oysters and two or three boxes of sardines, but nothing of the bread kind whatever. The hotelkeeper probably understood his business better than we did, and had declined to dissipate his evidently moderate capital by investing any part of it in articles not of prime necessity. Our wants being peculiar, we could not trade with him, but after an interchange of courtesies, passed on.[2]

Two miles further, we crossed, by a bad and difficult ford, Chapman's Creek, running south to the Smoky Hill, bordered by a thin streak of timber, and meandering through a liberal valley of gloriously rich prairie. Here we passed the last settler on our road to Pike's Peak. He has been here two or three years; has seventy-five acres fenced and broken, grew three thousand bushels of corn last year, has a fine stock of horses and cattle about him, with at least eight towheaded children under ten years old. His house, judged superficially, would be dear at fifty dollars, but I think he neither needs nor wishes to be pitied.

Our road bore hence north of west, up the left bank of Chapman's Creek, on which, twenty-three miles from Junction, we halted at Station 8, at 11 A.M., to change mules and dine. (This station should be five miles further on, and three or four miles further south, but cannot be for want

[2] Richardson gives a livelier account of the incident: "At a creek-crossing, a little tent beside our road is labeled 'grocery' in enormous letters. With keen appetites we awake the melancholy merchant who in green spectacles is sleeping soundly between two whiskey barrels.
" 'Have you any crackers?'
" 'Nary cracker.'
" 'Any bread?'
" 'Any *what*?'
" 'Bread.'
" 'No *Sir*' (indignantly), 'I don't keep a bakery.'
" 'Any ham?'
" 'No.'
" 'Any figs?'
" 'No.'
" 'Well, what *have* you?'
" 'Why, I have sardines, pickled oysters, smoking tobacco, and stranger, I have got some of the best whiskey you ever seen since you was born!' " Richardson: op. cit., p. 162.

of wood and water.) There is, of course, no house here, but two small tents and a brush arbor furnish accommodations for six to fifteen persons, as the case may be. A score of mules are picketed about on the rich grass; there is a rail-pen for the two cows; of our landlady's two sun-browned children (girls of ten and six respectively), one was born in Missouri, the other at Laramie. I was told that their father was killed by Indians, and that the station-keeper is her second husband. She gave us an excellent dinner of bacon and greens, good bread, applesauce and pie, and would have given us butter had we passed a few days later; but her cows, just arrived, have been overdriven, and need a few days rest and generous feeding. The water was too muddy—the prejudices of education would not permit me to drink it—the spring being submerged by the high water of the brook, which was the only remaining resource. She apologized for making us eat in her narrow tent rather than under her brush arbor, saying that the last time she set the table there the high prairie wind made a clean sweep of tablecloth and all upon it, breaking several of her not abundant dishes. I have rarely made a better dinner, though the violent rain of the second previous night came nigh drowning out the whole concern.

We were in the wagon again a few minutes before noon (the hours kept on the Plains are good), for we had thirty-five miles yet to make today, which, with a mule team, require a long afternoon. True, the roads are harder here, less cut up, less muddy, than in Eastern Kansas; but few men think how much up and down is saved them in traveling over a civilized region by bridges and causeways over watercourses. We still kept north of west for several miles, so as to cling to the high "divide" between Chapman's Creek and Solomon's Fork (another tributary of the Smoky Hill) so far as possible. Soon we saw our first antelope, and,

63

in the course of the afternoon, five others; but not one of them seemed to place a proper estimate on the value of our society. Two of them started up so near us as to be for a moment within possible rifle shot; but they widened the gap between us directly. We crossed many old buffalo trails and buffalo heads nearly reduced to the skeleton, but no signs that buffalo have been so far east this season. Two or three of the larger watercourses we crossed had here and there a cottonwood or stunted elm on its banks, but the general dearth of timber is fearful, and in a dry season there can be little or no water on this long thirty-five miles. But it must be considered that our route avoids the streams, and of course the timber, to the utmost. The creek on which we are encamped (a branch of Solomon's) is now a fair mill-stream, but in a dry time might doubtless be run through a nine-inch ring. It has considerable wood on its banks— say a belt averaging ten rods in width.

Twenty miles back, the rock suddenly changed entirely from the universal limestone of Kansas, east of Chapman's Creek, to a decaying red sandstone; the soil hence becomes sandy and much thinner; the grass is also less luxuriant, though in some places still good. For acres, especially on the higher ridges, there is little or no soil; rock in place or slightly disturbed nearly covering the surface. Through all this region, the furious rains, rushing off in torrents without obstruction, have worn wide and devious water-courses, but they are neither deep enough nor permanently wet enough to shelter timber. I reckon "claims" will not be greedily hunted nor bought at exorbitant prices hereabouts for some years yet.

Our hostess for the night has two small tents, as at No. 8, and gave us a capital supper, butter included; but she and her two children alike testify that, in one of the drenching thunderstorms so frequent of late, they might nearly as well have been out on the prairie, and that sleeping under such a visitation is an art only to be acquired by degrees. They have a log cabin going up, I am happy to say. Their tents were first located on the narrow bottom of the creek; but a rapidly rising flood compelled them, a few nights since, to scramble out, and move them to a higher bench of prairie. It would have been pitiful to have been turned out so, only the shelter they were enjoying was good for nothing.

I believe I have now descended the ladder of artificial life nearly to its lowest round. If the Cheyennes—thirty of whom stopped the last express down on the route we must traverse, and tried to beg or steal from it—shall see fit to capture and strip us, we shall probably have further experience in the same line; but for the present the progress I have made during the last fortnight toward the primitive simplictiy of human existence may be roughly noted thus:

May 12th—Chicago—Chocolate and morning newspapers last seen on the breakfast table.

23d—Leavenworth—Room bells and baths make their final appearance.

24th—Topeka—Beefsteak and washbowls (other than tin) last visible. Barber ditto.

26th—Manhattan—Potatoes and eggs last recognized among the blessings that "brighten as they take their flight." Chairs ditto.

27th—Junction City—Last visitation of a bootblack, with dissolving views of a board bedroom. Beds bid us good-bye.

28th—Pipe Creek—Benches for seats at meals have disappeared, giving place to bags and boxes. We (two passengers of a scribbling turn) write our letters in the express wagon that has borne us by day, and must supply us lodgings for the night. Thunder and lightning from both south and west give strong promise of a shower before morning.

Dubious looks at several holes in the canvas covering of the wagon. Our trust, under Providence, is in buoyant hearts and an India-rubber blanket. Good night.

7

THE HOME OF THE BUFFALO

Station 11, Pike's Peak Express,
Clear Creek, May 29, 1859

I ceased writing No. 6 last night at midnight at Station 9—the storm, which had been threatened since dark, just bursting in the wind and rain. The wind was a gale, but upset neither tents nor wagons; the rain fell for about an hour, then ceased, though a little more fell this morning, and we have had thunder and lightning at intervals through the day, and have it still, threatening showers before dawn. We rose early from our wagon bed this morning, had breakfast at six, and soon bade adieu to Pipe Creek, with its fringe of low elms and cottonwoods, such as thinly streak all the streams we have passed today that are large enough to protect timber from prairie fires. Very soon, were off the sandstone upon limestone again, which has been the only rock visible for the last forty miles, and this but sparingly. The soil is of course improved, but I think not equal to that of Eastern Kansas. The face of the country is slightly rolling—in one place, a level prairie eleven miles wide—but even this is cut and washed out by shallow watercourses, probably dry a good part of each summer. We have crossed many streams today, all making south for Solomon's Fork, which has throughout been from two to six miles from us on our left, its narrow belt of timber constantly sending out longer or shorter spurs up the creeks which feed it on either side.

The route has been from fifty to two hundred feet above the bed of the Fork, keeping out of all bottoms and marshes, but continually cut by watercourses, often with abrupt banks and miry beds, in one of which only were we stalled until an extra span of mules was sent from the other wagon to our aid. (The express wagons always go in pairs, for reciprocal aid and security.) I presume all the timber we have passed through since we left the Republican at Junction (and we are now one hundred and ten miles from it by our route, and perhaps one hundred in a straight line) would not form a belt half a mile wide, with but a few white oaks to render it of any value except for fuel. A low, long-limbed, twisty elm, forms three-fourths of all the wood we have seen this side of Junction; the residue is mainly cottonwood. The streams are usually clear, except where riled by recent showers, and springs are not infrequent. If well timbered, this country would be rather inviting. It is largely covered with the dead stalks of the wild sunflower, which is said to indicate a good soil for corn. The sunflower plant has not started this season.

On rising our first ridge this morning, a herd of buffalo was seen grazing on the prairie some three miles toward the Solomon; soon, more were visible; then others. At length, a herd of perhaps a hundred appeared on the north—the only one we saw on that side of our road during the day. Having been observed, they were heading down the valley of a small creek toward the Solomon. Just then, the tents and wagons of a body of encamped Pike's Peakers appeared right across a little creek; two men were running across the prairie on foot to get a shot at the buffalo; another was mounting a horse with like intent. The herd passed on a long, awkward gallop north of the tents and struck southwest across our road some forty rods ahead of us. A Sharp's rifle was leveled and fired at them by one of our party, but

67

seemed rather to hasten than arrest their progress. But one old bull shambled along behind in a knock-kneed fashion (having probably been lamed by some former party); and he was fired at twice by our marksmen as he attempted to cross the road—once when only fifteen rods distant. They thought they wounded him fatally, but he vanished from our sight behind a low hill, and their hasty search for him proved unsuccessful.

Thence nearly all day, the buffalo in greater or less numbers were visible among the bottoms of the Solomon on our right[1]—usually two to three miles distant. At length, about 5 P. M., we reached the crest of a "divide," whence we looked down on the valley of a creek running to the Solomon some three miles distant, and saw the whole region from half a mile to three miles south of our road, and for an extent of at least four miles east and west, fairly alive with buffalo. There certainly were not less than ten thousand of them; I believe there were many more. Some were feeding, others lying down, others pawing up the earth, rolling on it, etc. The novel spectacle was too tempting for our sportsmen. The wagons were stopped, and two men walked quietly toward the center of the front of the herd. Favored by a watercourse, they crept up to within fifty rods of the buffalo, and fired eight or ten shots into the herd, with no visible effect. The animals nearest the hunters retreated as they advanced, but the great body of the herd was no more disturbed or conscious of danger than if a couple of mosquitoes had alighted among them. After an hour of this fruitless effort, the hunters gave it up, alleging that their rifle was so foul and badly sighted as to be worthless. They rejoined us, and we came away, leaving nine-tenths of the vast herd exactly where we found them. And there they

[1] Greeley contradicts himself here. Earlier in this dispatch he says Solomon's Fork is on his left.

doubtless are sleeping at this moment, about three miles from us.

We are near the heart of the buffalo region. The stages from the west that met us here this evening report the sight of millions within the last two days. Their trails checker the prairie in every direction. A company of Pike's Peakers killed thirteen near this point a few days since. Eight were killed yesterday at the next station west of this by simply stampeding a herd and driving them over a high creek bank, where so many broke their necks. Buffalo meat is hanging or lying all around us, and a calf two or three months old is tied to a stake just beside our wagons. He was taken by rushing a herd up a steep creek bank, which so many could not possibly climb at once; this one was picked out in the melee as most worth having, and taken with a rope. Though fast-tied and with but a short tether, he is true game, and makes at whoever goes near him with desperate intent to butt the intruder over. We met or passed today two parties of Pike's Peakers who had respectively lost three oxen or steers, stampeded last night by herds of buffalo. The mules at the express stations have to be carefully watched to preserve them from a similar catastrophe—to their owners.

I do not like the flesh of this wild ox. It is tough and not juicy. I do not forget that our cookery is of the most unsophisticated pattern—carrying us back to the age of the building of the Pyramids, at least—but I would much rather see an immense herd of buffalo on the prairie than eat the best of them.

The herbage hereabout is nearly all the short, strong grass known as the buffalo grass, and is closely fed down; we are far beyond the stakes of the land surveyor—beyond the usual haunts of white men. The Santa Fé trail is far south of us; the California is considerably north. Very probably, the buffalo on Solomon's Fork were never hunted by white men till this spring. Should one of these countless herds take a fancy for a manhunt, our riflemen would find even the express wagons no protection.

Though our road is hardly two months old, yet we passed two graves on it today. One is that of an infant, born in a tent of the wife of one of the stationmasters on her way to his post, and which lived but a day; the other that of a Missourian on his way to Pike's Peak, who was accidentally shot in taking a rifle from his wagon. His party seems to have been singularly unfortunate. A camp or two further on, a hurricane overtook them and tore their six wagons into oven wood; they were able to make but three passable wagons out of the remains. Their loss in other property was serious, and they sustained much bodily harm. One more of them was buried a camp or two further on.

Those whom we meet here coming down confirm the worst news we have had from the Peak. There is scarcely any gold there; those who dig cannot average two shillings per day; all who can get away are leaving; Denver and Auraria are nearly deserted; terrible sufferings have been endured on the Plains, and more must yet be encountered; hundreds would gladly work for their board, but cannot find employment—in short, Pike's Peak is an exploded bubble, which thousands must bitterly rue to the end of their days. Such is the tenor of our latest advices. I have received none this side of Leavenworth that contradict them. My inform-ant says all are getting away who can, and that we shall find the region nearly deserted. That is likely, but we shall see.

A young clerk with whom I conversed at supper gave me a little less discouraging account; but even he, having frozen his feet on the winter journey out, had had enough of gold-hunting, and was going home to his parents in Indiana, to stick to school for a few years. I commended that as a wise resolution. Next morning, after we had started on our opposite ways, I was apprised by our conductor that said clerk was a woman! I had not dreamed of such a thing; but his more practical or more suspicious eyes had seen through her disguise at once. We heard more of her at Denver—quite enough more—but this may as well be left untold.

8

LAST OF THE BUFFALO

Station 13, Pike's Peak Express Co.,
Reisinger's Creek, May 31, 1859

I would rather not bore the public with buffalo. I fully realize that the subject is not novel—that Irving, and Cooper, and many others, have written fully and admirably upon it; and that the traveler's enthusiastic recital falls coldly on the ear of the distant, critical, unsympathizing reader. Yet I insist on writing this once more on buffalo, promising then to drop the subject, as we pass out of the range of the buffalo before night. All day yesterday, they darkened the earth around us, often seeming to be drawn up like an army in battle array on the ridges and adown their slopes a mile or so south of us—often on the north as well. They are rather shy of the little screens of straggling timber on the creek bottoms—doubtless from their sore experience of Indians lurking therein to discharge arrows at them as they went down to drink. If they feed in the grass of the narrow valleys and ravines, they are careful to have a part of the herd on the ridges which overlook them, and with them the surrounding country for miles. And, when an alarm is given, they all rush furiously off in the direction which the leaders presume that of safety.

This is what gives us such excellent opportunities for regarding them to the best advantage. They are moving northward, and are still mainly south of our track. Whenever alarmed, they set off on their awkward but effective canter to the great herds still south, or to haunts with which they are comparatively familiar, and wherein they have hitherto found safety. This necessarily sends those north of us across our roads often but a few rods in front of us, even when they had started a mile away. Then a herd will commence running across a hundred rods ahead of us, and, the whole blindly following their leader, we will be close upon them before the last will have cleared the track. Of course, they sometimes stop and tack, or, seeing us, sheer off and cross further ahead, or split into two lines; but the general impulse, when alarmed, is to follow blindly and at full speed, seeming not to inquire or consider from what quarter danger is to be apprehended.

What strikes the stranger with most amazement is their immense numbers. I know a million is a great many, but I am confident we saw that number yesterday. Certainly, all we saw could not have stood on ten square miles of ground. Often, the country for miles on either hand seemed quite black with them. The soil is rich, and well matted with their favorite grass. Yet it is all (except a very little on the creek bottoms, near to timber) eaten down like an overtaxed sheep pasture in a dry August. Consider that we have traversed more than one hundred miles in width since we first struck them, and that for most of this distance the buffalo have been constantly in sight, and that they continue for some twenty-five miles further on—this being the breath of their present range, which has a length of perhaps a thousand miles—and you have some approach to an idea of their countless myriads. I doubt whether the domesticated horned cattle of the United States equal the numbers, while they must fall considerably short in weight, of these wild ones. Margaret Fuller long ago observed that the Illinois prairies seemed to repel the idea of being new to civilized life and industry—that they, with their borders of trees and belts of timber, reminded the traveler rather of the parks and spacious fields of an old country like England —that you were constantly on the involuntary lookout for the chateaux, or at least the humbler farmhouses, which should diversify such a scene. True as this is or was of Illinois, the resemblance is far more striking here, where the grass is all so closely pastured and the cattle are seen in such vast herds on every ridge. The timber, too, aids the illusion, seeming to have been reduced to the last degree consistent with the wants of a grazing country, and to have been left only on the steep creek banks where grass would not grow. It is hard to realize that this is the center of a region of wilderness and solitude, so far as the labors of civilized man are concerned—that the first wagon passed through it some two months ago. But the utter absence of houses or buildings of any kind, and our unbridged, unworked road, winding on its way for hundreds of miles without a track other than of buffalo intersecting or leading away from it on either hand, bring us back to the reality.

I shall pass lightly over the hunting exploits of our party. A good many shots have been fired—certainly not by me; even were I in the habit of making war on nature's children, I would as soon think of shooting my neighbor's oxen as these great, clumsy, harmless creatures. If they were scarce, I might comprehend the idea of hunting them for sport; here, they are so abundant that you might as well hunt your neighbor's geese. And, while there have been several shots fired by our party at point-blank distance, I have reason for my hope that no buffalo has experienced any personal inconvenience therefrom. For this impunity, the foulness of the rifle has had to answer in part; the greenness of the sportsmen is perhaps equally responsible for it. But then we have had no horse or mule out of our regular teams, and the candid will admit that a coach-and-four is not precisely the fittest turn-out for a hunting party.

I write in the station tent (having been driven from our wagon by the operation of greasing its wheels, which was found to interfere with the steadiness of my hastily improvised table), with the buffalo visible on the ridges south and every way but north of us. They were very close down to us at daylight, until the increasing light revealed distinctly our position, since which they have kept a respectful distance. But a party of our drivers, who went back seven miles on mules last evening, to help get our rear wagon out of a gully in which it had mired and stuck fast, from which expedition they returned at midnight, report that they found the road absolutely dangerous from the crowds of buffalo feeding on either side, and running across it—that, the night being quite dark, they were often in great danger of being run over and run down by the headlong brutes. They were obliged to stand still for minutes, and fire their revolvers right and left, to save their lives and their mules.

The superintendent of this division, Mr. Fuller, had a narrow escape day before yesterday. He was riding his mule along our road, utterly unconscious of danger, when a herd of buffalo north of the road were stampeded by an emigrant train, and set off full gallop in a southwesterly direction, as usual. A slight ridge hid them from Mr. F.'s sight till their leader came full tilt against his mule, knocking him down, and going over him at full speed. Mr. F. of course fell with the dying mule, and I presume lay very snug by his side while the buffaloes made a clear sweep

74

over the concern—he firing his revolver rapidly, and thus inducing many of the herd to shear off on one side or the other. He rose stunned and bruised, but still able to make his way to the station—with an increased respect for buffalo, I fancy, and a disposition to give them a reasonably wide berth hereafter. But he has gone out this morning in quest of the mired coach, and our waiting for his return gives me this chance to write without encroaching on the hours due to sleep.

Two nights ago, an immense herd came down upon a party of Pike's Peakers camped just across the creek from this station, and (it being dark) were with difficulty prevented from trampling down tents, cattle, and people. Some fifty shots were fired into them before they could be turned. And now our stationmaster has just taken his gun to scare them off so as to save our mules from a stampede.

But the teams have returned with the missing coach, and I must break off and pack to go on.

Station 15, Prairie Dog Creek, May 31, evening

We have made fifty-five miles since we started about nine this morning, and our present encampment is on a creek running to the Republican, so that we have bidden a final adieu to Solomon's Fork, and all other affluents of the Smoky Hill branch of the Kansas. We traveled on the "divide" between this and the northern branch of the Kansas for some miles today, and finally came over to the waters of that stream (the Republican), which we are to strike some eighty miles further on. We are now just halfway from Leavenworth to Denver, and our coach has been a week making this distance; so that with equal good fortune we may expect to reach the land of gold in another week. The coaches we met here tonight have been just a week on the

75

way, having (like us) lost a day, but not, like us, by high water: their bother was with wild Indians, Arapahoes mainly, whom they report to be in great numbers on our route—not hostile to us, but intent on begging or stealing, and stopping the wagons peremptorily till their demands are complied with. They are at war with the Pawnees, and most of their men are now on the warpath; their women and children are largely camped around the express company's stations, living as they best may. The Pawnees, I believe, are mainly or entirely south of our road. The Arapahoes boast of triumphs and slaughters which, I am tempted to hope, have been or will be reciprocated. Indian wars with each other are, in our day, cruel and cowardly plundering forays, fitted to excite only disgust.

As we left Station 14 this morning, and rose from the creek bottom to the high prairie, a great herd of buffalo were seen in and around our road, who began to run first north, then south, many standing as if confused and undecided which course to take, and when at last they all started southward, we were so near them that our driver stopped his mules to let the immense impetuous herd pass without doing us any harm. Our sportsman's Sharp was not loaded at the time; it afterward was, and fired into a herd at fair distance, but I did not see anything drop. After this, they were seen in greater or less numbers on the ridges and high prairie, mainly south of us, but they either kept a respectful distance or soon took one. We have not seen one for the last twenty-five miles; but they are now considerably further this way than they were a few days since; and as every foot of the way thus far, and (I hear) further, is carpeted with buffalo grass, not here eaten down, and as buffalo paths and other evidences that this is their favorite feeding ground are everywhere present, I presume they will be here in the course of a week. But enough of them. And

76

let me here proffer my acknowledgements to sundry other quadrupeds with whom I have recently formed a passing acquaintance.

The prairie wolf was the first of these gentry to pay his respects to us. He is a sneaking, cowardly little wretch, of a dull or dirty white color, much resembling a small, short-bodied dog set up on pretty long legs. I believe his only feat entitling him to rank as a beast of prey consists in sometimes, when hard pressed by hunger, digging out a prairie dog and making a meal of him. His usual provender is the carcass—no matter how putrid—of any dead buffalo, mule, or ox that he may find exposed on the prairies. He is a paltry creature.

But the gray wolf—who is also a denizen of the prairies—(I think we have seen at least a dozen of the species today)—is a scoundrel of much more imposing caliber. He delights to lurk around the outskirts of a herd of buffalo, keeping out of sight and unsuspected in the ravines and creek timber, so far as possible; and woe to the unlucky calf that strays (which he seldom does) outside of the exterior line of defense formed by the bulls. If very large and hungry, the gray wolf will sometimes manage to cut a cow off from the herd, and, interposing between her and her companions, detain or drive her further away, until she is beyond the hope of rescue, when her doom is sealed. His liveliest hope, however, is that of finding a buffalo whom some hunter has wounded, so that he cannot keep up with the herd, especially should it be stampeded. Let him once get such a one by himself, and a few snaps at his hamstrings, taking excellent care to keep out of the way of his horns, insures that the victim will have ceased to be a buffalo, and become mere wolf meat before another morning.

It is impossible for a stranger to the prairies to realize the impudence of these prairie lawyers. Of some twenty of them that I have seen within the last two days, I think not six have really run from us. One that we saw just before us, two hours ago, kept on his way across the prairie, stopping occasionally to take a good look at us, but not hurrying himself in the least on our account, though for some minutes within good rifle range. Once today, our superintendent sent a ball after one who was making very deliberate time away from us, hitting him in a quarter where the compliment should have expedited his movements; but it did not seem to have that effect. It is very common for these wolves to follow at night a man traveling the road on a mule, not making any belligerent demonstrations, but waiting for whatever may turn up. Sometimes the express wagons have been followed in this way, but I think that unusual. But this creature is up to anything wherein there is a chance for game.

The prairie dog is the funny fellow of these parts—frisky himself, and a source of merriment to others. He dens in villages or towns, on any dry, grassy ground—usually on the dryest part of the high prairie—and his hole is superficially a very large anthill, with the necessary orifice in its center. On this anthill sits the proprietor—a chunky little fellow, in size between a gray squirrel and a rabbit—say about half a woodchuck. When we approach, he raises the cry of danger—no bark at all, but something between the piping of a frog on a warm spring evening, and the noise made by a very young puppy—then drops into his hole and is silent and invisible. The holes are not very regularly placed, but some thirty feet apart; and when I say that I believe we have today passed within sight of at least three square miles of these holes, the reader can guess how many of these animals must exist here, even supposing that there is usually but one to each hole. I judge that there cannot be less than a hundred square miles of prairie-dog towns within the present buffalo range.

That the prairie dog and the owl—of a small, brown-backed, white-bellied species—do live harmoniously in the same hole, I know, for I have seen it. I presume the owl pays for his lodgings like a gentleman, probably by turning in some provisions toward the supply of the common table. If so, this is the most successful example of industrial and household association yet furnished. That the rattlesnake is ever admitted as a third partner, I indignantly deny.[1] No doubt he has been found in the prairie dog's home—it would be just like him to seek so cozy a nest—but he doubtless entered like a true border ruffian, and contrived to make himself a deal more free than welcome. Politeness, or (if you please) prudence, may have induced the rightful owner to submit to a joint tenancy at will—the will of the tenant, not that of the rightful landlord—but no consent was ever given, unless under constraint of that potent logic which the intruder carries in his head, and warning whereof proceeds from the tip of his tail.

Of antelope, I have seen many, but not so near at hand as I could wish. I defer speaking of them, in the hope of a better acquaintance.

A word now of the face of the country:

For more than a hundred miles back, I have seen no stone, and think there is none, except at a great depth. Solomon's Fork, where we left its vicinity, is now a stream two rods wide, running but four to six inches of water over a bed of pure sand, at a depth of some three or four hundred feet below the high prairie level of the country. I infer that there is no rock in place for at least that depth. The subsoil of the prairies is generally a loamy clay, resting on a bed of sand. The violent though not frequent rains of this region form sheets of water, which rush down the slopes into the watercourses, which they rapidly swell into torrents, which, meeting no resistance from rocks or roots

[1] A bit later he eats these words.

of trees, are constantly deepening or widening the ravines which run down to the creeks on every side. These gullies or gorges have originally steep, perpendicular banks, over which, in times of heavy rain, sheets of water go tumbling and roaring into the bottom of the ravines, washing down the sodden, semi-liquid banks, and sending them to thicken the waters of the Kansas and the Missouri. Thus the prairie, save some narrow, irregular ridges, or "divides," is gradually scooped and worn into broader or narrower valleys, some of which have three or four little precipices at intervals up their sides, where they formerly had but one, and will eventually have none. For still the soil is washing away and running off to the Gulf of Mexico; and if this country should ever be cultivated, the progress of this disaster would be materially accelerated. It needs to be timbered before it can be fit for the habitation of civilized man. But still a few low cottonwoods and elms along the margins of the larger streams—not a cord of wood in all to each square mile— are all the timber that is be seen. I hear of some poor oak on the broader streams, and an occasional white ash, but do not see them.

The prairie wind shaking the wagon so that I write in it with difficulty, bespeaks a storm at hand. Adieu!

9

THE AMERICAN DESERT

Station 18, Pike's Peak Express Co., June 2, 1859

The clouds, which threatened rain at the station on Prairie Dog Creek, whence I wrote two days ago, were dissipated by a violent gale, which threatened to overturn the heavy wagon in which my fellow passengers[1] and I were courting sleep—had it stood broadside to the wind, it must have gone over. It is customary, I learn, to stake down the wagons encamped on the open prairie; in the valleys of the creeks, where the company's stations are located, this precaution is deemed superfluous. But the winds which sweep the high prairies of this region are terrible; and the few trees that grow thinly along the creek bottoms rarely venture to raise their heads above the adjacent bluffs, to which they owe their doubtful hold on existence.

For more than a hundred miles back, the soil has been steadily degenerating, until here, where we strike the Republican, which has been far to the north of us since we left it at Fort Riley, three hundred miles back, we seem to have reached the acme of barrenness and desolation. We left this morning, Station 17, on a little creek entitled Gouler, at least thirty miles back, and did not see a tree and but one bunch of low shrubs in a dry watercourse throughout our dreary morning ride, till we came in sight of the Republican, which has a little—a very little—scrubby cottonwood nested in and along its bluffs just here; but there is none beside for miles, save a little lurking in a ravine which makes down to the river from the north. Of grass there is little, and that little of miserable quality—either a scanty furze or coarse alkaline sort of rush, less fit for food than physic. Soil there is none but an inch or so of intermittent grass-root tangle, based on what usually seems to be a thin stratum of clay, often washed off so as to leave nothing but a slightly argillaceous sand. Along the larger watercourses—this one especially— this sand seems to be as pure as Sahara can boast.

The dearth of water is fearful. Although the whole region

[1] In describing the wreck a bit later, Greeley speaks of "my fellow *passenger*." There is no evidence that any persons other than he, Richardson, and driver were on the stage. It is possible, though unlikely, that there were some short-haul passengers between stations.

is deeply seamed and gullied by watercourses—now dry, but in rainy weather millstreams—no springs burst from their steep sides. We have not passed a drop of living water in all our morning's ride, and but a few pailfuls of muddy moisture at the bottoms of a very few of the fast-drying sloughs or sunken holes in the beds of dried-up creeks. Yet there has been much rain here this season, some of it not long ago. But this is a region of sterility and thirst. If utterly unfed, the grass of a season would hardly suffice, when dry, to nourish a prairie fire.

Even the animals have deserted us. No buffalo have been seen this year within many miles of us, though their old paths lead occasionally across this country; I presume they pass rapidly through it, as I should urgently advise them to do; not a graywolf has honored us with his company to-day—he prefers to live where there is something to eat—the prairie dog also wisely shuns this land of starvation; no animal but the gopher (a little creature, between a mouse and a ground squirrel) abounds here; and he burrows deep in the sand and picks up a living, I cannot guess how; while a few hawks and an occasional prairie wolf (coyote) lives by picking here and there a gopher. They must find him disgustingly lean.

I would match this station and its surroundings against any other scene on our continent for desolation. From the high prairie over which we approach it, you overlook a grand sweep of treeless desert, through the middle of which flows the Republican, usually in several shallow streams separated by sandbars or islets—its whole volume being far less than that of the Mohawk at Utica, though it has drained above this point an area equal to that of Connecticut. Of the few scrubby cottonwoods lately cowering under the bluffs at this point, most have been cut for the uses of the station, though logs for its embryo house are drawn from a little clump, eight miles distant. A broad bed of sand indicates that the volume of water is sometimes a hundredfold its present amount, though it will doubtless soon be far less than it now is. Its average depth cannot now exceed six inches. On every hand, and for many miles above and below, the country above the bluffs is such as we have passed over this morning. A dead mule—bitten in the jaw this morning by a rattlesnake—lies here as if to complete the scene. Off the five-weeks-old track to Pike's Peak, all is dreary solitude and silence.

Speaking of rattlesnakes—I hasten to retract the skepticism avowed in a former letter as to the usual and welcome residence of these venomous serpents in the prairie dog's burrow. The evidence of the fact is too direct and reliable to be gainsayed. A credible witness testifies that he and others once undertook to drown out a prairie dog in his domicile, and, when sufficient water had been rapidly poured in, out came a prairie dog, an owl, and a rattlesnake all together. In another case, a tremendous rain raised a creek so that it suddenly overflowed a prairie-dog town, when the general stampede of prairie dogs, owls, and rattlesnakes was a sight to behold. It is idle to attempt holding out against facts; so I have pondered this anomaly until I think I clearly comprehend it. The case is much like that of some newspaper establishments, whose proprietors, it is said, find it convenient to keep on their staff "a broth of a boy" from Tipperary, standing six feet two in his stockings and measuring a yard or more across the shoulders, who stands ready, with an illegant brogue, a twinkle in his eye, and a hickory sapling firmly grasped in his dexter fist, to respond to all choleric, peremptory customers, who call of a morning, hot with wrath and bristling with cowhide, to demand a parley with the editor. The coyote is a gentleman of an inquiring, investigating turn, who is an adept at excavation, and whose fondness

for prairie dog is more ardent than flattering. To dig one out
and digest him would be an easy task, if he were alone in his
den, or with only the owl as his partner; but when the firm
is known or strongly suspected to be Prairie Dog, Rattlesnake & Co., the coyote's passion for subterranean researches
is materially cooled. The rattlesnake is to the concern what
the fighting editor is to the journalistic organizations aforesaid. And thus, while my faith is enlarged, is my reason
satisfied.[2]

A word now on the antelope. I liked him when I first saw
him, days ago; I then wished for a better acquaintance, which
wish has since been gratified; and since I dined with him
(that is, off of him), my esteem has ripened into affection.
Of the many antelopes I have seen, I judge a majority considerably larger than the deer of our eastern forests—not so
tall nor (perhaps) so long, but heavier in body, while hardly
less swift or less graceful in motion. He is the only animal
I have seen here that may justly boast of either grace or
beauty. His flesh is tender and delicate—the choicest eating
I have found in Kansas. Shy and fleet as he is, he is the
chief sustenance at this season of the Indians out of the present buffalo range. An old hunter assures me that, with all
his timidity, he is easily taken by the knowing. To follow
him is absurd; his scent is too keen, his fear too great; but
go upon a high prairie, to a knoll or swell whence you can
overlook fifteen or twenty square miles; there crouch in a
hollow or in the grass, and hoist your handkerchief, or some
red, fluttering scarf on a light pole, which you wave gently
and patiently in the air; soon the antelope, if there be one
within sight, perceives the strange apparition: his curiosity is
excited; it masters his caution; he makes toward the strange

[2] It is for the reader to decide whether Greeley really became convinced that the rattlesnake lives with the owl and the prairie dog, or
just pretended to reverse himself for the sake of his rather labored
joke.

object, and keeps drawing nearer and nearer till he is within fifteen or twenty rods. The rest requires no instruction.

Station 21, June 3, evening, 1859

Since I wrote the foregoing, we have traveled ninety miles up the south branch of the Republican (which forks just above Station 18) and have thus pursued a course somewhat south of west. In all these ninety miles, we have passed just two live streams making in from the south—both together running scarcely water enough to turn a grindstone. In all these ninety miles, we have not seen wood enough to make a decent pig-pen. The bottom of the river is perhaps half a mile in average width; the soil in good part clay and covered with a short, thin grass; the bluffs are naked sand-heaps; the rock, in the rare cases where any is exposed, an odd conglomerate of petrified clay with quartz and some specks that resemble cornelian. Beside this, in some of the bluffs, where clay overlies and is blended, under peculiar circumstances, with the sand below it, a sort of rock seems to be formed or in process of formation. Water is obtained from the apology for a river, or by digging in the sand by its side; in default of wood, corrals (cattle-pens) are formed at the stations by laying up a heavy wall of clayey earth flanked by sods, and thus excavating a deep ditch on the inner side, except at the portal, which is closed at night by running a wagon into it. The tents are sodded at their bases; houses of sods are to be constructed so soon as may be. Such are the shifts of human ingenuity in a country which has probably not a cord of growing wood to each township of land.

Six miles further up, this fork of the Republican emerges from its sandy bed, in which it has been lost for the twenty-five miles next above. Of course, it loses in volume in passing

85

through such a land of drought. Probably thirty times today we have crossed the broad sandy beds of creeks running down from the high prairies—creeks which in winter and early spring are sweeping torrents, but now are wastes of thirsty sand. Thus has it been for ninety miles—thus is it for many miles above and I presume many also below. The road from Leavenworth to Denver had to be taken some fifty miles north of its due course to obtain even such a passage through the American desert; on a direct line from the head of Solomon's Fork, it must have passed over some two hundred miles of entire absence of wood and water.

I have seen, during the last three or four days, several bands of wild Indians—Arapahoes, Cheyennes, Kioways, Sioux, etc.—mainly the two former. Of these, the Arapahoes have been the most numerous and repulsive. Their children swarmed around us at Station 16—the men being mainly absent on a marauding expedition against the Pawnees—the women staying in their lodges. The young ones are thorough savages—their allowance of clothing averaging six inches square of buffalo skin to each, but so unequally distributed (as is the case with worldly goods in general) that the majority have a most scanty allowance. A large Cheyenne village is encamped around Station 19, where we stopped last night; and we have been meeting squads of these and other tribes several times a day. The Kioways are camped some eight miles from this spot. They all profess to be friendly, though the Cheyennes have twice stopped and delayed the express wagons on pretence of claiming payment for the injury done them in cutting wood, eating grass, scaring away game, etc. They would all like to beg, and many of them are deemed not disinclined to steal. We are to pass through several more encampments, but expect no trouble from them. The Cheyennes are better clad, and seem to have more self-respect than the Arapahoes, but they are

86

all low in the scale of intellectual and moral being, and must fade away unless they can be induced to work. More of them hereafter.

The unusual dullness of this letter is partly explained by an accident. Two evenings since, just as we were nearing Station 17, where we were to stop for the night, my fellow passenger and I had a jocular discussion on the gullies into which we were so frequently plunged, to our personal discomfort. He premised that it was a consolation that the sides of these gullies could not be worse than perpendicular; to which I rejoined with the assertion that they could be and were—for instance, where a gully, in addition to its perpendicular descent, had an inclination of forty-five degrees or so to one side of the track. Just then, a violent lurch of the wagon to one side, then to the other, in descending one of these jolts, enforced my position. Two minutes later, as we were about to descend the steep bank of the creek intervale, the mules acting perversely (being frightened, I fear, by Indians), my friend stepped out to take them by the head, leaving me alone in the wagon. Immediately we began to descend the steep pitch, the driver pulling up with all his might, when the left rein of the leaders broke, and the team was in a moment sheared out of the road and ran diagonally down the pitch. In a second, the wagon went over, hitting the ground a most spiteful blow. I of course went over with it, and when I rose to my feet as soon as possible, considerably bewildered and disheveled, the mules had been disengaged by the upset and were making good time across the prairie, while the driver, considerably hurt, was getting out from under the carriage to limp after them. I had a slight cut on my left cheek and a deep gouge from the sharp corner of a seat in my left leg below the knee, with a pretty smart concussion generally, but not a bone started nor a tendon strained, and I walked away to the station as firmly as ever, leaving the superintendent and my fellow passenger to pick up the pieces and guard the baggage from the Indians who instantly swarmed about the wreck. I am sore yet, and a little lame, but three of four day's rest—if I can ever get it—will make all right.[3] This is the first and only accident that has happened to the express line, though it has run out some thirty passage wagons from Leavenworth, and perhaps half so many back from Denver, over a track where there was no track six weeks ago. And this was the result of a casualty for which neither driver nor company was to blame.

Three days hence, I hope to be at Denver (one hundred and eighty-five miles distant), whence our latest advices are very cheering to the hearts of the legions of faint and weary gold-seekers we have passed on the way. I trust, for their sakes, that this news will prove fully true.

[3] Richardson's more colorful account doesn't quite square with Greeley's in all details. "Descending an abrupt hill, our mules, terrified by meeting three savages, broke a line, ran down a precipitous bank, upsetting the coach which was hurled upon the ground with a tremendous crash, and galloped away with the fore-wheels. I sprang out in time to escape being overturned. From a mass of cushions, carpet-sacks and blankets soon emerged my companion, his head arising above the side of the vehicle like that of an advertising boy from his frame of pasteboard. Blood was flowing profusely from cuts in his cheek, arm and leg; but his face was serene and benignant as a May morning. He was soon rescued from his cage, and taken to Station Seventeen, a few yards beyond, where the good woman dressed his galling wounds." Richardson: op. cit., p. 173.

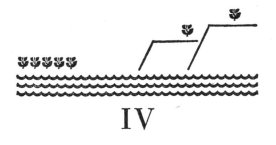

IV

COLORADO

Dispatches 10 through 15

In the weeks preceding Greeley's arrival there on June 6, 1859, newborn Denver was in imminent danger of going the way of many a Western boom town. Disgruntled and empty-handed gold-seekers were heading back home about as fast as the eager newcomers came pouring in. By mid-May it seemed likely that Denver's population would be smaller by the end of the summer than it had been a year earlier.[1] Many Eastern editors had already picked up the cry of "Hoax!" and newspapers carried lurid stories of the suffering and violence brought on by the desperate plight of the "Pikers."

[1] Robert L. Perkin: *The First Hundred Years: An Informal History of Denver and the Rocky Mountain News* (New York: Doubleday and Co.; 1959), p. 97.

89

*Fighting a game but seemingly hopeless one-man battle
to stem the eastward tide was William H. Byers, founder and
editor of the* Rocky Mountain News, *first paper in the region
(and still going strong after more than a hundred years'
continuous publication). Byers used cajolery, ridicule, indignation, humor, and every other form of persuasion at his
command—coining a new word, "gobacks," in the process—
but without noticeable effect. Then, by remarkable coincidence, two things happened almost at once: rich new strikes
were made in the mountains west of Denver, and Horace
Greeley arrived in town.*

*So stiff and sore he had to be lifted from his mule, Greeley
went to the diggings, saw the gold for himself, collaborated
with two other journalists in writing a report on the spot,
and sent the story off at once to Byers back in Denver. Byers
rushed into print with an "extra," printed on brown wrap-
ping paper because he had no regular newsprint at the time,
and Denver was saved.*

"The News *extra sped eastward along the lines of returning emigrants, and the name of Greeley was magic," writes
the historian of the* Rocky Mountain News. *"The great* Tribune *crusader . . . would never lend himself to a hoax. The
report, Richardson wrote, 'was widely copied throughout the
country as the first specific, disinterested and trustworthy
account of the newly-discovered placers.' The brown-paper
broadside, an ugly little sheet, had changed the prospects of
an infant city from dismal to bright."* [2]

*No hint of his role in this drama, or even of the drama it-
self, is found in Greeley's journal.*

[2] Perkin: op. cit., p. 119.

10

GOOD-BYE TO THE DESERT

Denver, June 6, 1859

My last, I believe, was written at Station 21, ninety miles
up the Republican from the point at which the Leavenworth
Express Company's road strikes that river in the great
American desert. Six miles farther up, the stream disappears
in the deep, thirsty sands of its wide bed, and is not seen
again for twenty-five miles. Even a mile or two below its
point of disappearance, I learn that recent excavations in
its bed to a depth of eight feet have failed to reach water.
Its reappearance below this point is marked, and seems to
be caused by the timely junction of a small tributary from
the south, which appears to flow over a less thirsty bed,
and pours into the devouring sands of the Republican a
small but steady stream, aided by which the river begins
to reappear, first in pools, and soon in an insignificant but
gradually increasing current. At the head of this "sink,"
the stream disappears in like manner to that of its emergence.
Here is Station 22, and here are a so-called spring, and one
or two considerable pools, not visibly connected with the
sinking river, but doubtless sustained by it. And here the
thirsty men and teams, which have been twenty-five miles
without water on the Express Company's road, are met
by those which have come up the longer and more southerly
route by the Smoky Hill, and which have traveled *sixty*
miles since they last found water or shade. This is a sore
trial for weary, gaunt, heavy-laden cattle, and doubtless
proves fatal to many of them. The Pike's Peakers from the
Smoky Hill whom I met here had driven their ox teams
through the sixty miles at one stretch, the time required

being two days and the intervening night. From this point westward, the original Smoky Hill route is abandoned for that we had been traveling, which follows the Republican some twenty-five miles further. Its bed is often dry, or only moistened by little pools exuding from the meager current which filters slowly through the deep sands below. Where the bed is narrow and the channel under one bank, the petty stream is seen creeping slowly away to the Kansas, the Missouri, the Mississippi, the Gulf of Mexico. Of course there are seasons when the river runs above ground throughout, and others when the "sink" is far longer than now.

The face of the country remains as I have already described it, save in the greater scarcity of wood and water. The bluffs are usually low, and the dry creeks which separate them are often wide reaches of heavy sand, most trying to the ill-fed teams. There is little grass on the rolling prairie above the bluffs, and that little generally thin, dead, worthless. Some of the dry-creek valleys have a little that is green but thin, while the river bottom—often half a mile wide— is sometimes tolerably grassed, and sometimes sandy and sterile. Of wood, there is none for stretches of forty or fifty miles: the corrals are made of earth, and consist of a trench and a mud or turf wall; one or two station houses are to be built of turf if ever built at all; and at one station the fuel is brought sixty miles from the pineries further west. Even the grasses are often coarse and rushy, or so alkaline as to be injurious to cattle; the more common plants seem to be wild sage and wild wormwood. The cactus—which had begun to appear some two hundred miles back—grows common, but is dwarfed by the pervading sterility; the Spanish nettle and prickly pear are abundant further on. But little rock is seen, and that looks like a volcanic conglomerate. Yet the river, such as it is, is the life of this region; the ground squirrel of the prairies digs his holes profusely in its vicinage; the hawk and the raven circle and swoop in pursuit of him; the antelope often looks down from the ridges, and is hunted with success; the bark of the coyote is heard; the gray wolf prowls fearless and ferocious, and does not hesitate to rob cows of their young calves in spite of the desperate maternal resistance, and even to attack and disable ponies. The harness of the mules which draw the express wagons have been often gnawed and injured as they hung up beside the tents, in which half a dozen men were sleeping, by these impudent miscreants. They may easily be shot by anyone who will bait and patiently, skillfully hunt them.

A ride over a rolling "divide" of some twenty miles brought us to the Big Sandy, running southwest to become tributary (when it has anything to contribute) to the Arkansas. Like the Republican, it is sometimes a running stream, sometimes a succession of shallow pools, sometimes a waste of deep, scorching sand. A few paltry cottonwoods, a few bunches of low willow, may have graced its banks or those of some dry creek running in to it, in the course of the twenty miles or so that we followed up its northern bank, but I do not now remember any. I recollect only that the grass at intervals along its narrow bottoms seemed a little better than on the upper course of the Republican. One peculiarity of the Big Sandy I had not before observed—that of a thin, alkaline incrustation—mainly of soda, I believe—covering many acres of the smoother sands in its dry bed. Hence I infer that the water of its stagnant pools must be prejudicial to man or beast. At length we crossed its deep, trying sand and left it behind us, passing over a high "divide," much cut up by gullies through which the water of the wet seasons tears its way to the Arkansas on the south or the Platte on the north, until we struck, at five last evening, the first living tributary to the Platte—a little

93

creek called Beaver, which I have not seen on any map. It is about ten miles east of the Bijou, with which it probably unites before reaching the Platte.

After leaving the valley of Big Sandy, the grass of the uplands becomes better, and is no longer confined to the watercourses. It spreads in green luxuriance up the southward slopes of considerable hills, which seems to be owing to vast drifts of snow in winter, swept over and off the tops of hills by the fierce prairie winds, and piled up here to a height of fifteen or twenty feet, to be slowly dissolved by the warmer suns of the spring months, and thus give rise to an aftergrowth of grass which contrasts strongly with the surrounding sterility.

At Beaver Creek we saw, for the first time in many weary days—for more than two hundred miles at the least—a clump of low but sturdy cottonwoods, thirty or forty in number—part of them laid low by the devastating axe, but still giving hope that the desert was nearly past. And, six or seven miles further, just as night was falling, we came in sight of pines, giving double assurance that the mountains were at hand. Pike's Peak in the west-southwest, and Long's Peak in the west-northwest (the latter nearly the direction of Denver), had stood revealed to us hours before, by the gleam of their snowy diadems, as the morning sun dispelled the chill mists of the preceding night; but their majesty was a bleak and rugged one;[1] while the pines, though but scattered clumps of the short and scrubby variety known in New England and the south as pitch pine, lent a grace and hospitality to the landscape which only the weary and wayworn, who have long traversed parched and shadeless deserts, can appreciate. They grow here mainly in steep

[1] The stagecoach was now in the vicinity of present-day Limon, Colorado, approximately 185 air miles from Long's Peak and 80 miles from Pike's Peak.

ravines, and often show marks of fire which the bareness of the surrounding prairies—sterile as "pine plains" are apt to be—renders to me inexplicable. Possibly, the fires that scorched them were kindled in the leafy carpet spread beneath them by the trees themselves.

This is but the northern outskirt of the pine region, which stretches far south, through Arkansas and beyond, soon thickening into forests and widening to a breadth of some sixty miles. Scattered as it is, I could hardly repress a shout on meeting it. And it was a pleasure to see, last evening, the many parties of wayworn gold-seekers encamped beside our way, after their long journey through a woodless region, surrounding great, ruddy, leaping fires of the dead pitchwood, and solacing themselves for their long privation by the amplest allowance of blaze and warmth; for the climate of the American desert is terrible. Be the day ever so hot in the sun's unsoftened glare, the night that follows is sure to be chill and piercing, driving the mosquitoes and buffalo gnats to their hiding places directly after sunset. The fierce prairie wind searches to the marrow (ice froze a quarter of an inch thick on the Plains on the 26th of May), and a shower at this season is very apt to be accompanied by hail as well as thunder and lightning. I trust our country has no harsher climate, save high among her grandest mountains.

From the Bijou to Cherry Creek—some forty miles— I can say little of the country, save that it is high rolling prairie, deeply cut by several streams, which run northeastwardly to join the Platte, or one of its tributaries just named. We passed it in the night, hurrying on to reach Denver, and at sunrise this morning stopped to change mules on the bank of Cherry Creek, twelve miles south of this place (which is situated at the junction of the creek with the south fork of the Platte). The foothills of the Rocky Moun-

95

tains seemed but a few miles west of us during our rapid ride down the smooth valley of the Cherry Creek, which has a fine belt of cottonwood only, but including trees of immense size—not less than three to four feet in diameter. The soil of the adjacent prairie seems light and sandy, but well grassed, and capable of yielding oats, potatoes, etc.; but the elevation (hardly less than six thousand feet), and the proximity of the Rocky Mountains, whose snow-covered crests, gleaming between and over the foothills, seem hardly twenty miles distant, must ever render the growth of corn difficult, if not absolutely impossible. Wheat, I understand, has been grown fifty to eighty miles south of this, with moderate success. Still, if the adjacent gold mines realize the sanguine expectations now entertained here, this region will require millions on millions' worth of food from the rich prairies and bottoms of Kansas proper, Nebraska, and Missouri, and we shall need but the Pacific railroad to open up a most beneficent home trade, and give the rich valley of the Missouri and its immediate tributaries better markets than those of the east.

And I fervently trust that the fond expectations of these gold-seekers, however chastened, may not be disappointed. For the sake of the weary, dusty, footsore thousands I have passed on my rapid journey from civilized Kansas to this point, I pray that gold may be found here in boundless extent, and reasonable abundance. Throughout the next six weeks, they will be dropping in here, a hundred or more per day; and I trust that they are not to be sent home disappointed, spirit-broken, penniless. If they must recross the great desert with their slow-moving teams, may they be enabled to do so with lighter hearts and heavier purses.

For the very mothers who bore them would hardly recognize their sons now toiling across the Plains, and straggling into this place, hideously hirsute, recklessly ragged, barefoot, sun-browned, dust-covered, and with eyes shielded (where they have them) by goggles from the glare of the prairie sun, reflected from the desert clay. A true picture of gold-seekers setting out from home, trim and jolly, for Pike's Peak, and of those same gold-seekers, sober as judges, and slow-moving as their own weary oxen, dropping into Denver, would convey a salutary lesson to many a sanguine soul. Nay, I have in my mind's eye an individual who rolled out of Leavenworth, barely thirteen days ago, in a satisfactory rig, and a spirit of adequate self-complacency, but who—though his hardships have been nothing to theirs— dropped into Denver this morning in a sobered and thoughtful frame of mind, in dust-begrimed and tattered habiliments, with a patch on his cheek, a bandage on his leg, and a limp in his gait, altogether constituting a spectacle most rueful to behold. It is likely to be some time yet before our fashionable American spas and summer resorts for idlers will be located among the Rocky Mountains.[2]

As to gold, Denver is crazy. She has been low in the valley of humiliation, and is suddenly exalted to the summit of glory. The stories of days' works, and rich leads that have been told me today—by grave, intelligent men— are absolutely bewildering. I do not discredit them, but I shall state nothing at second-hand where I may know if I will. I have come here to lay my hand on the naked, indisputable facts, and I mean to do it. Though unfit to travel, I start for the great diggings (fifty miles hence nearly due west in the glens of the Rocky Mountains) tomorrow morning.

---

[2] The tone suggests sarcasm, but the words indicate that Greeley correctly foresaw Colorado's future as a vacation spot.

11

THE KANSAS[1] GOLD-DIGGINGS

In the Rocky Mountains,
Gregory's Diggings, June 9, 1859

We left Denver at six yesterday morning, in a wagon drawn by four mules, crossing immediately by a rope ferry the south fork of the Platte. This fork is a swift, clear, cold stream, now several feet deep and some twenty rods wide, but fordable except when snows are melting in the mountains. Many gold-seekers' wagons were waiting to cross, and more were momently arriving, so that the ferryman at least must be making his pile out of the diggings. Henceforward, our way lay northwest for fifteen miles, across a rolling and well-grassed prairie, on which one or two farms had been commenced, while two or three persons have just established "ranches"—that is, have built each his corral, in which cattle are herded at night, while allowed to run at large on the prairie during the day: $1.50 per month is the usual price per head for herding in this way, and the cattle are said to do very well. The miners leave or send back their cattle to herd on these prairies, while they prosecute their operations in the mountains where feed is generally scarce.

Reaching Clear Creek (properly Vasquer's Fork), a cold, swift, rocky-bottomed stream, which emerges just above through a deep, narrow canyon from the Rocky Mountains, we left our wagons, saddled the mules and forded the creek (and it was all our mules could do to stem its impetuous current), ascended a gentle, grassy slope to the foot of the

---

[1] So called because they lay in the southern part of present Colorado, which was Kansas Territory under the Kansas-Nebraska Act of 1854.

Rocky Mountains—which had for an hour seemed almost within a stone's throw on our left. Now they were to be faced directly, and the prospect was really serious. The hill on which we were to make our first essay in climbing, rose to a height of one thousand six hundred feet in a little more than a mile—the ascent for most of the distance being more than one foot in three. I never before saw teams forced up such a precipice; yet there were wagons with ten or twelve hundred weight of mining tools, bedding, provisions, etc., being dragged by four to eight yoke of oxen up that giddy precipice, with four or five men lifting at the wheels of each. The average time consumed in the ascent is some two hours. Our mules, unused to such work, were visibly appalled by it; at first they resisted every effort to force them up, even by zigzags. My companions all walked, but I was lame and had to ride, much to my mule's intense disgust. He was stubborn, but strong, and in time bore me safely to the summit.

New as this rugged road is—it was first traversed five weeks ago today—death had traveled it before me. A young man, shot dead while carelessly drawing a rifle from his wagon, lies buried by the roadside on this mountain. I have heard of so many accidents of this nature—not less than a dozen gold-seekers having been shot in this manner during the last two months—that I marvel at the carelessness with which firearms are everywhere handled on this side of the Missouri. Had no single emigrant across the Plains this season armed himself, the number of them alive at this moment would have been greater than it is.

We traveled some two miles along the crest of this mountain, then descended, by a pitch equally sharp with the ascent, but shorter, to a ravine, in which we rested our weary animals and dined. That dinner—of cold ham, bread and cheese—was one of the best relished of any I ever shared. Resaddling, we climbed another precipice a little less steep—and so up and down for ten miles, when we descended into the narrow valley of a little branch of Clear Creek, and thenceforward had ten miles of relatively smooth going, crossing from one valley to another over hills of moderate elevation and easy ascent.

A wilderness of mountains rose all around us, some higher, some lower, but generally very steep, with sharp, narrow ridges for their summits. Some of them are thinly grassed, between widely scattered trees up their sides and on their tops; but they are generally timbered, and mainly with yellow pine, some of it quite large, but more of it small and apparently young. High on the mountains, this pine is short and scraggy, while in the ravines it grows tall and shapely, but averages not more than a foot in diameter. Hurricanes have frequently swept these mountains, prostrating the pines by scores; fires have ravaged and decimated them; still, pines on the summits, pine on the hillsides, pines even in the ravines, are all but universal. The balsam fir grows sparingly in the ravines; hemlock, also, is reported, though I have not seen it: but the quaking asp or aspen— which seems but a more delicate species of cottonwood—is thick-set in the ravines, and sometimes appears on the more moderate acclivities, as do gooseberry bushes in the glens. Brooks of the purest water murmur and sing in every ravine; springs abound; the air is singularly pure and bracing; the elk, black-tailed deer and mountain sheep are plentiful, except where disturbed by the inrush of emigration; grouse are common and bold: the solitude was sylvan and perfect until a few weeks ago. All is now being rapidly changed, and not entirely for the better.

We had a smart shower, with thunder and lightning, during the afternoon, which compelled us to halt a few minutes. Another such this afternoon, indicates that it is a habit of the country. I am told, however, that though thunder is common, rain is generally withheld at this season, or confined to a mere sprinkle.

Night fell upon us, while yet six or seven miles from the diggings, and we camped in the edge of the pines, on the brow of a gentle acclivity, with a prospect of grass as well as water for our weary, hungry beasts down the slope south of us. Mine had fallen to her knees in the last water-course we had passed, very nearly throwing me over her head; had she done it, I am sure I had not the strength left to rise and remount, and hardly to walk the remaining half mile. As it was, I had to be lifted tenderly from my saddle and laid on a blanket, with two more above me, where I lay while the fire was built, supper prepared, and a lodge of dry poles and green pine boughs hastily erected. I was too tired to eat, but the bright, leaping flame from the dry pines heaped on our fire gradually overcame the shivering, which was about the only sign of vitality I showed when first laid down, and I at length resumed the perpendicular by an effort, and took my place in our booth, where sleep but fitfully visited me during that bright, cool, short summer night. But this left me more time to rub my chafed and stiffened limbs, so that, when breakfast was called in the morning, I was ready, appetite included, and prepared to dispel the apprehensions of those who had predicted, on seeing me taken off my mule, that I must be left there for at least a day. By six o'clock, we were again in the saddle, and pushing on, over a stony but rather level tableland, which extended for two or three miles, thickly covered with young pines and aspens, to the next ravine, whence the road leads up a short, steep hill, then down a very long, equally steep one, to Ralston's Fork of Clear Creek—being as rapid and rock-bottomed as where we had crossed the main creek the day before thirty miles below, but with only one-third the volume of water, so that we forded it easily without a wet foot. A little runnel coming in from the west directly at the Ford, with its natural translucency changed to milky whiteness by the running of its waters through sluices in which the process of gold-washing was going forward, gave us assurance that we were in immediate proximity to the new but already famous workings called, after their discoverer, Gregory's Diggings.*

I shall not here speak of their pecuniary success or promise, though I have visited, during the day, a majority of those which have sluices already in operation, and received reports from my fellow visitors from nearly all the others. Having united with them in a statement—to be herewith forwarded—of what we saw and learned, I refer those who feel any interest in the matter to that statement. What I propose here to do is to give the reader some idea of the place and its general aspects.

The little brook which here joins Clear Creek from the west starts at the foot of mountains three or four miles distant, and runs in a usually narrow ravine between generally steep hills from five hundred to fifteen hundred feet high. Gregory's lead is very near its mouth; half a mile above seems the heart of the present mining region, though there are already sluices in operation at intervals for at least two miles up the runnel, and others are soon to be started at intervals above them. Three or four miles southwest from its mouth are Russell's Diggings,[2] where coarse gold is procured, but I was unable to visit them. Prospecting is actively going forward in every direction, and vague reports of lucky

---

* Now (October) known as Mountain City.

[2] The Russell brothers—William Green, Dr. Levi J., and J. Oliver— were also, like John Gregory, from the gold region of northern Georgia. The first of the three, known as Green Russell, was married to a Cherokee woman and wore his beard in two long braids, which he tucked into his shirt front.

hits or brilliant prospects are started on this side or on that, but I have not been able to verify them. It is no disparagement to the others to say that, though mining is carried on at various points within a radius of thirty miles from this spot, Gregory's Diggings are today the chief hope of gold-mining in the Rocky Mountains.

Six weeks ago, this ravine was a solitude, the favorite haunt of the elk, the deer, and other shy denizens of the profoundest wildernesses, seldom invaded by the footsteps of man. I believe this strip of country has long been debatable land between the Utes and the Arapahoes, which circumstances combined with its rarely accessible situation to secure its wild tenants against human intrusion and persecution. I hear that the Arapahoes say that a good "lodgepole trail"—that is, one which a pony may traverse with one end of the lodgepoles on his back, the other trailing behind him—exists from this point to the open prairie where Clear Creek debouches from the mountains—a trail which doubtless winds along the steep sides of the ravines and avoids the rugged heights necessarily traversed by the miner's wagon road. Should these diggings justify their present promise, I doubt not a road will in time be made, reducing by one half—say five thousand feet—the present aggregate of ascent and descent between this and Denver. But an unworked wagon road must avoid the sides of these steepbanked ravines, running square up the faces and along the crests of the mountains, so that this spot is destined to remain barely accessible for at least another year.

This narrow valley is densely wooded, mainly with the inevitable yellow pine, which, sheltered from the fierce winds which sweep the mountaintops, here grows to a height of sixty or eighty feet, though usually but a foot to eighteen inches in diameter. Of these pines, log cabins are constructed with extreme facility, and probably one hundred are now being built, while three or four hundred more are in immediate contemplation. They are covered with the green boughs of the pines, then with earth, and bid fair to be commodious and comfortable. As yet, the entire population of the valley—which cannot number less than four thousand, including five white women and seven squaws living with white men—sleep in tents, or under booths of pine boughs, cooking and eating in the open air. I doubt that there is as yet a table or chair in these diggings, eating being done around a cloth spread on the ground, while each one sits or reclines on mother earth. The food, like that of the Plains, is restricted to a few staples—pork, hot bread, beans and coffee forming the almost exclusive diet of the mountains; but a meatshop has just been established, on whose altar are offered up the ill-fed and well-whipped oxen who are just in from a fifty days' journey across the plains, and one or two cows have been driven in, as more would be if they could here been subsisted. But these mountains are mainly wooded, while the open hillsides are so dry during summer that their grass is very scanty. It is melancholy to see so many overworked and half-starved cattle as one meets or passes in this ravine and on the way hither. Corn is four dollars per bushel in Denver, and scarce at that; oats are not to be had; there is not a ton of hay within two hundred miles, and none can ever be brought hither over the present road at a cost below forty dollars per ton. The present shift of humane owners is to herd their oxen or mules on the rich grass of the nearest prairies for a week or so, then bring them in here and keep them at work for a week or more, letting them subsist on browse and a very little grass, and then send them down the mountain again. This, bad as it is, seems the best that can be done. Living of all kinds will always be dear at these mines, where American flour is now selling at the rate of forty-four dollars per barrel, and bacon is worth fifty cents per pound; sugar ditto.

I presume less than half the four or five thousand people now in this ravine have been here a week; he who has been here three weeks is regarded as quite an old settler. The influx cannot fall short of five hunderd per day, balanced by an efflux of about one hundred. Many of the latter go away convinced that Rocky Mountain gold-mining is one grand humbug. Some of them have prospected two or three weeks, eating up their provisions, wearing out their boots—and finding nothing. Others have worked for the more fortunate for one dollar per day and their board and lodging—certainly not high wages when the quality of the living is considered. And I feel certain that, while some—perhaps many —will realize their dreams of wealth here, a far greater number will expend their scanty means, tax their powers of endurance, and then leave, soured, heartsick, spirit-broken. Twenty thousand people will have rushed into this ravine before the 1st of September, while I do not see how half of them are to find profitable employment here. Unless, therefore, the area of the diggings shall meantime be greatly enlarged—of which there is no assurance—I cannot imagine how half the number are to subsist here, even up to that early setting in of winter which must cause a general paralysis of mining, and consequently of all other Rocky Mountain industry. With the gold just wrested from the earth still glittering in my eyes—and one company has taken out today, at a cost of not more than twenty-five dollars, a lump (condensed by the use of quicksilver) which looks like a steelyard poise and is estimated as worth five hundred and ten dollars—I adhere to my long-settled conviction that, next to outright and indisputable gambling, the hardest (though sometimes the quickest) way to obtain gold is to mine for it; that a good farmer or mechanic will usually make money faster, and of course immeasurably easier, by sticking to his own business than by deserting it for gold-digging; and that the man who, having failed in some other pursuit, calculates on retrieving his fortunes by gold-mining, makes a mistake which he will be likely to rue to the end of his days.

We had a famous gathering a few rods from this tent this evening. The estimate of safe men puts the number present at fifteen hundred to two thousand. Though my name was made the excuse for it, brief and forcible addresses were made by several others, wherein mining, postal, and express facilities, the Pacific railroad, the proposed new Rocky Mountain State, temperance, gambling, etc., etc., were discussed with force and freedom. Such a gathering of men suddenly drawn hither from every section, and nearly every state, in a glen where the first axe was raised, the first tent pitched by white men, less than six weeks ago, should have inspired the dullest speaker with earnestness, if not with eloquence.

Mining quickens almost every department of useful industry. Two coal pits are burning close at hand. A blacksmith has set up his forge here, and is making a good thing of sharpening picks at fifty cents each. A volunteer post office is just established, to which an express office will soon attach itself. A provision store will soon follow, then groceries, then dry goods, then a hotel, etc., until within ten years the tourist of the continent will be whirled up to these diggings over a longer but far easier road winding around the mountaintops rather than passing over them, and will sip his chocolate and read his New York paper—not yet five days old—at the Gregory House, in utter unconsciousness that this region was wrested from the elk and the mountain sheep so recently as 1859.

Denver, June 10, 1859

We left the diggings yesterday morning, and came down to the foot of the mountains, in spite of a drizzling rain from

noon to three or four o'clock, which at one time threatened
a heavy shower. We made a poor shelter of a buffalo skin
and a rubber blanket, stretched across a fallen tree, and there
waited half an hour; but, finding the rain neither stopped
nor grew violent, we saddled up and came on. Two accidents,
which might have proved serious, happened to members of
our party—the first to Mr. Villard, of Cincinnati,[3] who,
riding at some distance from all others, was thrown by his
mule's saddle slipping forward and turning under him, so
that he fell heavily on his left arm, which was badly bruised,
and thence was dragged a rod with his heel fast in the stirrup. His mule then stopped; but when I rode up behind him,
I dared not approach him lest I should start her, and waited
a moment for the friend who, having heard his call for help,
was coming up in front. Mr. V. was released without further
injury, but his arm is temporarily useless. The other casualty
happened to Mr. Kershaw, of New York,[4] who, riding to
my assistance at Clear Creek crossing at nightfall, was
thrown by his mule's starting at the rush of a savage dog,
and considerably injured, though he is nearly well today. It
would have been to me a source of lasting sorrow had his fall
resulted in more serious damage.

When we reached Clear Creek on our way up three
mornings since, though the current rushing from the mountains looked somewhat formidable, I charged it like a Zouave,
and was greeted with three ringing shouts from the assembled Pike's Peakers, as I came up, gay and dripping, on
the north shore. But now, though the water was but a few
inches higher, the starch was so completely taken out of me
by those three days' rough experience in the mountains, that
I had neither strength nor heart for the passage. I felt that

[3] Henry Villard, reporter for the Cincinnati *Daily Commercial*, more
famous as the builder of the Northern Pacific Railroad.

[4] This is the only mention of Mr. Kershaw, and there is no further
clue to his identity.

the least stumble of my mule over the round, slippery stones that fill the channel would fling me, and that I was unable to stand a moment in that rushing torrent. So, driving in my mule after the rest of the party, and seeing her reach the south bank safely, though with great difficulty—breaking a girth and spilling saddle, blanket, etc., into the water—I betook myself to a spot, half a mile upstream, where the creek is split by islets into three channels, and where a rude footbridge of logs affords a dry-shod passage. Here I was met by my friend with his mule, and in a few minutes rode to our wagon, beside which we found supper in an emigrant tent and lodging in several, at four o'clock this morning harnessed up and drove into Denver—just three whole men out of a party of six, and all as weary and care-worn as need be, but all heartily gratified with our experience of three days in the Rocky Mountains.

12

THE PLAINS—THE MOUNTAINS

Denver, June 15, 1859

I know few greater contrasts than that between the region which stretches hundreds of miles eastward from this spot toward the Missouri, and is known as *The Plains*, and that which overlooks us on the west and, alike by its abrupt and sharp-ridged foothills seeming just at hand, and its glittering peaks of snow in the blue distance, vindicates its current designation, *The Mountains*. Let me elucidate:

The Plains are nearly destitute of human inhabitants. Aside from the buffalo range—which has been steadily narrowing ever since Daniel Boone made his home in Kentucky, and is now hardly two hundred miles wide—it affords little sustenance and less shelter to man. The antelope are seldom seen in herds—three is the highest number I observed together, while one, or at most two, is a more common spectacle. One to each mile square would be a large estimate for all that exist on the plains. Elk are scarcely seen at all, even where they have hardly ever been hunted or scared. Of deer, there are none, or next to none. For the Plains are the favorite haunt of beasts and birds of prey—of the ravenous and fearless gray wolf, of the coyote, the raven, and the hawk —the first hanging on the flanks of every great herd of buffalo, ready to waylay any foolish calf or heedless heifer that may chance to stray for water or fresher grass beyond the protection of the hard-headed and chivalrous patriarchs, behind whose vigilant ranks there is comparative safety, and counting as their property any bull, even, whom wounds or disease or decrepitude shall compel to fall behind in the perpetual march. For, while a stray buffalo, or two, or three, may linger in some lonely valley for months—for all winter, perhaps—the great herds which blacken the earth for miles in extent cannot afford to do so—they are so immensely numerous and find their safety in traveling so compactly that they must keep moving or starve. Avoiding, so far as possible, the wooded ravines of the slender watercourses, where experience has taught them to dread the lance-like arrow of the lurking Indian, they keep to the high "divides," or only feed in the valleys while they have these well covered by sentinel bulls to give warning of any foe's approach. Take away the buffalo, and the Plains will be desolate far beyond their present desolation; and I cannot but regard with sadness the inevitable and not distant fate of these noble and harmless brutes, already crowded into a breadth of country too narrow for them, and continually hunted, slaughtered, decimated, by the wolf, the Indian, the white man. They could have stood their ground against all in the absence of firearms, but "villainous salpeter" is too much for them. They are bound to perish; I trust it may be oftener by sudden shot than by slow starvation.

Wood and water—the prime necessities of the traveler as of the settler—are in adequate though not abundant supply for a hundred miles and more on this as they are throughout on the other side of the buffalo range; at length they gradually fail, and we are in a desert indeed. No spring, no brook, for a distance of thirty to sixty miles (which would be stretched to more than a hundred* if the few tracks called roads were not all run so as to secure water so far as possible)—rivers which have each had fifty to a hundred miles of its course gradually parched up by force of sun and wind, and its waters lost in their own sands, so that the weary, dusty traveler vainly digs for hours in their dry beds in quest of drink for his thirsty cattle—rivers which dare not rise again till some friendly brook, having its source in some specially favored region, pours in its small but steady tribute, moistens the sands of the river bed, and encourages its waters to rise to the surface again. In one case, an emigrant assures me that he dug down to the bedrock of one of these rivers, yet found all dry sand.

I know not that I can satisfactorily account, even to myself, for the destitution of wood which the Plains everywhere present, especially the western half of them. The poverty of the soil will not suffice, for these lands, when sufficiently moistened by rain or thawing snowdrifts, produce grass, and are not so sterile as the rocky hills, the pebbly knolls, of New England, which, nevertheless, produce wood rapidly and abundantly. On the prairies of Illinois, Missouri, and eastern Kansas, the absence of wood is readily accounted

---

* Since writing the above, I learn by a newly arrived Pike's Peaker that the waterless stretch of desert is already a hundred miles long, and that every day's sun is extending it.

for by the annual fires which, in autumn or spring, sweep over nearly every acre of dead grass, killing every tree sprout that may have started up from scattered seeds or roots running from the timber in the adjacent ravine beneath the matted grass. But here are thousands of acres too poorly grassed to be swept by the annual fires—on which the thinly scattered reed stalks and bunch grass of last year shake dryly in the fierce night winds—yet not a tree nor shrub relieves the sameness, the bareness, the desolation, of thousands after thousands of acres—not a twig, a scion, gives promise of trees that are to be. For a time, the narrow ravine or lowest intervale of the frequent streams were fairly timbered with cottonwood, and low, sprawling elm, with a very little oak, or white ash at long intervals intermixed; but these grew gradually thinner and feebler until nothing but a few small cottonwoods remained, and these skulking behind bluffs, or in sheltered hollows at intervals of twenty to forty miles. Once in ten or twenty miles, a bunch of dwarf willows, perhaps two feet high, would be found cowering in some petty basin washed out by a current of water many years ago; but these, like the cottonwoods, are happy if able to hold their own; indeed, I have seen much evidence that wood was more abundant on the Plains a hundred years ago than it now is. Dead cottonwoods, of generous proportions, lie in the channels of dry brooks on which no tree nor shrub now grows; and, at one or more stations of the express company, near the sink of the Republican, they find dead pine eight miles up a creek, where no living pine has been seen for generations. I judged that the desert is steadily enlarging its borders and at the same time intensifying its barrenness.

The fierce drought that usually prevails throughout the summer doubtless contributes to this, but I think the violent and all but constant winds exert a still more disastrous potency. High winds are of frequent, all but daily, occurrence here, within a dozen miles of the great protecting bulwark of the Rocky Mountains; while, from a point fifty miles eastward of this, they sweep over the Plains almost constantly, and at times with resistless fury. A driver stated on our way up, with every appearance of sincerity, that he had known instances of tires being blown off from wagon wheels by the tornadoes of the Plains; and, hard to swallow as that may seem, I have other and reliable assurance that when the Missourians' camp on the express road was swept by a hurricane five or six weeks ago, so that, after the wreck, but three decent wagons could be patched up out of their six, as I have already narrated, one of the wheel tires was not only blown off but nearly straightened out! There is almost always a good breeze at midday and after, on the Plains; but, should none be felt during the day, one is almost certain to spring up at sunset, and blow fiercely through the night. Thus, though hot days, or parts of days, are frequent on the Plains, I have experienced not even a moderately warm night. And thus trees are not; mainly because the winds uproot or dismember them, or so rock and wrench them while young, that their roots cannot suck up even the little nourishment that this soil of baking clay resting on porous sand would fain afford them. Thus the few shoots that cleave the surface of the earth soon wither and die, and the broad landscape remains treeless, cheerless, forbidding.

But the dearth of water and wood on the Plains is paralleled by the poverty of shrubbery and herbage. I have not seen a strawberry leaf—far from me be the presumption of looking for a berry!— since I left the Missouri three weeks ago; and the last blackberry bramble I observed grew on Chapman's Creek—at all events, the other side of the buffalo range. A raspberry cane has not blessed my sight these three weary weeks, nor aught else that might be hoped to bear an old-fashioned fruit, save the far-off blackberries aforesaid, and two or three doubtful grapevines on some creek a great way back. The prickly pear, very rare and very green, is the only semblance of fruit I discovered on the Plains; a dwarfish cactus, with its leaves close to the ground; the Spanish nettle—a sort of vegetable porcupine—a profusion of wild sage, wild wormwood, and other such plants, worthless alike to man and beast, relieved by some well-gnawed grass in the richer valleys of winter watercourses (the flora usually very scanty and always coarse and poor)—such are my recollections of the three hundred miles or so that separate the present buffalo range from the creeks that carry snow water to the Platte and the pines that herald our approach to the Rocky Mountains.

THE ROCKY MOUNTAINS

And now all changes, but slowly, gradually. The cactus, the Spanish nettle, the prickly pear continue, even into and upon the mountains; but the pines, though stunted and at first scattered, give variety, softness and beauty to the landscape, which becomes more rolling, with deeper and more frequent valleys, and water in nearly all of them; the cottonwoods along the streams no longer skulk behind bluffs or hide in casual hollows; you may build an honest campfire without fear of robbing an embryo county of its last stick of wood, and water your mules generously without drying up some long, pretentious river, and condemning those who come after you to weary, thirsty marches through night and day. The cottonwoods, as you near the wind-quelling range of protecting heights, which rise, rank above rank, to the westward (the more distant still white-robed with snow) grow large and stately—some of them sixty to seventy feet high, and at least three feet in diameter; the unwooded soil ceases to be desert and becomes prairie once more; but still this is in the main a sandy, thinly grassed region, which can-

113

not compare with the prairies of Illinois, of Iowa, or eastern Kansas.

There seems to be as rich and deep soil in some of the creek bottoms, especially those of the South Platte, as almost anywhere; and yet I fear the husbandman is doomed to find even this belt of grassed and moderately rolling land, which stretches along the foot of the mountains to a width of perhaps twenty miles, less tractable and productive than fertile. It lies at such an elevation—from five thousand to six thousand feet above the ocean level—that, though its winters are said to be moderate, its springs cannot be early. There was a fall of a foot of snow in this region on the 26th of May, when ice formed to a quarter-inch thickness on the Plains; and when summer suddenly sets in, about the 1st of June, there are hot suns by day, and cool, strong winds by night, with a surfeit of petty thunder squalls, but little or no rain. The gentle rain of last Thursday in the mountains fell, for a short time, in sheets just at their feet—say for a breadth of five miles—and there ceased. Hardly a drop fell within five miles west, or for any distance east of this place, though the earth was soaked only ten miles further west. Hence, the enterprising few who have commenced farms and gardens near this point tell me that their crops have made no progress for a week or two, and can make none till they have rain. I trust wheat and rye will do well here whenever they shall be allowed a fair chance; barley and oats, if sowed very early on deeply plowed land, may do tolerably; but corn, though it comes up well and looks rank at present, will hardly ripen before frost, even should it escape paralysis by drought; while potatoes, peas, and most vegetables will probably require irrigation, or yield but sparingly. Yet, should the gold mines justify their present promise, farming, in the right localities at the base of these mountains, even by the help of irrigation, will yield—to those who bring to it the requisite sagacity, knowledge, and capital—richer rewards than elsewhere on earth. Everything that can be grown here will command treble or quadruple prices for years; and he who produces anything calculated to diversify and improve the gross, mountainous diet of salt pork, hot bread, beans, and coffee, now necessarily all but universal in this region, will be justly entitled to rank with public benefactors.

And the Rocky Mountains, with their grand, aromatic forests, their grassy glades, their frequent springs, and dancing streams of the brightest, sweetest water, their pure, elastic atmosphere, and their unequalled game and fish, are destined to be a favorite resort and home of civilized man. I never visited a region where physical life could be more surely prolonged or fully enjoyed. Thousands who rush hither for gold will rush away again disappointed and disgusted, as thousands have already done; and yet the gold is in these mountains, and the right men will gradually unearth it. I shall be mistaken if two or three millions are not taken out this year, and some ten millions in 1860, though all the time there will be, as now, a stream of rash adventurers heading away from the diggings, declaring that there is no gold there, or next to none. So it was in California and in Australia; so it must be here, where the obstacles to be overcome are greater, and the facilities for getting home decidedly better. All men are not fitted by nature for gold-diggers; yet thousands will not realize this until they have been convinced of it by sore experience. Any good phrenologist should have been able to tell half the people who rushed hither so madly during the last two months that, if these mountains had been half made of gold, they never would get any of it except by minding their own proper business, which was quite other than mining. And still the long procession is crossing the Platte and Clear Creek, and pressing up the Hill of Difficulty in mad pursuit of gold, whereof not one-fifth will carry back to the states so much as they brought away. New leads will doubtless be discovered, new veins be opened, new diggings or districts become the rage—for it were absurd to suppose that little ravine known as Gregory's, running to Clear Creek, the sole depository of gold worth working in all this region—and in time the Rocky Mountains will swarm with a hardy, industrious, energetic white population. Not gold alone, but lead, iron, and (I think) silver or cobalt, have already been discovered here, and other valuable minerals, doubtless will be, as the mountains are more thoroughly explored—for as yet they have not been even run over. Those who are now intent on the immediate organization and admission of a new state may be too fast, yet I believe the Rocky Mountains, and their immediate vicinity —say between Fort Laramie on the north, and Taos on the south—will within three years have a white population of one hundred thousand, one half composed of men in the full vigor of their prime, separated by deserts and waste places from the present states, obliged to rely on their own resources in any emergency, and fully able to protect and govern themselves. Why not let them be a state so soon as reasonably may be.

Mining is a pursuit akin to fishing and hunting, and, like them, enriches the few at the cost of the many. This region is doubtless foreordained to many changes of fortune; today, giddy with the intoxication of success—tomorrow, in the valley of humiliation. One day, report will be made on the Missouri by a party of disappointed gold-seekers, that the "Pike's Peak humbug" has exploded, and that everybody is fleeing to the states who can possibly get away; the next report will represent these diggings as yellow with gold. Neither will be true, yet each in its turn will have a certain thin substratum of fact for its justification. Each season will see its thousands turn away disappointed, only to give place

116

to others thousands, sanguine and eager as if none had ever failed. Yet I feel a strong conviction that each succeeding month's researches will enlarge the field of mining operations, and diminish the difficulties and impediments which now stretch across the gold-seeker's path, and that, ten years hence, we shall be just beginning fairly to appreciate and secure the treasures now buried in the Rocky Mountains.

13

"LO! THE POOR INDIAN!"

Denver, June 16, 1859

I have been passing, meeting, observing and trying to converse with Indians almost ever since I crossed the Missouri. Eastern Kansas is checkered with their reservations— Delaware, Kaw, Ottawa, Osage, Kickapoo, Potawatomie and others—while the buffalo range, and all this side belong to, and are parceled among the Cheyennes, the Arapahoes, and the Apaches—or perhaps among the two former only, as Indian boundaries are not very well defined. At all events, we have met or passed bands of these three tribes, with occasional visitors from the Sioux on the north, and the Comanches on the south—all these tribes having for the present a good understanding. The Utes, who inhabit the mountains, and are stronger and braver than any one of the three tribes first named, though hardly a match for them all, are at war with them; the Arapaho chief, Left Hand, assures me that his people were always at war with the Utes—at least, he has no recollection, no tradition, of a time when they were at peace. Some two or three hundred lodges of Arapahoes are encamped in and about this log city, calculating that the presence of the whites will afford some protection to their wives and children against a Ute onslaught while the braves are off on any of their fighting—that is, stealing—expeditions. An equal or larger body of Utes are camped in the mountains, some forty or fifty miles west, and the Arapaho warriors recently returned in triumph from a war party, on which they managed to steal about a hundred horses from the Utes, but were obliged to kill most of them in their rapid flight, so that they only brought home forty more than they took away. They are going out again in a day or two, and have been for some days practising secret incantations and public observances with reference thereto. Last midnight, they were to have had a grand war dance, and to have left on the warpath today; but their men, sent out after their horses, reported that they saw three Utes on the plain, which was regarded as premonitory of an attack, and the braves stood to their arms all night, and were very anxious for white aid in case of a Ute foray on their lodges here in Denver. Such an attack seems very improbable, and I presume the three Utes who caused all this uproar were simply scouts or spies, on the watch for just such marauding surprise parties as our Arapaho neighbors are constantly meditating. I do not see why they need take even this trouble. There are points on the mountain range west of this city where a watchman with a sharp eye and a good glass would command the entire plain for fifty miles north, south, and east of him, and might hence give intelligence of any Arapaho raid at least a day before a brave entered the mountains. For, though it is true that Indians on the warpath travel or ride mainly by night, I find that the Arapahoes do this only after they have entered on what they consider disputed or dangerous ground —that they start from their lodges in open day, and only advance under cover of darkness after they are within the shadows of the mountains. Hence, the Utes, who are confessedly the stronger, might ambush and destroy any

Arapaho force that should venture into their Rocky Mountain recesses, by the help of a good spyglass, and a little white forecast.

But the Indians are children. Their arts, wars, treaties, alliances, habitations, crafts, properties, commerce, comforts, all belong to the very lowest and rudest ages of human existence. Some few of the chiefs have a narrow and short-sighted shrewdness, and very rarely in their history, a really great man, like Pontiac or Tecumseh, has arisen among them; but this does not shake the general truth that they are utterly incompetent to cope in any way with the European or Caucasian race. Any band of schoolboys, from ten to fifteen years of age, are quite as capable of ruling their appetites, devising and upholding a public policy, constituting and conducting a state or community, as an average Indian tribe. And, unless they shall be treated as a truly Christian community would treat a band of orphan children providentially thrown on its hands, the aborigines of this country will be practically extinct within the next fifty years.

I have learned to appreciate better than hitherto, and to make more allowance for, the dislike, aversion, contempt wherewith Indians are usually regarded by their white neighbors, and have been since the days of the Puritans. It needs but little familiarity with the actual, palpable aborigines to convince anyone that the poetic Indian—the Indian of Cooper and Longfellow—is only visible to the poet's eye. To the prosaic observer, the average Indian of the woods and prairies is a being who does little credit to human nature— a slave of appetite and sloth, never emancipated from the tyranny of one animal passion save by the more ravenous demands of another. As I passed over those magnificent bottoms of the Kansas which form the reservations of the Delaware, Potawatomies, etc., constituting the very best cornlands on earth, and saw their owners sitting around the doors of their lodges at the height of the planting season and in as good, bright planting weather as sun and soil ever made, I could not help saying, "These people must die out—there is no help for them. God has given this earth to those who will subdue and cultivate it, and it is vain to struggle against His righteous decree." And I yesterday tried my powers of persuasion on Left Hand—the only Arapaho chief who talks English—in favor of an Arapaho tribal farm, say of two hundred acres for a beginning, to be broken and fenced by the common efforts of the tribe, and a patch therein allotted to each head of a family who would agree to plant and till it—I apprehend to very little purpose. For Left Hand, though shrewd in his way, is an Indian, and every whit as conservative as Boston's Beacon Street or our Fifth Avenue. He knows that there is a certain way in which his people have lived from time immemorial, and in which they are content still to live, knowing and seeking no better. He may or may not have heard that it is the common lot of prophets to be stoned and of reformers to be crucified; but he probably comprehends that squaws cannot fence and plow, and that braves are disinclined to any such steady, monotonous exercise of their muscles. I believe there is no essential difference in this respect between braves of the red and those of the white race, since even our country's bold defenders have not been accustomed to manifest their intrepidity in the corn-fields along their line of march, save in the season of roasting ears; and the verb "to soldier" has acquired, throughout Christendom in all its moods and tenses, a significance beyond the need of a glossary. Briefly, the brave, whether civilized or savage, is not a worker, a producer; and where the men are all braves, with a war always on hand, the prospect for productive industry is gloomy indeed. If, then, the hope of Indian renovation rested mainly on the men, it would be slender enough. There is little probability that the present generation of braves can be weaned from the traditions and the habits in which they find a certain personal consequence and immunity from daily toil, which stand them instead of intelligence and comfort. Squalid and conceited, proud and worthless, lazy and lousy, they will strut out or drink out their miserable existence, and at length afford the world a sensible relief by dying out of it.

But it is otherwise with the women. Degraded and filthy as they are, beyond description or belief, they bear the germ of renovation for their race, in that they are neither too proud nor too indolent to labor. The squaw accepts work as her destiny from childhood. In her father's lodge, as in that wherein she comes in turn to hold a fifth or sixth interest in a husband (for all Indians are polygamists in theory, and all who have means or energy become such in practice) she comprehends and dutifully accepts drudgery as her "peculiar institution." She pitches and strikes the tent, carries it from one encampment to another, gathers and chops the wood, and not only dresses and cooks the game which forms the family's food (when they have any) but goes into the woods and backs it home, when her lord returns with the tidings that he has killed something. Tanning or dressing hides, making tents, clothing, moccasins, etc., all devolve on her. Under such a dispensation, it is not difficult to believe that she often willingly accepts a rival in the affections of her sullen master, as promising a mitigation rather than an aggravation of the hardships of her lot.

And yet even the Indian women are idle half their time, from sheer want of anything to do. They will fetch water for their white neighbors, or do anything else whereby a piece of bread may be honestly earned; and they would do ten times more than they do, if they could find work and be reasonably sure of even a meager reward for it.

I urge, therefore, that in future efforts to improve the

condition of the Indians, the women be specially regarded and appealed to. A conscientious, humane, capable Christian trader, with a wife thoroughly skilled in household manufactures and handicraft, each speaking the language of the tribe with whom they take up their residence, can do more good than a dozen average missionaries. Let them keep and sell whatever articles are adapted to the Indians' needs and means, and let them constitute and maintain an industrial school, in which the Indian women and children shall be freely taught how to make neatly and expeditiously not only moccasins, but straw hats, bonnets, and (in time) a hundred other articles combining taste with utility. Let a farm and garden be started so soon as may be, and vegetables, grain, fruits given therefrom in exchange for Indian labor therein, at all times when such labor can be made available. Of course, the school, though primarily industrial, should impart intellectual and religious instruction also, wisely adapted in character and season to the needs of the pupils, and to their perception of those needs. Such an enterprise, combining trade with instruction, thrift with philanthropy, would gradually mould a generation after its own spirit—would teach them to value the blessings of civilization before imposing on them its seeming burdens; and would, in the course of twenty years, silently transform an indolent savage tribe into a civilized Christian community. There may be shorter modes of effecting this transformation, but I think none surer.

Doubtless, such an enterprise demands rare qualities in its head—that of patience prominent among them. The vagrancy of the Indians would prove as great an obstacle to its success as their paltry but interminable wars. Very often, in the outset, the apostle of industry and civilization would find himself deserted by all his pupils, lured away by the hope of success elsewhere in marauding or hunting. But let him, having first deliberately chosen his location, simply persevere, and they will soon come round again, glad enough to find food that may be had even for solid work; for all I can learn impels me to believe that hunger is the normal state of the Indian, diversified by transient interludes of gluttony. Meat is almost his only food; and this, though plentiful at seasons, is at others scarcely obtainable in the smallest quantities, or dried to the toughness of leather. The Indian likes bread as well as the white; he must be taught to prefer the toil of producing it to the privation of lacking it. This point gained, he will easily be led to seek shelter, clothing, and all the comforts of civilized life, at their inevitable cost; and thus his temporal salvation will be assured. Otherwise, his extermination is inexorably certain, and cannot long be postponed.

14

THE GOLD IN THE ROCKY MOUNTAINS

Denver, June 20, 1859

For some ten years past, vague stories affirming or implying the existence of gold in our country's principal chain of mountains, have from time to time reached the public ear; but they seemed to rest on very slight or insecure foundations, and attracted but limited and transient attention. An Indian's, or trapper's, or trader's bare assertion that, in traversing the narrow ravines and precipitous heights of our American Switzerland, he had picked up a piece of quartz lustrous with gold, or even a small nugget of the pure metal, was calculated to attract little attention while California was unfolding her marvelous treasures, and while the fact stood forth clear and unquestioned that not one pound of the precious dust from all the region watered by the Missouri's mountain tributaries had ever been known to swell the world's aggregate of the all-desired metal, and not one company, or individual even, was known to be seeking the yellow idol on this side of the backbone of our continent. So far as I can learn, the first three parties ever organized to search for gold in all this Rocky Mountain region were fitted out in the spring of 1858, from the Cherokee nation from Missouri, and from Kansas (Lawrence) respectively; and these, though they carried home or sent home large stories of the auriferous character of the country they "prospected," took with them precious little gold. But their reports aroused a spirit of gold-seeking adventure in others, so that the ensuing (last) fall witnessed a rush of three or four hundred, mainly men of broken fortunes from the dead mushroom "cities" of Nebraska and Kansas, to the region watered by the South Platte and the more northerly sources of the Arkansas. For some reason, this point—the junction of Cherry Creek with the South Platte—became the focus of the gold hunt; here those who staid through the autumn and winter busied themselves in putting up log cabins, and writing home to their friend in the states accounts of the richness of this region in gold—a metal which, except in very minute quantities, they had seen but with the eye of faith. I doubt that three thousand dollars' worth of gold in every shape had been taken out by the five or six hundred seekers who came to this region in hot pursuit of it, down to the first day of last month—May, 1859. I doubt it, not merely because I have never seen any reliable accounts of that much gold being sent or received from here prior to that date, but because the gold does not exist where it had almost exclusively been sought down to that day. Cherry Creek, though its extreme sources are near Pike's Peak, is so headed off from the mountains by the South

Platte that I can hardly realize that is should bring down any gold at all; and, at best, washing for gold the sands of either of these streams near their junction seems to me much like washing the banks of the Amazon, in Maritime, Brazil, for the gold of the Andes. Yet nearly all the gold-hunting of this region, up to last month, had been done in the sands of these creeks, most of it miles distant from the mountains. There is testimony that several dollars' worth of dust per day to the hand was thus washed out in certain happily chosen spots; but such successes were transient, and, despite all the glowing accounts set forth in letters to the states, it is clear that all the gold-washing done throughout this region up to last month had not paid an average of fifty cents per day's work, while the cost of each man's subsistence, while thus employed, cannot have fallen short of a dollar per day. And the high waters of the streams preclude advantageous washing in the spring, even were gold far more abundant and enduring in their sands than it has yet been proved.

Such was the actual state of things when the first flood of gold-seeking immigration began to pour in upon Auraria and Denver two months or more ago. Many of the seekers had left home with very crude ideas of gold-digging, impelled by glowing bulletins from writers who confounded sanguine expectations with actual results, and at best spoke of any casual realization of five to ten dollars from a day's washing as though it were a usual and reliable reward of gold-seeking industry throughout this region. Many who came were doubtless already wearied and disgusted with the hardships of their tedious journey—with sleeping in wet blankets through storms of snow and hurricanes of hail, and urging hollow and weary cattle over immense, treeless plains, on which the grass had hardly started. Coming in thus weather-beaten, chafed and soured, and finding but a handful of squalid adventurers living in the rudest log huts, barred out from the mountains by snow and ice, and precluded from washing the sands of the streams on the plains by high water, they jumped at once to the conclusion that the whole thing was a humbug, got up by reckless speculators to promote selfish ends. They did not stop to reason, much less to explore; but, spurred by a laudable even if untimely longing to "see Nancy and the children," they turned their cattle's heads eastward and rushed pell-mell down the Platte, sweeping back nearly all they met. I estimate the number who have started for Pike's Peak this season and turned back at not less than forty thousand, and their positive loss by the venture (in time, clothing and money) at not less than an average of fifty dollars each—or, in all, two millions of dollars.

Meantime, a few of the pioneers of this region—mainly experienced gold-miners from Georgia, California, and even Australia—were quietly proceeding to prospect the mountains, so fast as the disappearance of snow and ice would permit—and, before the snow was fairly off the hither ranges, while it still lay solid and deep on the central and higher chain, Mr. J. H. Gregory, a veteran Georgia gold-digger, had struck the lead on a branch of Vasquer's Fork (Clear Creek) some thirty miles west of this place by an air line and forty-five by trail, which has since been the main focus and support of the gold fever. Other leads have since been opened in the same ravine and its vicinity; Mr. Green Russell (another Georgian) is reported to be doing exceedingly well in his "gulch diggings" three miles southwest of Gregory's; we have various reports of good leads struck at sundry points ten to fifteen miles west, south and north of Gregory's; and we have a further report that quartz of marvelous richness in gold has been found on the other side of the snowy range, some sixty miles west of Gregory's, and

126

not far from the Middle Park, whence the water flows to Grand River, and thence, through the Colorado, into the Gulf of California.

I indorse none of these reports as absolutely true, though all but the last are probably so. Tens of thousands will vainly ransack these mountains for gold through weeks and months, and leave them at last ragged and despondent, as hundreds are leaving them now; yet rich leads will continue to be struck, veins to be opened, sluices to be constructed, through years to come; and I shall not be disappointed to find the district yet prospected a mere corner of the Rocky Mountain gold region, of which the center is very probably a hundred miles north or south of this point. It may be north of Laramie even. All that has yet been done toward the thorough development of the gold-producing capacity of the Rocky Mountains is very much what tickling an elephant's ear with a pin would be toward dissecting him.

But will disemboweling these mountains in quest of gold *pay?* A very pregnant question. I answer—it will pay some; it will fail to pay others. A few will be amply and suddenly enriched by finding "leads" and selling "claims"; some by washing those "claims"; other some by supplying the mountains with the four apparent necessaries of mining life—whisky, coffee, flour, and bacon; others by robbing the miners of their hard earnings through the instrumentality of cards, roulette, and the "little joker;" but ten will come out here for gold for every one who carries back so much as he left home with, and thousands who hasten hither flushed with hope and ambition will lay down to their long rest beneath the shadows of the mountains, with only the wind-swept pines to sigh their requiem. Within this last week, we have tidings of one young gold-seeker committing suicide, in a fit of insanity, at the foot of the mountains; two more found in a ravine, long dead and partially devoured by wolves; while five others, with their horse and dog, were overtaken, some days since, while on a prospecting tour not far from Gregory's, by one of those terrible fires which, kindled by the culpable recklessness of some camping party, finds ready aliment in the fallen pine leaves which carpet almost the entire mountain region, and are fanned to fury by the fierce gales which sweep over the hilltops, and thus were all burned to death, and so found and buried, two or three days since—their homes, their names, and all but their fearful fate, unknown to those who rendered them the last sad offices. Ah! long will their families and friends vainly await and hope for the music of footsteps destined to be heard no more on earth! Thus, Death seems to be more busy and relentless on these broad, breezy plains, these healthful, invigorating mountains, than even in the crowded city or the rural district thick-sown with venerable graves.

It is my strong belief that gold is scarely less abundant in the Rocky Mountains than in California, though it seems, for many reasons, far less accessible. It is:

1. Much further from the seaboard, or from any navigable water or means of easy approach.

2. Belted by deserts and by regions on which little or no rain falls in summer, so that food, and almost every necessary of life, will here be permanently dearer than in California.

3. So elevated (six thousand feet and over above tidewater) that little can be done at mining for a full half of each year.

4. Most of the gold which has been broken down and washed out of the veins by watercourses has been so swept along and dispersed by the fierce mountain torrents that very little of it can be profitably washed out; hence, mining here must be mainly confined to veins, and will thus

involve blasting, raising by windlass, etc., etc., and so require large investments of capital for its energetic and successful prosecution. While, therefore, I believe that these
mountains will soon be yielding gold at the rate of many
millions per annum, I say most emphatically to the poor
men who want gold and are willing to work for it, This
is not the country for you! Far better seek wealth further
east through growing wheat, or corn, or cattle, or by any
kind of manual labor, than come here to dig gold. One man
may possibly acquire wealth faster in this gold lottery than
in New England or Kansas; but let one thousand poor men
come hither to mine, while the same number resolve to win
a competence by eminent industry and frugality in the
East, and the latter will assuredly have more wealth at five
years' end than the former—and will have acquired it with
far less sacrifice of comfort, health and life.

And here let me say, in closing up the subject, that I
think the report made by Messrs. Richardson, Villard and
myself, of what we saw and learned at Gregory's Diggings
is fully justified by more recent results. For example: we
gave the first four days' product of W. Defrees & Co. from
Indiana (running one sluice) at $66, $80, $95, and $305
respectively—the four following days not returned. I have
since obtained them; and they range as follows: $257, $281,
$203, $193—or $388 more than those of the four days for
which we gave the returns. This company then sold out
their claim for $7,000, and on the 8th of June opened a
sluice on another, which in four days produced as follows:
$31, $205, $151, $213. Another Indiana company, miscalled
Sopris, Henderson & Co., in our report, ran two sluices on
the 9th and 10th, realizing about $450 per day, and on the
11th had three sluices in operation for the first, and cleaned
up $1,009 (really worth about $900) from the product of
that day's labor of twelve men. Some scores are doing well,

though few quite so well as this; but of the thousands who are doing nothing—at least, realizing nothing—who shall report? Some of these issue daily from the mountains, out of provisions, out of means, out of heart; and, between this and snowfall, thousands like them will come out, still more hungry, weary, forlorn, and take their way down the Platte as gaunt and disconsolate as men ever need be. But this, and much more, will not dissuade new thousands from rushing to take their places, so long as it is known that the Rocky Mountains contain gold.

P. S. A friend just in from the mountains, who had a narrow escape from the flames, confirms our worst rumors of disaster and death. He says not less than *fifteen** men have fallen victims to the conflagration, which is still raging, and threatens even the dense crowd of tents and cabins at Gregory's. My friend informs me that the fire began very near where we camped during my first weary night in the mountains, and would seem to have been purposely set by reckless simpletons curious to see the woods in a blaze! He thinks the victims were generally, if not uniformly, smothered before the fire reached them—the dense, pitchy smoke at once shrouding the vision and obstructing respiration. He says the flames swept through the pines and above their tops to a height of two hundred feet, with a roar and a rush appalling even to look on. He was obliged to run his mule at her utmost speed for two or three miles, in order to effect his escape. If this drought continues—as it is likely to do for months—the mountains this side of the snowy range will be nearly burned over for at least fifty miles north and south of the Gregory trail, driving out all that is left of game, killing much of the timber, and rendering the country every way more inhospitable—a most superfluous proceeding.

I hear of still further discoveries further up in the moun-

* Another friend just arrived says certainly *seventeen*.

tains—some of them gulch or watercourse diggings, which are said to pay very well. They have just begun to work the sand of Clear Creek at the point where it issues from the mountains. Another friend just from Gregory's says he fears the victims of the fires now raging in that quarter will number *one hundred*. The limbs of the green pines are burned off close to the trunks, and the columns of roaring flame seem to fill the sky. The Gregory settlement was in some danger when my informants left it yesterday.

15

WESTERN CHARACTERS

Denver, June 21, 1859

I know it is not quite correct to speak of this region as "Western," seeing that it is in fact the center of North America and very close to its backbone. Still, as the terms "Eastern" and "Western" are conventional and relative— Castine being "Western" to a Bluenose, and Carson Valley "Eastern" to a Californian—I take the responsibility of grouping certain characters I have noted on the Plains and in or about the mountains as "Western," begging that most respectable region which lies east of the buffalo range—also that portion which lies west of the Colorado—to excuse the liberty.

The first circumstance that strikes a stranger traversing this wild country is the vagrant instincts and habits of the great majority of its denizens—perhaps I should say, of the American people generally, as exhibited here. Among any ten whom you successively meet, there will be natives of New England, New York, Pennsylvania, Virginia or Georgia, Ohio or Indiana, Kentucky or Missouri, France,

Germany, and perhaps Ireland. But, worse than this; you cannot enter a circle of a dozen persons of whom at least three will not have spent some years in California, two or three have made claims and built cabins in Kansas or Nebraska, and at least one spent a year or so in Texas. Boston, New York Philadelphia, New Orleans, St. Louis, Cincinnati, have all contributed their quota toward peopling the new gold region. The next man you meet driving an ox team, and white as a miller with dust, is probably an ex-banker or doctor, a broken merchant or manufacturer from the old states, who has scraped together the candle ends charitably or contemptuously allowed him by his creditors on settlement, and risked them on a last desperate cast of the dice by coming hither. Ex-editors, ex-printers, ex-clerks, ex-steamboat men, are here in abundance—all on the keen hunt for the gold which only a few will secure. One of the stations at which we slept on our way up—a rough tent with a cheering hope (since blasted) of a log house in the near future—was kept by an ex-lawyer of Cincinnati and his wife, an ex-actress from our New York Bowery—she being cook. Omnibus drivers from Broadway repeatedly handled the ribbons; ex-border ruffians from civilized Kansas —some of them of unblessed memory—were encountered on our way, at intervals none too long. All these, blended with veteran mountain men, Indians of all grades from the tamest to the wildest, half-breeds, French trappers and *voyageurs* (who have generally two or three Indian wives apiece), and an occasional Negro, compose a medley such as hardly another region can parallel. Honolulu, or some other port of the South Sea Islands, could probably match it most nearly.

The old mountaineers form a caste by themselves, and they prize the distinction. Some of them are Frenchmen, or Franco-Americans, who have been trapping or trading in and around these mountains for a quarter of a century, have wives and children here, and here expect to live and die. Some of these have accumulated property and cash to the value of two hundred thousand dollars, which amount will not easily be reduced, as they are frugal in everything (liquor sometimes excepted), spend but a pittance on the clothing of their families, trust little, keep small stocks of goods, and sell at large profits. Others came years ago from the states, some of them on account each of a "difficulty" wherein they severally killed or savagely maimed their respective antagonists under circumstances on which the law refuses to look leniently; whence their pilgrimage to and prolonged sojourn here, despite enticing placards offering five hundred dollars or perhaps one thousand dollars for their safe return to the places that knew them once, but shall know them no more. This class is not numerous, but is more influential than it should be in giving tone to the society of which its members form a part. Prone to deep drinking, soured in temper, always armed, bristling at a word, ready with the rifle, revolver or bowie knife, they give law and set fashions which, in a country where the regular administration of justice is yet a matter of prophecy, it seems difficult to overrule or disregard. I apprehend that there have been, during my two weeks' sojourn, more brawls, more fights, more pistol shots with criminal intent in this log city of one hundred and fifty dwellings, not three-fourths completed nor two-thirds inhabited, nor one-third fit to be, than in any community of no greater numbers on earth. This will be changed in time—I trust within a year, for the empty houses are steadily finding tenants from the two streams of emigration rolling in daily up the Platte on the one hand, down Cherry Creek on the other, including some scores of women and children, who generally stop here, as all of them should; for life in the mountains is yet horribly rough. Public religious worship, a regular mail and other civilizing influences, are being established; there is a gleam of hope that the Arapahoes—who have made the last two or three nights indescribably hideous by their infernal war whoops, songs and dances—will at last clear out on the foray against the Utes they have so long threatened, diminishing largely the aggregate of drunkenness and riot, and justifying expectations of comparative peace. So let me close up my jottings from this point—which circumstances beyond my control have rendered so voluminous—with a rough ambrotype of

LIFE IN DENVER

The rival cities of Denver and Auraria front on each other from either bank of Cherry Creek, just before it is lost in the South Platte. The Platte has its sources in and around the South Park of the Rocky Mountains, a hundred miles southwest of this point; but Cherry Creek is headed off from them by that river, and, winding its northward course of forty or fifty miles over the Plains, with its sources barely touching the mountains, is a capricious stream, running quite smartly when we came here, but whose broad and thirsty sands have since drank it all up at this point, leaving the log footbridges which connect the two cities as useless as an icehouse in November. The Platte, aided by the melting of the snows on the higher mountains, runs nearly full-banked, though the constant succession of hot suns and dry winds begins to tell upon it; while Clear Creek (properly Vasquer's Fork), which issues directly from the mountains just above its crossing on the way to the Gregory diggings, is nearly at its highest, and will so remain till the inner mountains are mainly denuded of their snowy mantles. But, within a few days, a footbridge has been completed over the Platte, virtually abolishing the ferry and saving considerable time and money to gold-seekers and travelers; while

134

another over Clear Creek precludes not only delay but danger—several wagons having been wrecked and two or three men all but drowned in attempts to ford its rapid, rocky current. Thus the ways of the adventurous grow daily smoother; and they who visit this region ten years hence will regard as idle tales the stories of privation, impediment, and "hairbreadth'scapes" which are told, or might be, by the gold-seekers of 1859.

Of these rival cities, Auraria is by far the more venerable —some of its structures being, I think, fully a year old, if not more. Denver, on the other hand, can boast of no antiquity beyond September or October last. In the architecture of the two cities there is, notwithstanding, a striking similarity— cottonwood logs, cut from the adjacent bottom of the Platte, roughly hewed on the upper and under sides, and chinked with billets of split cottonwood on the inner, and with mud on the outer side, forming the walls of nearly or quite every edifice which adorns either city. Across the center of the interior, from shorter wall to wall, stretches a sturdy ridgepole, usually in a state of nature, from which "shooks," or split saplings of cottonwood, their split sides down, incline gently to the transverse or longer sides; on these (in the more finished structures) a coating of earth is laid; and, with a chimney of mud-daubed sticks in one corner, a door nearly opposite, and a hole beside it representing or prefiguring a window, the edifice is complete. Of course, many have no earth on their covering of shooks, and so are liable to gentle inundation in the rainy season; but, though we have had thunder and lightning almost daily, with a brisk gale in most instances, there has been no rain worth naming such here for weeks, and the unchinked, barely shook-covered houses, through whose sides and roofs you may see the stars as you lie awake nights, are decidedly the cooler and airier. There is a new hotel nearly finished in Auraria, which has a second-story (but no first-story) floor; beside this, mine eyes have never yet been blessed with the sight of any floor whatever in either Denver or Auraria. The last time I slept or ate with a floor under me (our wagon box and mother earth excepted) was at Junction City, nearly four weeks ago. The Denver House, which is the Astor House of the gold region, has walls of logs, a floor of earth, with windows and roof of rather flimsy cotton sheeting; while every guest is allowed as good a bed as his blankets will make. The charges are no higher than at the Astor and other first-class hotels, except for liquor—twenty-five cents a drink for dubious whisky, colored and nicknamed to suit the taste of customers, being the regular rate throughout this region. I had the honor to be shaved there by a nephew (so he assured me) of Murat, Bonaparte's king of Naples—the honor and the shave together costing but a paltry dollar. Still, a few days of such luxury surfeited me, mainly because the main or drinking room was also occupied by several blacklegs as a gambling hall, and their incessant clamor of "Who'll go me twenty? The ace of hearts is the winning card. Whoever turns the ace of hearts wins the twenty dollars," etc., etc., persisted in at all hours up to midnight, became at length a nuisance, from which I craved deliverance at any price. Then the visitors of that drinking and gambling room had a careless way, when drunk, of firing revolvers, sometimes at each other, at other times quite miscellaneously, which struck me as inconvenient for a quiet guest with only a leg and a half, hence in poor condition for dodging bullets. So I left.

"How do you live in Denver?" I inquired of a New York friend some weeks domiciled here, in whose company I visited the mines. "O, I've jumped a cabin," was his cool, matter-of-course reply. As jumping a cabin was rather beyond my experience, I inquired further, and learned that, finding an uninhabited cabin that suited him, he had quietly entered and spread his blankets, eating at home or abroad as opportunity might suggest. I found, on further inquiry, that at least one-third of the inhabitations in Denver and Auraria were desolate when we came here (they have been gradually filling up since), some of the owners having gone into the mountains, digging or prospecting, and taken their limited supply of household goods along with them; while others, discouraged by the poor show of mining six weeks ago, when even the nearer mountains were still covered with snow and ice, rushed pell-mell down the Platte with the wild reflux of the spring emigration, abandoning all but what they could carry away. It is said that lots and cabins together sold for twenty-five dollars—so long as there were purchasers; but these soon failing, they were left behind like campfires in the morning, and have since been at the service of all comers.

So, in company with a journalizing friend, I, too, have "jumped a cabin," and have kept to it quite closely, under a doctor's care, for the last week or ten days. It is about ten feet square, and eight feet high, rather too well chinked for summer, considering that it lacks a window, but must be a capital house for this country in winter. I board with the nearest neighbor; and it is not my landlady's fault that the edible resources of Denver are decidedly limited. But even these are improving. To the bread, bacon, and beans, which formed the staple of every meal a short time ago, there have been several recent additions; milk, which was last week twenty-five cents per quart, is now down to ten, and I hear a rumor that eggs, owing to a recent increase in the number of hens, within five hundred miles, from four or five to twelve or fifteen, are about to fall from a dollar a dozen to fifty cents per dozen. On every side, I note signs of progress—improvement—manifest destiny: there was a man about the city yesterday with lettuce to sell, and I am credibly assured that there will be green peas next month— actually peas!—provided it should rain soakingly meantime —whereof a hazy, lowering sky would seem just now to afford some hope. (P. S. The hope has vanished.) But I— already sadly behind, and nearly able to travel again—must turn my back on this promise of luxuries, and take the road to Laramie today, or at furthest tomorrow.

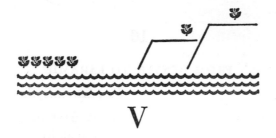

V

DENVER TO SALT LAKE CITY

Dispatches 16 through 19

Lively and interesting as Denver might be, California was the destination and it was a long way off. Greeley hired D. B. Wheelock to take him by wagon over the rough and empty reach of country along the edge of the Rockies to Ft. Laramie. The westbound stage departed Laramie June 30 with the New York editor, its sole passenger, perched atop seventeen sacks of mail. Greeley soon discovered to his indignation that sixteen of them were filled with franked mail from Washington destined for the constituents of a Mormon Congressman. Greeley reached Salt Lake City on July 11, three weeks out of Denver, having had occasion en route to observe at first hand the white man's traffic in Indian girls and bad whisky.

16

FROM DENVER TO LARAMIE

Fort Laramie, June 27, 1859

I left Denver at 3 P. M. on Tuesday, 21st inst. There are two roads thence to this point: that usually preferred follows down the east fork of the South Platte some forty miles, crossing that river near St. Vrain's (deserted) Fort, thus avoiding several rapid and difficult creeks, and crossing Cache-la-Poudre near its mouth, where, like nearly all these streams, it is broader and shallower than where it issues from the Rocky Mountains. My guide had expected to take this route till the last moment, when he learned that the South Platte was entirely too high to be forded near St. Vrain's Fort, or anywhere else, and that there was now no ferryboat for two hundred miles below Denver; hence he had no choice but to take the upper or mountain route. So we crossed the Platte directly at Denver, and Clear Creek some three or four miles below the road to Gregory's Diggings, by a bad, difficult ford, embellished by some half dozen deep, ugly "sloughs" in the bottom on either side, the creek being so high that the bottom was flooded in part, and very miry. This high water cut us off from a purposed call on a hunter in the bottom, of whom we had expected to obtain fresh meat for our journey. We pushed on ten miles further, and camped for the night opposite Boulder City, a log hamlet of some thirty habitations,[1] covering the entrance to Boulder Diggings, twelve miles westward in the mountains. Here we found four wagons, two of them with horse teams, each conveying the luggage of four or five men who, having

---

[1] Now a city of approximately 40,000 and the site of the University of Colorado.

taken a look at this gold region, had decided to push on for California, most of them, I believe, through what is known as the Cherokee Trail, which forms a part of the shortest practicable route from Denver to Salt Lake. I was strongly tempted at Denver to join one or these parties, and go through this pass—had I stood firmly on both feet, I think I should have done it, saving distance, though losing time. We all camped for the night beside a small brook, the rippling of whose waters over its pebbly bed fell soothingly on the drowsy ear. I had the wagon to myself for a bed chamber, while my three companions spread their buffalo skin and blankets on the grass, and had the vault of heaven for their ceiling. The night was cool and breezy; our mules were picketed on the grass at a short distance; our supper of fried pork and pilot bread had not surfeited us; and we slept quietly till the first dawn of day, when our mules were quickly harnassed, and we left our fellow campers still torpid, pushing on fifteen miles, and crossing two deep, swift, steep-banked creeks (St. Vrain's Fork, and a branch of Thompson's Creek) before stopping for feed and breakfast. After two hours' rest, we harnessed up, and made twenty miles more before stopping, at the crossing of the other fork of Thompson's Creek for dinner. Here we found a caravan moving from Missouri to California, which reminded me of the days of Abraham and Lot. It comprised six or seven heavy wagons, mainly drawn by oxen, with a light traveling carriage and pair of horses conveying the patriarch's family, some two or three hundred head of cows, steers, and young cattle, with three or four young men on horseback driving and keeping the herd. Girls were milking, women cooking or washing, children playing—in short, here was the material for a very fair settlement, or quite an imposing Kansas City. While we were snoozing, they hitched up and moved on before us, but we

141

very soon overtook and passed them. There are scores of such caravans now on the various roads to California, many of which will see very hard times ere they reach Carson Valley, and some still harder before they get fairly across the Sierra Nevada. Many of them are behind time; the feed—for most of the way scanty at best—has been devoured by the cattle ahead of them, and the drought forbids the growth of more until September, in which month snow begins to fall heavily on the Sierra Nevada. And it will not tend to rouse their flagging spirits to meet—as I am well assured they must—similar caravans of people, who, having tried California to their full satisfaction, are now moving back to Missouri again. Was there ever another such vagrant, restless, discontented people, pretending to be civilized, as ours!

Pushing on steadily over a reasonably level country, though crossed by many deep and steep-banked dry gullies, and perhaps one petty living stream, we stood at 5 p. m. on the south bank of Cache-la-Poudre, seventy miles from Denver, and by far the most formidable stream between the South Platte and the Laramie.[2] Our conductor was as brave as mountaineer need be, but he was wary as well, and had seen so many people drowned in fording such streams, especially the Green River branch of the Colorado, on which he spent a year or two, that he chose to feel his way carefully. So he waited and observed for an hour or more, meantime sending word to an old French mountaineer friend from Utah, who has pitched his tent here, that his help was

---

[2] At this point he was not far from the future site of Greeley, Colorado. It was founded just ten years later, in 1869, by Nathan C. Meeker, an idealistic former Fourierist whose enthusiasm for a colony of "temperance men ambitious to establish a good society" in the Far West found ready response in Greeley. "Go ahead," he told Meeker, "and I will back you in the *Tribune*." Then, characteristically, he gave Meeker some advice: "Have no rum and no fences in your colony." Hale: op. cit., p. 309. Greeley is now a prospering city of some 30,000.

142

wanted. There had been a ferry boat at this crossing till two nights before, when it went downstream, and had not since been heard of. A horseman we met some miles below, assured us that there was no crossing; but this we found a mistake—two men mounted on strong horses crossing safely before our eyes, and two heavy-laden ox wagons succeeding them in doing the same, save that one of them stuck in the stream, and the oxen had to be taken off and driven out, being unable to pull it while themselves were half buried in the swift current. But these crossings were made from the other side, where the entrance was better and the current rather favored the passage; the ox wagons were held to the bottom by the weight of their loads, while our "ambulance" was light, and likely to be swept downstream. At length our French friend appeared, mounted on a powerful horse, with an Indian attendant on another such. He advised us to stay where we were for the night, promising to come in the morning with a heavy ox team and help us over. As this, however, involved a loss of at least ten miles on our next day's drive, our conductor resolved to make an attempt now. So the Frenchman on his strong horse took one of our lead mules by the halter and the Indian took the other, and we went in, barely escaping an upset from going down the steep bank obliquely, and thus throwing one side of our wagon much above the other; but we righted in a moment and went through—the water being at least three feet deep for about a hundred yards, the bottom broken by the boulders, and the current very strong. We camped so soon as fairly over, lit a fire, and, having obtained a quarter of antelope from our French friend, proceeded to prepare and discuss a most satisfactory supper. Table, of course, there was none, and we had unluckily lost our fork; but we had still two knives, a sufficiency of tin-cups and plates, with an abundance of pork and pilot bread, and an old bag for tablecloth which had evidently seen hard service, and had gathered more dirt and blood in the course of it than a tablecloth actually needs. But the antelope ham was fresh, fat, and tender; and it must have weighed less by three pounds when that supper was ended than when its preparation was commenced.

By the way, there was a discussion at supper between my three companions—all mountaineers of ripe experience—as to the relative merits of certain meats, of which I give the substance for the benefit of future travelers through this wild region. Buffalo I found to be a general favorite, though my own experience of it makes it a tough, dry, wooden fiber, only to be eaten under great provocation. I infer that it is poorer in spring than at other seasons, and that I have not been fortunate in cooks. Bear, I was surprised to learn, is not generally liked by mountaineers—my companions had eaten every species, and were not pleased with any. The black-tailed deer of the mountains is a general favorite; so is the mountain hen or grouse; so is the antelope, of course; the elk and mountain sheep less decidedly so. None of our party liked horse, or knew any way of cooking it that would make it really palatable, though of course it has to be eaten occasionally, for necessity hath no law—or rather, is its own law. Our conductor had eaten broiled wolf, under compulsion, but could not recommend it; but he certified that a slice of cold boiled dog—*well* boiled, so as to free it from rankness, and then suffered to cool thoroughly—is tender, sweet and delicate as lamb. I ought to have ascertained the species and age of the dog in whose behalf this testimony was borne—for a young Newfoundland or King Charles might justify the praise, while it would be utterly unwarranted in the case of an old cur or mastiff—but the opportunity was lost, and I can only give the testimony as I received it.

Cache-la-Poudre seems to be the center of the antelope

country. There are no settlements, save a small beginning just at this ford, as yet hardly three months old, between Denver, seventy miles on one side, and Laramie, one hundred and thirty on the other. The North Platte and the Laramie, both head in the mountains, forty to eighty miles due west of this point, thence pursuing a generally north course for more than a hundred miles among the hills, which are here lower and less steep than further south. The bold, high, regular front displayed by the Rocky Mountains for at least a hundred (and, I believe, for two hundred) miles south of the Cache-la-Poudre, hence gradually melts away into a succession of softer, rounder, lower hills; snow disappears; the line between the mountains and the plains is no longer straight and sharply defined; and the still waters of the plain have for some miles an alkaline appearance, beside being very scarce in summer. The Cherokee Trail plunges into the mountains on the north side of and very near to Cache-la-Poudre; and henceforth we overtake no emigrants moving westward—none of any sort—but meet a few in wagons making for Boulder City or the Gregory Diggings. Since we crossed Clear Creek, on which there is on this trail a decent fringe of cottonwood, we had seen but the merest shred of small cottonwoods and some shrub willow at wide intervals along the larger watercourses; but the pine still sparsely covered the face of the Rocky Mountains. Cache-la-Poudre has quite a fair belt of cottonwood; thenceforth there is scarcely a cord of wood to a township for the next fifty or sixty miles; and the pine is no longer visible on the hills near us, because they expose little rock, and hence are swept by the annual fires. The high prairie on either side is thinly, poorly grassed, being of moderate fertility at best, often full of pebbles of the average size of a goose egg, and apparently doomed to sterility by drought. This region, though inferior in soil, and less smooth in surface, is not dissimilar in its topography to Lombardy, and, like it, will in time be subjected to systematic irrigation,[3] should the Rocky Mountain gold mines prove rich and extensive. Some of the streams crossed by our road might easily be so dammed at their egress from the mountains as to irrigate miles in width to the South Platte, forty or fifty miles distant; and, at the prices which vegetables must always command here should the gold mines prove inexhaustible, the enterprise would pay well. I was told at Cache-la-Poudre that encouraging signs of gold had been obtained on that stream, though it had only begun to be prospected.

We were up and away betimes, still over thinly grassed, badly watered prairie, rather level in its general outlines, but badly cut by steep-banked watercourses, now dry. Some shallow ponds are also formed here in the wet season, but the last of them had just dried up. We drove fifteen miles, and stopped for breakfast on a feeble tributary of Cache-la-Poudre, named Box Elder, from a small tree which I first observed here, and which is poorer stuff, if possible, than cottonwood. This is the only tributary which joins the Cache-la-Poudre below its egress from the mountains. All the streams of this region are largest where they emerge from the mountains, unless re-enforced below by other streams having a like origin; the thirsty prairie contributes nothing, but begins to drink them up from the time they strike it. The smaller streams are thus utterly absorbed in the course of five to ten miles, unless they happen sooner to be lost in some larger creek. Drought, throughout each summer, is the inexorable and desolating tyrant of the plains.

Rising from the valley of Box Elder, we passed over a divide, and were soon winding our way among the buttes, or irregular, loosely aggregated hills, which form a prominent

[3] This region did indeed come under extensive irrigation, as Greeley predicted.

146

feature of the next seventy or eighty miles, and which I must try to give some idea of.

The soil of this region, like that of the Plains generally, is mainly clay, with some sand and gravel intermixed —the gravel probably washed from the mountains. Here, though not at a distance from the mountains, loose, water-rounded stones, from the size of a pigeon's egg up to that of a man's head, are often, though by no means uniformly, intermingled with the soil, especially near the beds of streams. These stones are of various kinds and colors, including quartz, indicating a mountain origin. But there seems to be no underlying rock in place—that is, none at any depth attained by the deepest watercourses—and the soil, when sodden by the pouring rains of winter and early spring, seems unable to oppose any resistance to the washing, wearing influence of every stream or rill. The average level of the Plains would seem to have once been at least forty or fifty feet higher than at present, the greater part of the earth to that depth having been gradually worn away and carried down the streams to the Missouri and lower Mississippi. But there are localities which, from one cause or another, more or less obstinately resist this constant abrasion; and these are gradually moulded into hills by the abstraction annually proceeding all around them. Some of them have been washed down to so gentle a slope that grass covers them completely, and prevents further loss; but the greater number are still being gullied, washed and worn away by the influence of each violent rain. Others have living streams at their base, which, having once taken a sheer against them, are continually increasing the acuteness of their angles and gouging more and more decidedly into their banks, occasionally flinging down tons of undermined earth into their channels to be gradually carried off, as so much has already been. In such places, the buttes are nearly

147

perpendicular and square-faced; but they are more apt to be circular, and steeper near the summit than below. In some instances, the earth is of a bright vermilion color; in others, partly thus and partly white—giving the buttes a variegated and fantastic appearance, like that of the Pictured Rocks of Lake Superior. When first seen from a distance, the ensemble of the red buttes is very striking. But the white clay, as it is gradually washed away, leaving surfaces almost or quite perpendicular exposed to the action of sun, air and water, is, by some occult agency, gradually hardened into a kind of rock, of which long ranges of perpendicular bluffs are composed, sometimes miles in extent, but broken and disturbed at intervals by the intervention of watercourses or other influences.

After leaving Box Elder, our road gradually ascended, winding among the rounded and less regularly arranged buttes first described above, but passing no water but a single spring and little available grass, until it descends a long hill to a fork of Howard's Creek, twenty miles from Box Elder. Here we stopped for dinner at 3 P. M. beside two or three wagons of Pike's Peakers, from whom we obtained a generous supply of fresh bread and another antelope ham, very much to the improvement of our edible resources. (I may as well explain here that all the emigrants we met going into the Kansas diggings had started from the Missouri, on the north side of the Platte, and had failed to cross at Shinn's Ferry, sixty-five miles up the latter stream, supposing that they could do so at Fort Kearney, or some other point below the forks; but, in the absence of ferries, the high water had headed them off, and forced them clear up to Laramie, whence they were now working southward, having lost fully two hundred miles by neglecting to cross the Platte where they might have done so.) In all this region, it is a settled maxim that you must cross (if you can) a stream directly upon reaching it, if your way lies across it, never camping before you do so, lest a sudden rise should obstruct your passage for days. Many have lost a fortnight's weary travel by failing to heed this rule in spirit with regard to the Platte.

We moved again at five, passing over a high ridge and into a broad valley, with rounded hills on the west, and a range of such precipitous clay-rock bluffs as I have tried to describe on the east. These bluffs were broken through at intervals, and the streams that came down the hills on the west ran out at the brooks, after traversing the valley for two or three miles, and flowed away east to join Howard's Fork and the South Platte. Our trail here bore considerably west of north, evidently to reach the mouth of the Cheyenne Pass. We had hoped to make our next camp at that point; but night fell upon us before reaching it, and we stopped on a little run where we found water and good grass, close under the mountains, and in one of the loneliest spots I ever beheld. Not a tree nor shrub was visible, nor had been for miles; yet, it was not difficult to gather dry sticks enough to cook our supper, proving what I have elsewhere observed, that wood was formerly more common in all this region than now. We had all turned in by nine, and were doing very well, when a rush by one of our mules apprised us that he was loose, having broken his lariat; he was soon caught and made fast, and we all addressed ourselves to slumber again. In an hour, however, there was a fresh alarm, and not without reason, for three of our mules had gone, we could not tell whither. The first impression was that a band of Cheyennes, who were known to be encamped in the mountains very near us, had, unsuspected by us, been watching our progress from their heights, and had stolen down under cover of the deep darkness, unfastened, and started our mules with intent to run them off. This was not an agree-

able view of the case, as we could hope neither to recover
nor replace our faithful animals for at least a week. However, a little watching of the mule still fast convinced our
conductor that the others had started back on the road we
had traversed, which was a route the Cheyennes were most
unlikely to take, while so near their hiding places in the
mountains. So two of our men started on the back-track,
but returned in an hour unsuccessful. Then the remaining
mule was saddled and bridled—and he had to be thrown
down twice before he would submit to the operation—when
our conductor mounted him, expecting to be instantly thrown
by the perverse beast, unused to the saddle, but he was
happily disappointed, and started down the road on a brisk
trot. By this time there was moonlight; and he found all
the missing mules a little beyond the point to which he had
previously proceeded on foot, and brought them back in
triumph. It was now break of day, and we resolved to feed
and breakfast for once before starting. We did so, and moved
on at 6 A. M., reaching Camp Walbach, at the mouth of
the Cheyenne Pass, in less than half an hour.

Let me halt here a moment to illustrate the military and
public land systems of the United States. It last year entered
the head of some genius connected with the War Department that the public interest or safety required the establishment of a military post at this point, and one was accordingly planted and maintained there throughout last
winter. Of course, buildings were required to shelter the
officers, soldiers, and animals in that severe climate, and
they were accordingly erected, some of the timber being
transported from Laramie—a distance of fully eighty miles.
In the main, however, they are built of pine logs from the
adjacent mountains, the crevices being plastered with mud.
In the spring, the troops were very properly withdrawn,
leaving half a dozen good serviceable houses and a su-

perior horse shed and corral untenanted. Hereupon, three lazy louts have squatted on the premises, intending to start a city there, and to hold and sell the government structures under a claim of pre-emption! I need hardly say that, in the absence of any United States survey, with the Indian title still unextinguished, this claim is most impudent; but that will not prevent their asserting it, and I fear with success. The private interest on one side will be strong, with none on the other; they can threaten to exert a political influence, favorably or adversely, as the case may be, to those whom they find in power; if they are only tenacious enough, impudent enough, they will probably carry their point. Yet, they might as fairly pre-empt the White House at Washington, should they ever chance to find it vacant.

We drove on across a badly gullied region, wherein are the heads of Horse Creek—the first stream on our route that runs to the North Platte—and struck the Chugwater just where it emerged from the mountains, about 11 A.M. Thence, we followed down this creek more than forty miles, crossing it four times, and finally leaving it on our left to cross the Laramie River, eight or ten miles above this place.

The Chugwater is a rapid, muddy millstream, running in a deep, narrow, tortuous channel, and constantly gouging into one bank or the other, except where the willows and some other small shrubs oppose the resistance of their matted roots to the force of the current. The rocky hills sometimes crowd the stream closely, compelling the road to make a circuit over the high prairie adjacent to avoid the impracticable canyons through which the stream frets and foams on its devious way. The red buttes are numerous and conspicuous on the upper course of this creek—the ochry earth or rock which gives them their peculiar color being accounted a rich iron ore. On the lower bottoms of this stream, we found far better grass than elsewhere on this journey. But the day was hot, and our mules suffered so much from mosquitoes and flies that they ate fitfully and sparingly where we halted for dinner, and again where we stopped for the night. We were unable to stop where the grass was best, because we could not there get our animals down the steep creek bank to water.

We made our last camp at a point thirty miles from this post, having made one hundred and sixty miles in three days' steady travel, hampered by the necessity of finding grass and water for our beasts. With grain, I think they would easily have made sixty-five miles per day. We stopped beside a stone-and-mud shanty of very rude construction, where a Frenchman had this spring made a small dam across the Chugwater, so as to irrigate and fence (by a ditch) a small piece of intervale, on which he had attempted to grow some grains and vegetables, with rather poor promise of success. He was absent, and no person or domestic animal to be seen about his place. The night was uncommonly warm for this region—the mosquitoes a good deal more attentive than obliging. We rose early again, came on ten miles for breakfast, passing almost continually between two rows of magnificent buttes, often looking in the distance like more or less ruined castles; one of them reminded me strongly of the Roman Coliseum. Two miles after breakfast, we crossed the Chugwater for the last time, and left it running north to the Laramie, while we struck a more easterly course for this place. Two miles further on, we came to a most excellent spring—the first I had seen since I emerged from the Rocky Mountains, by Clear Creek, two weeks before. I had been poisoned by brook water—often warm and muddy —so long that I could hardly get enough of this. We now passed over twelve or fifteen miles of high, rolling, parched, barren prairie, and halted for dinner by a little brook—the only one that crosses our trail between Chugwater and Laramie—after which we drove down opposite this place in an hour, but were obliged to go two miles below, and pay $2.50 bridge toll to get across the Laramie, now very high, and looking decidedly larger at their junction than the North Platte itself.

I have been tediously minute in my record of this cross-march to reach the high road to California, because some kind friends have remonstrated with me against the fancied perils of my journey, as if I were running recklessly into danger. I believe this portion of my route is at least as perilous as any other, being the only part not traversed by a mail stage or any public conveyance, and lying wholly through a region in which there are not a dozen white settlers, all told, while it is a usual battleground between hostile tribes of Indians. But we were never in any shadow of danger; and, though I was compelled to economize steps in order to complete the healing of my lame leg, I have rarely had a more pleasant journey. Let anyone who wishes an independent and comfortable ride just run up to Denver and ask my friend D. B. Wheelock to harness up his four-mule team to the Rockaway wagon and take him over to Laramie, and if he does not enjoy a fine prospect, bracing breezes, a lively pace and excellent company, then he will be less fortunate than I was.

17

LARAMIE TO SOUTH PASS

South Pass, Rocky Mountains, July 5, 1859

I exhausted all the possibilities of obtaining a lodging in Laramie before applying to the commander of the post; but no one else could (or would) afford me a shelter on any terms; so I made a virtue of necessity, and applied to Captain Clark, who at once assigned me a room—there being few troops there at present—and for the five days I remained there I slept between a floor and a roof, after five weeks' experience of the more primitive methods of keeping cold and storm at bay. I was treated with more than hospitality —with generous kindness—by Captain Clark, Lieutenants Hascall and Follet, and Dr. Johns—and yet the long tarry became at length irksome, because I had already lost too much time, and was most anxious to be moving westward. Finally, the mail stage from the East hove in sight on the morning of June 30th, but halted just across Laramie River all day, repairing coach; and it was 8 P.M. when it started— I alone perched on the summit of its seventeen mailbags as passenger—he who had thus far filled that exalted post kindly giving way for me, and agreeing to take instead the slower wagon that was to follow next morning. We forded the swollen Laramie two miles above the fort, in the last vestige of twilight—had the usual trouble with mules turning about in mid-stream, tangling up the team, and threatening to upset the wagon—but overcame it after a while, got safely out, drove on fifteen miles to Warm Spring—a fountain which throws out half water enough for a gristmill, all which is drunk up by the thirsty sands through which it takes its course, before it can reach the Platte, only three or four miles distant. We camped here till daylight, then lost two hours in hunting up our mules, which had been simply tied in pairs, and allowed to go at large in quest of the scanty grass of that region. They were found at last, and we went on our way rejoicing.

I shall not weary my readers with a journal of our travels for the last four days. Hitherto, since I left civilized Kansas, I had traversed routes either newly opened, or scarcely known to the mass of readers; but from Laramie I have followed the regular California and Oregon Overland Trail, already many times described, and by this time familiar to hundreds of thousands. Suffice it that, for over two hundred miles from Laramie, it traverses a region substantially described in my notes of my journey from the buffalo range to Denver, and from Denver to Laramie; a region, for the most part, rainless in summer and autumn, yet on whose soil of more or less sandy clay, lacking support from ridges of underlying rock, has been more seamed, and gouged, and gullied, and washed away, by the action of floods and streams than any other on earth—a region of bluffs and buttes, and deep ravines, and intervales, and shallow alkaline lakelets, now mainly dried up, and streams running milky, even when low, with the clay gullied from their banks, and sent off to render the Missouri a river of mud, and to fertilize the bottoms of the lower Mississippi. Occasionally, but not so frequently as south of Laramie, the clay hills, hardened into rock by some alchemy of nature, present the perpendicular fronts and ruinous-castle aspects already described—in a few instances, the scanty creeks which make their way from the mountains to the North Platte or the Sweetwater run through narrow canyons of such rock; but usually each creek has washed out for itself a wide valley, and the bluffs or buttes, where they exist, are distant many miles on one side, if not on both. In a few places, the mountains are so near that their thinly scattered, stunted, scraggy yellow pines are plainly seen—are even close beside us; but usually the prospect is composed of rolling prairie very scantily grassed and often thickly covered for miles on miles by the everlasting sagebrush of this desolate region. This is not an anomaly, as might be supposed—the stem lives for years, perhaps centuries, though the shoots and leaves die* every autumn. Another shrub, less

* I guess this is a mistake; further observation induces me to believe that the sagebrush is an evergreen.

common, but which often thickly covers hundreds of acres, is the greasewood—a low, prickly bush, growing in bunches, like the sagebrush, and looking like a bad imitation of the English privet. Besides these two miserable shrubs, the dry land, other than the mountains, for hundreds of miles, produces a very little burnt-up grass in patches, and a good many ill-favored weeds of no known or presumed value. Of wood, the Platte and its more easterly tributaries have, at intervals, a shred of the eternal cottonwood of the plains, much of it the more scrubby and worthless species known as bitter cottonwood, with very little of the equally worthless box elder—and that is all. But, one hundred and forty miles this side of Laramie, we leave the Platte, which here comes from the south, and strike nearly forty miles across a barren "divide" to its tributary, the Sweetwater, which we find just by Independence Rock, quite a landmark in this desolate region, with several low mountains of almost naked rock around it, having barely soil enough in their crevices to support a few dwarfish pines. Five miles above this is the Devil's Gate—a passage of the Sweetwater, through a perpendicular canyon, some twenty-five feet wide, and said to be six hundred feet high—a passage which must have been cut while the rock was still clay. Here a large party of Mormons were caught by the snows, while on their way to Salt Lake, some years since, and compelled to encamp for the winter, so scantily provided that more than a hundred of them died of hunger and hardship before spring. Many more must have fallen victims had not a supply train from Salt Lake reached them early in the season. And here is a fountain of cold water—the first that I had seen for more than a hundred miles, though there is another on the long stretch from the Platte to the Sweetwater, which is said to be good, but a drove of cattle were making quite too free with it when we passed. Here the weary crowds of emigrants to California were to gather yesterday for a celebration of the "glorious fourth," and I was warmly invited to stop and participate, and I now heartily wish I had, since I find that all our haste was in vain.

It was midnight of the 3rd, when we reached the mail-route station known as the Three Crossings, from the fact that so many fordings of the Sweetwater (here considerably larger than at its mouth, forty miles or more below) have to be made within the next mile. We had been delayed two hours by the breaking away of our two lead mules, in crossing a deep watercourse after dark—or rather by the fruitless efforts of our conductor to recover them. I had been made sick by the bad water I had drunk from the brooks we crossed during the hot day, and rose in a not very patriotic, certainly not a joyful mood, unable to eat, but ready to move on. We started a little after sunrise; and, at the very first crossing, one of our lead mules turned about and ran into his mate, whom he threw down and tangled so that he could not get up; and in a minute another mule was down, and the two in imminent danger of drowning. They were soon liberated from the harness, and got up, and we went out; but just then an emigrant on the bank espied a carpetbag in the water—mine, of course—and fished it out. An examination was then had, and showed that my trunk was missing—the boot of the stage having been opened the night before, on our arrival at the station, and culpably left unfastened. We made a hasty search for the stray, but without success, and after an hour's delay our conductor drove off, leaving my trunk still in the bottom of Sweetwater, which is said to be ten feet deep just below our ford. I would rather have sunk a thousand dollars there. Efforts were directed to be made to fish it out; but my hope of ever seeing it again is a faint one. We forded Sweetwater six times yesterday after that, without a single mishap; but I have hardly yet become reconciled to the loss of my trunk, and, on the whole, my fourth of July was not a happy one.

Our road left a southerly bend of Sweetwater after dinner, and took its way over the hills, so as not to strike the stream again till after dark, at a point three miles from where I now write. We passed, on a high divide some miles before the Three Crossings of the Sweetwater, a low swamp or meadow known as Ice Springs, from the fact that ice may be obtained here at any time by digging down some two or three feet into the frosty earth. We met several wagonloads of come-outers from Mormonism on their way to the states in the course of the afternoon; likewise, the children of the Arkansas people killed two years since, in what is known as the Mountain Meadows massacre. We are now nearly at the summit of the route, with snowy mountains near us in several directions, and one large snowbank by the side of a creek we crossed ten miles back. Yet our yesterday's road was no rougher, while it was decidedly better, than that of any former day this side of Laramie, as may be judged from the fact that, with a late start, we made sixty miles with one (six-mule) team to our heavy-laden wagon. The grass is better for the last twenty miles than on any twenty miles previously; and the swift streams that frequently cross our way are cold and sweet. But, unlike the Platte, the Sweetwater has scarcely a tree or bush growing on its banks; but up the little stream on which I am writing, on a box in the mail company's station tent, there is glorious water, some grass, and more wood than I have seen so close together since I emerged from the gold diggings on Vasquer's Fork, five hundred miles away. A snowbank, forty rods long and several feet deep, lies just across the brook; the wind blows cold at night; and we had a rain squall—just rain enough to lay the dust—yesterday afternoon. The mail agent whom we met here has orders not to run into Salt Lake ahead of time; so he keeps us over here today, and will then take six days to reach Salt Lake, which we might reach in four. I am but a passenger, and must study patience.

A word on the Salt Lake mail. Of the seventeen bags on which I have ridden for the last four days and better, at least sixteen are filled with large bound books, mainly Patent Office reports, I judge—but all of them undoubtedly works ordered printed at the public cost—*your* cost, reader!—by Congress, and now on their way to certain favored Mormons, franked (by proxy) "Pub. Doc. *Free*, J. M. Bernhisel, M. C." I do not blame Mr. B. for clutching his share of this public plunder, and distributing it so as to increase his own popularity and importance; but I do protest against this business of printing books by wholesale at the cost of the whole people for free distribution to a part only. It is every way wrong and pernicious. Of the one hundred ninety thousand dollars per annum paid for carrying the Salt Lake mail, nine-tenths is absorbed in the cost of carrying these franked documents to people who contribute little or nothing to the support of the government in any way. Is this fair? Each Patent Office report will have cost the treasury four or five dollars by the time it reaches its destination, and will not be valued by the receiver at twenty-five cents. Why should this business go on? Why not "reform it altogether?" Let Congress print whatever documents are needed for its own information, and leave the people to choose and buy for themselves. I have spent four days and five nights in close contact with the sharp edges of Mr. Bernhisel's "Pub. Doc."—have done my very utmost to make them present a smooth or at least endurable surface; and I am sure there is no slumber to be extracted therefrom unless by reading them, a desperate resort, which no rational person would recommend. For all practical purposes, they might as well—now that the printer has been paid for them—be where I heartily wish they were—in the bottom of the sea.

18

SOUTH PASS TO BRIDGER

Big Sandy, Oregon,[1] *July 6, 1859*

I wrote last from the mail company's station tent in Quaking Asp Canyon, at the east end of the South Pass, three miles off the direct and well-beaten road from the Missouri to Salt Lake, and so to California, which was formerly the road to Oregon as well. But Col. Lander, at the head of a U. S. exploring and pioneer party, has just marked and nearly opened a new road through the canyon aforesaid, which makes a northern cutoff, and strikes the old Oregon Trail some fourteen miles south of Fort Hall, saving sixty miles on the journey to Oregon, and striking through to California on a northerly route, which I think passes to the north of Honey Lake, and thence over the Sierra down one of the forks of the Yuba. I cannot, of course, say that this is better than the old route, but it can hardly be more destitute of grass, while the naked fact that it divides the travel affords cheering hope of a mitigation of the sufferings and hardships of the long journey. I missed seeing Col. Lander, to my regret; but I am sure he is doing a good work, for which thousands will have reason to bless him. At all events, a great majority of the California, with all the Oregon emigration, are turning off on the new route, and I pray that they may find on it food for their weary, famished cattle, and a safe journey to their chosen homes.

Though the elevation of the pass is nearly 8,000 feet above the ocean level, I never endured heat exceeding that of yesterday in and about the station tent. The sun rose clear,

[1] Greeley meant Oregon *Territory*, no doubt, but Big Sandy (in present Wyoming) was not within the boundaries of the Oregon Territory.

as it almost always does here in summer, soon dispelling the chill which attends every night in this region; and by nine o'clock the heat was most intense. But the afternoon brought clouds, a wind and a petty rain squall, and the following night was cold enough to still any mosquitoes but those of the Rocky Mountains. I suspect these would sing and bite even with the mercury at zero.

Toward evening, I climbed the hill on the east of the canyon, and obtained from its summit a wide prospect, but how desolate! These hills are of volcanic formation, a kind of coarse slate, the strata upheaved almost perpendicularly, the surface shattered and shingly, with veins of hard quartz running across them. There is scarcely a bushel of soil to each square rod, of course no grass, and little vegetation of any kind. To the north, say ten to twenty miles away, is a snow-streaked range of the Rocky Mountains; to the south, some miles across the Sweetwater, are lower and less barren hills, with some snowbanks and some wood—quaking asp and yellow pine—on their northern slopes. The Sweetwater heads among the mountains to the north and northwest. There is a little well-gnawed grass on its immediate banks and on those of its tributaries—on the high rolling land which fills all beside of the wide space between the mountains north and those south, there is not a mule feed to each acre. Some greasewood at intervals, the eternal sagebrush, and a few weeds, with the quaking asp and yellow pine aforesaid, and a thick tangle of bitter cottonwood (which is a bad caricature of our swamp alder) thatching portions of a few of the smaller streams, comprise the entire vegetation of this forlorn region.

We started at seven this morning, came down to the old Salt Lake, Oregon, and California Trail at the Sweetwater, crossed and left that creek finally, and traversed a slightly rolling country for seven miles to the Twin Buttes, two low, clay-topped mounds which mark the point from which the water runs easterly to the Gulf of Mexico, and westerly to the Pacific. If anyone has pictured to himself the South Pass as threading some narrow, winding, difficult, rocky mountain gorge, he is grievously mistaken. The trail through the South Pass is the best part of the route from Atchison to California; the clay has here been almost wholly washed away and carried off, so that the road passes over a coarse, heavy, gravelly sand, usually as compact and smooth as the best illustrations of the genius of McAdam. I never before traversed forty-five miles of purely natural road so faultless as that through the South Pass which I have traveled today. But this tract would be good for roads, as it seems absolutely good for nothing else. The natural obstacles to constructing a railroad through this region are not comparable to those overcome in the construction of the Camden and Amboy.

Passing the Twin Buttes—the distance between the mountains on the north and the hills on the south being not less than thirty miles, and thenceforth westward rapidly widening—we ran down the side of a dry, shallow watercourse some five miles, to a wet, springy marsh or morass of fifteen or twenty acres, covered with poor, coarse grass, in which are found the so-called Pacific Springs. The water is clear and cold, but bad. Perhaps the number of dead cattle, of which the skeletons dot the marsh, made it so distasteful to me. At all events, I could not drink it. This bog is long and narrow; and from its western end issues a petty brook, which takes its way southwestwardly to the Sandy, Green River, the Colorado and the Gulf of California. Hence, toward the south and west, no hills are visible—nothing but a sandy, barren plain, mainly covered with the miserable sagebrush.

Twelve miles further on, we crossed *Dry* Sandy—not quite dry at this point, but its thirsty sands would surely drink the last of it a mile or so further south. Five miles beyond this, the old and well-beaten Oregon Trail strikes off to the northwest, while our road bends to the southwest. We are now out of the South Pass, which many have traversed unconsciously, and gone on wondering and inquiring when they should reach it. Seven miles further brought us to *Little* Sandy, and eight more to *Big* Sandy, whereon is the station at which, at 4 P.M., we (by order) stopped for the night. All these creeks appear to rise in the high mountains many miles north of us, and to run off with constantly diminishing volume, to join the Colorado at the south. Neither has a tree on its banks that I have seen—only a few low willow bushes at long intervals—though I hear that some cottonwood is found on this creek ten miles above. Each has a "bottom" or intervale of perhaps four rods in average width, in which a little grass is found, but next to none on the high sandy plains that separate them. Drought and sterility reign here without rival.

Fort Bridger,[2] *Utah, July 8, 1859*

We crossed Big Sandy twice before quitting it—once just at the station where the above was written, and again eighteen miles further on. Twelve miles more brought us to Green River—a stream here perhaps as large as the Mohawk at Schenectady or the Hudson at Waterford. It winds with a rapid, muddy current through a deep, narrow valley, much of it sandy and barren, but the residue producing some grass with a few large cottonwoods at intervals, and some worthless bushes. There are three rope ferries within a short distance, and two or three trading posts, somewhat frequented by Indians of the Snake tribe. Eighteen miles more of perfect desolation brought us to the next mail company's station

[2] Utah Territory, now in Wyoming.

163

on Black's Fork, at the junction of Ham's Fork, two large millstreams that rise in the mountains south and west of this point, and run together into Green River. They have scarcely any timber on their banks, but a sufficiency of bushes—bitter cottonwood, willow, choke cherry, and some others new to me—with more grass than I have found this side of the South Pass. On these streams live several old mountaineers, who have large herds of cattle which they are rapidly increasing by a lucrative traffic with the emigrants, who are compelled to exchange their tired, gaunt oxen and steers for fresh ones on almost any terms. R. D., whose tent we passed last evening, is said to have six or eight hundred head, and, knowing the country perfectly, finds no difficulty in keeping them through summer and winter by frequently shifting them from place to place over a circuit of thirty or forty miles. J. R., who has been here some twenty-odd years, began with little or nothing, and has quietly accumulated some fifty horses, three or four hundred head of neat cattle, three squaws, and any number of half-breed children. He is said to be worth seventy-five thousand dollars, though he has not even a garden, has probably not tasted an apple nor a peach these ten years, and lives in a tent which would be dear at fifty dollars. I instance this gentleman's way of life not by any means to commend it, but to illustrate the habits of a class. White men with two or three squaws each are quite common throughout this region, and young and relatively comely Indian girls are bought from their fathers by white men as regularly and openly as Circassians at Constantinople. The usual range of prices is from forty to eighty dollars—about that of Indian horses. I hear it stated that, though all other trade may be dull, that in young squaws is always brisk on Green River and the North Platte. That women so purchased should be discarded or traded off, as satiety or avarice may suggest, and that they should desert or deceive their purchasers on the slightest temptation, can surprise no one. I met an Irishman on Big Sandy whose squaw had recently gone off with an Indian admirer, leaving him two clever, bright, half-breed children of seven and five years. I trust that plank in the Republican national platform which affirms the right and duty of Congressional prohibition, not only of slavery in the territories, but of polygamy also, is destined to be speedily embodied in a law.

We passed yesterday the two places at which a body of Mormons late in 1857 surprised and burned the supply trains following in the rear of the federal troops sent against them. The wagons were burned in corral, and the place where each stood is still distinctly marked on the ground. It seems incredible, yet I am assured it is undoubtedly true, that none of the military officers who were severally dispatched from Kansas, late that season on the road to Salt Lake without a commander and with no definite instructions, was directed to afford any protection or give any feed to these important towns. It is lamentable that presidents and secretaries of war are not subject to court-martial.

We have for the last two days been passing scores of good log or ox chains—in one instance, a hundred feet together— which, having been thrown away by California emigrants to lighten the loads of their famished, failing cattle, have lain in the road for months, if not years, passed and noted by thousands, but by none thought worth picking up. One would suppose that the traders, the herdsmen, the Indians, or some other of the residents of this region, would deem these chains worth having, but they do not. I had already become accustomed to the sight of wagon tire, wagon boxes, etc., rejected and spurned in this way; but good, new chains thus begging for owners, I have only noted this side of the South Pass. They are said to be still more abundant further on.

This morning, I was agreeably surprised by a greeting

from three acquaintances I made in Denver, who invited me to share their outfit and journey to California, who left Denver the morning before I did, and besides whom I camped my first night on the road to Laramie. They are just through the Cherokee Trail, entering the mountains at Cache-la-Poudre and crossing Green River by a ferry some thirty miles below the point which I did. They were detained one day making a raft on which to ferry their wagon over the North Platte, and found some rough places in the mountains; at one of which they were obliged to unhitch their horses and let their wagon down a steep pitch by ropes. They found the water of Bitter Creek—along which lies their road for a hundred miles or so—bitter indeed; and in some places grass was deficient; but their horses look nearly as well as when they left Denver. Their route has of course been some two hundred and fifty miles shorter than mine, and they will reach Salt Lake scarcely a day behind me. I wish I had been able to accompany them on their rugged and little-traveled route.

On the other side of the pass, we had mainly clear, hot days; on this side, they are cloudy and cool. We had a little shower of rain with abundance of wind night before last, another shower last night, and more rain is now threatened. Yet all old residents assure me that rain in summer is very rare throughout this region.

We stop tonight at a point only one hundred miles from Salt Lake, with two rugged mountains to cross, so that we are not to reach that stopping place till Monday.

19

FROM BRIDGER TO SALT LAKE

Salt Lake City, Utah, July 11, 1859

Fort Bridger, whence my last was sent, may be regarded as the terminus in this direction of the Great American Desert. Not that the intervening country is fertile or productive, for it is neither; but at Bridger its character visibly changes. The hills we here approach are thinly covered with a straggling growth of low, scraggy cedar; the sagebrush continues even into this valley, but it is no longer universal and almost alone; grass is more frequent and far more abundant. Black's Fork, which, a few miles below, runs whitish with the clay wash of the desert, is here a clear, sparkling mountain torrent, divided into half a dozen streams by the flat, pebbly islets on which the little village—or rather post—is located; while, twelve miles up its course, an improvement of 500 acres, begun some years since by the Mormons, has this season been put under cultivation, with flattering prospects. Oats, barley, potatoes, peas, etc., are the crops sought; and the enterprising growers have contracts for the supply of Fort Bridger at prices which will insure them a liberal return in case they realize even a moderate yield. This may seem a small matter; but I doubt that there are, in all, 500 acres more under cultivation in the 250,000 square miles or more lying between the forks of the Platte on the east, the Salt Lake Basin on the west, the settlements of New Mexico on the south, and the Yellow Stone on the north. Yet in this radius are included several military posts at which every bushel of grain consumed costs an average of $5, while potatoes and other edible roots would command nearly as good prices, could they be had. There are herdsmen at intervals throughout all this region who have each their hundreds of heads of cattle, but who hardly know the taste of a potato or turnip, who have never planted nor sowed an acre, and never contemplated the possibility of growing an apple or cherry, though they expect to live and die in this region. I trust, therefore, that the Fort Bridger enterprise will succeed, and that it will incite to like experiments in the vicinity of each wilderness post. The present enormous cost of our military service in this immense desert may thus be slightly compensated by proving the great desert not absolutely worthless, and creating a basis of civilization for its rude, nomadic, lawless, but hardy, bold, and energetic pioneers.

From Fort Bridger (named after an Indian trader who first settled here; then settled as an outpost and relief station by the Mormons when they began to people this valley, but abandoned by them on the approach, late in '57, of the army, by which it has since been held) the Salt Lake Trail rises over a high, broad ridge, then descends a very steep, rocky, difficult hill to Big Muddy, a branch of Black's Fork, where —12 miles from Bridger—is the mail company's station, at which we had expected to spend the night. But the next drive is 60 miles, and our new conductor wisely decided to cut a piece off of it that evening, as the road at the other end was hazardous in a dark night. So we moved on a little after sundown, rising over another broad ridge, and, after narrowly escaping an upset in a gully dug in the trail by that day's violent shower, camped 15 miles on, a little after 11 P.M. The sky was densely clouded; the moon nearly down; it was raining a little and blowing more, as we lay down to rest, most of us under the sullen sky. An hour or more thereafter, our mules (which were simply tied in pairs by long ropes and thus turned out to graze) were somehow disturbed, and our stagemen challenged and stood ready to repel the supposed depredator. He proved, however, to be a friend, traveling on muleback from Bridger to this place, who had wandered off the trail in the deep darkness, and perhaps been carried among our animals by the fondness of his own for congenial society; so all was soon right, and the newcomer unsaddled, pulled off his blankets, and was soon couched among us. At daylight we were all astir, and drove down to Bear River, only three or four miles distant, for breakfast.

We halted before crossing, beside what is here called a grocery, the only other structure on that side of the river being a blacksmith's shop (consisting, I believe, of a bellows and anvil under the open sky), to which some part of our rigging was sent for repair, while we prepared and ate breakfast. There were two or three men sleeping in wet blankets on the grass, who rose and made a fire on our appearance. The grocery was irregularly constructed of boxes which had once contained goods, but, having fulfilled that end, were thus made useful afresh. I suppose it was six feet high, and five by eight in diameter, though no two of its sides were of the same height. An old tent cloth for covering completed the edifice, from which we obtained sardines, canned lobster, and prepared coffee which was said to contain sugar and cream, but which was voted by our drinkers a swindling humbug. I believe these articles exhausted the capabilities of the concern; but, as we had bread, we needed no more. Some of our party thought otherwise, however; they called for whisky or some kindred beverage, and were indignantly disgusted at its non-production. They had become inured to groceries containing nothing that could by possibility be eaten; but a grocery devoid of some kind of "rot," as the fiery beverage was currently designated, was to them a novel and most distasteful experience. However, a man was at once dispatched across the creek to a similar establishment, but more happily furnished, whence he soon returned with the indispensable fluid (price $3 for a flask containing perhaps a pint and a half of some diabolic alcoholic concoction, wherein the small modicum of genuine whisky had taken to itself seven other devils worse than the first), and our breakfast was finished to general satisfaction.

A word here on the liquor traffic throughout this region. A mercantile firm in this city, in order to close out promptly its extra stock of liquors, offers to sell whisky at the extraordinarily low price of $3.50 per gallon. I believe the common price from Laramie westward to the Sierra Nevada is $8 per gallon; but it is usually sold to consumers by the bottle, holding less than a quart, for which the charge is $2 up to $3.50, but seldom below $2.50. And such liquor! True, I have not tasted it, but the smell I could not escape, and I am sure a more wholesome potable might be compounded of spirits of turpentine, aqua fortis, and steeped tobacco. Its look alone would condemn it—soapy, ropy, turbid, it is within bounds to say that every pint of it contains as much deadly poison as a gallon of pure whisky. And yet fully half the earnings of the working men (not including the Mormons, of whom I have yet seen little) of this whole region are fooled away on this abominable witch-broth and its foster-brother tobacco, for which they pay $1 to 2.50 per pound! The log-tavern-keeper at Weber, of whom our mailboys have brought their next supply of "rot," apologetically observed, "There a'n't nothing bad about this whisky; the only fault is, it isn't good." I back that last assertion with my whole heart.

Fording Bear River—here a swift, rocky-bottomed creek, now perhaps forty yards wide, but hardly three feet deep— we rose gradually through a grassy valley, partially inclosed by high, perpendicular stone buttes, especially on the right. The stone (evidently once clay) outposts of one of the buttes are known as The Needles. We thence descended a long, steep hill into the valley of Lost Creek—why "lost," I could not divine, as the creek is plainly there—a fair trout brook, running through a grassy meadow, between high hills, over which we made our way into the head of Echo Canyon, down which we jogged some twenty miles to Weber River.

This canyon reminded me afresh that evil and good are strongly interwoven in our early lot. Throughout the desolate region which stretches from the Sweetwater nearly or quite to Bridger, we had in the main the best natural road I ever traveled—dusty, indeed, and, in places, abrupt and rough, but equal in the average to the carefully made and annually repaired roads of New England. But in this fairly grassed ravine, hemmed in by steep, picturesque bluffs, with springs issuing from their bases, and gradually gathering into a trout brook as we neared the Weber, we found the "going decidedly bad," and realized that in the dark it could not but be dangerous. For the brook, with its welcome fringe of yellow, choke cherry, service berry, and other shrubs, continually zigzagged from side to side of the canyon, compelling us to descend and ascend its precipitous banks, and cross its sometimes miry bed, often with a smart chance of breaking an axle, or upsetting.

We stopped to feed and dine at the site of General Well's camp during the Mormon War of 1857–8, and passed, ten miles below, the fortifications constructed under his orders in that famous campaign. They seem childish affairs, more suited to the genius of Chinese than of civilized warfare. I cannot believe that they would have stopped the federal troops, if even tolerably led, for more than an hour.

We reached our next station on the Weber a little after 5 P.M. and did not leave till after an early breakfast next (yesterday) morning. The Weber is, perhaps, a little larger than the Bear, and runs through a deep, narrow, rugged valley, with no cultivation so far as we saw it. Two groceries, a blacksmith's shop, and the mail station, are all the habitations we passed in following down it some four or five miles

171

to the shaky polebridge, on which we crossed, though it is usually fordable. We soon after struck off up a rather steep, grassy watercourse which we followed to its head, and thence took over a "divide" to the head of another such, on which our road wound down to East Canyon Creek, a fair, rapid, trout brook, running through a deep, narrow ravine, up which we twisted, crossing and recrossing the swift stream, until we left it, greatly diminished in volume, after tracking it through a mile or so of low, swampy timber, and frequent mudholes, and turned up a little runnel that came feebly brawling down the side of a mountain. The trail ran for a considerable distance exactly in the bed of this petty brooklet —said bed consisting wholly of round, water-worn granite boulders, of all sizes, from that of a pigeon's egg up to that of a potash kettle; then the ravine widened a little, and the trail wound from side to side of the watercourse as chances for a foothold were proffered by one or the other. The bottom of this ravine was poorly timbered with quaking asp, and balsam fir, with some service berry, choke cherry, mountain currant, and other bushes; the whole ascent is four miles, not very steep, except for the last half mile; but the trail is so bad that it is a good two hours' work to reach the summit. But, that summit gained, we stand in a broad, open, level space on the top of the Wasatch range, with the Uintah and Bear Mountains on either hand, forming a perfect chaos of wild, barren peaks, some of them snowy, between which we have a glance at a part of the Salt Lake Valley, some thirty miles distant, though the city, much nearer, is hidden by intervening heights, and the lake is likewise concealed further to the right. The descent toward the valley is steeper and shorter than the ascent from the side of Bear River—the first half mile so fearfully steep that I judge few passengers ever rode down it, though carriage wheels are uniformly chained here. But, though the southern face of these moun-

tains is covered by a far more luxuriant shrubbery than the
northern, among which oaks and maples soon make their
appearance for the first time in many a weary hundred miles,
none of these seem ever to grow into trees; in fact, I saw
none over six feet high. Some quaking asps, from ten to
twenty-five feet high, the largest hardly more than six inches
through, cover patches of these precipitous mountainsides,
down which, and over the low intervening mountain, they
are toilsomely dragged fifteen or twenty miles to serve as
fuel in this city, where even such poor trash sells for fifteen
to twenty dollars per cord. The scarcity and wretchedness of
the timber—(I have not seen the raw material for a decent
ax helve growing in all my last thousand miles of travel)—
are the great discouragement and drawback with regard to
all this region. The parched sandy clay, or clayey sand of the
plains disappeared many miles back; there has been rich,
black soil, at least in the valleys, ever since we crossed the
Weber River, but the timber is still scarce, small, and poor,
in the ravines, while ninety-nine-hundredths of the surface
of the mountains is utterly bare of it. In the absence of coal,
how can a region so unblessed ever be thickly settled, and
profitably cultivated?

The descent of the mountain on this side is but two miles
in length, with the mail company's station at the bottom.
Here (thirteen miles from the city, twenty-seven from Bear
River) we had expected to stop for the night; but our new
conductor, seeing that there were still two or three hours of
good daylight, resolved to come on. So, with fresh teams, we
soon crossed the "little mountain"—steep, but hardly a mile
in ascent, and but half a mile in immediate descent—and ran
rapidly down some ten miles through the narrow ravine
known as Emigration Canyon, where the road, though much
traversed by Mormons as well as emigrants and merchant
trains, is utterly abominable; and, passing over but two or

three miles of intervening plain, were in this city just as twilight was deepening into night.

SALT LAKE CITY wears a pleasant aspect to the emigrant or traveler, weary, dusty, and browned with a thousand miles of jolting, fording, camping, through the scorched and naked American desert. It is located mainly on the bench of hard gravel that slopes southward from the foot of the mountains toward the lake valley; the houses—generally small and of one story—are all built of adobe (sun-hardened brick), and have a neat and quiet look; while the uniform breadth of the streets (eight rods) and the "magnificent distances" usually preserved by the buildings (each block containing ten acres, divided into eight lots, giving a quarter of an acre for buildings and an acre for garden, fruit, etc., to each householder) make up an ensemble seldom equaled. Then the rills of bright, sparkling, leaping water which, diverted from the streams issuing from several adjacent mountain canyons, flow through each street and are conducted at will into every garden, diffuse an air of freshness and coolness which none can fail to enjoy, but which only a traveler in summer across the Plains can fully appreciate. On a single business street, the post office, principal stores, etc., are set pretty near each other, though not so close as in other cities; everywhere else, I believe, the original plan of the city has been wisely and happily preserved. Southward from the city, the soil is softer and richer, and there are farms of (I judge) ten to forty or sixty acres; but I am told that the lowest portion of the valley, nearly on a level with the lake, is so impregnated with salt, soda, etc., as to yield but a grudging return for the husbandman's labor. I believe, however, that even this region is available as a stock range—thousands on thousands of cattle, mainly owned in the city, being pastured here in winter as well as summer, and said to do well in all seasons. For, though snow is never absent from the mountain chains which shut in this valley, it seldom lies long in the valley itself.

The pass over the Wasatch is, if I mistake not, eight thousand three hundred feet above the sea level; this valley, about four thousand nine hundred. The atmosphere is so pure that the mountains across the valley to the south seem but ten or fifteen miles off; they are really from twenty to thirty. The lake is some twenty miles westward; but we see only the rugged mountain known as Antelope Island, which rises in its center and seems to bound the valley in that direction. Both the lake and valley wind away to the northwest for a distance of some ninety miles—the lake receiving the waters of Weber and Bear Rivers behind the mountains in that direction. And then there are other valleys like this, nested among the mountains south and west to the very base of the Sierra Nevada. So there will be room enough here for all this strange people for many years.

But of the Mormons and Mormonism, I propose to speak only after studying them; to which end I remain here several days longer.

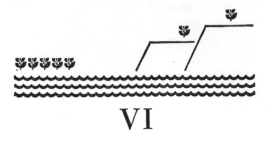

VI

UTAH

Dispatches 20 through 23

By 1859 the Mormons were well-established in Utah. Salt Lake City was already noted for its wide streets, orderly plan, and neat appearance. Greeley stayed more than a week before pushing on across the desert. Here occurred the famous interview with Brigham Young. Although not the prototype of the newspaper interview, another of America's many contributions to journalism, it ranks among the early notable specimens of the form.[1] The history of American journalism offers few scenes to match this confrontation be-

[1] "James Gordon Bennett is commonly given credit for the first interviews—the outgrowth of his questions to Rosina Townsend, madam of a 'fancy house' in New York in which, in 1836, a sensational murder had occurred." Mitchell V. Charnley: *Reporting* (New York: Henry Holt & Co.; 1959), p. 206.

tween the greatest editor and the most controversial religious leader of the day.

Also notable in the Utah dispatches is Greeley's disquisition on the Mormon religion and its most distinctive feature, polygamy. Greeley undoubtedly was aware of the news value inherent in that subject. This must have been one of the most avidly read of all his letters.

The dispatch from Camp Floyd, the much-discussed U. S. army post in Utah, is a brilliant example of interpretive reporting. It could serve young journalists to this day as a model demonstration of how to marshal the significant facts and raise the relevant questions on a sticky issue in the domain of public affairs.

20[1]

TWO HOURS WITH BRIGHAM YOUNG

Salt Lake City, Utah, July 13, 1859

My friend Dr. Bernhisel,[2] late delegate in Congress, took me this afternoon, by appointment, to meet Brigham Young, President of the Mormon Church, who had expressed a willingness to receive me at 2 P.M. We were very cordially welcomed at the door by the president, who led us into the second-story parlor of the largest of his houses (he has three), where I was introduced to Heber C. Kimball, General Wells, General Ferguson, Albert Carrington, Elias Smith, and several other leading men in the church, with two full-grown

[1] Erroneously numbered 21 in Saxton, Barker & Co. edition, 1860. All subsequent chapters in that volume perpetuate the error. Its number 22 is actually the twenty-first letter, etc.

[2] In his caustic remarks about Dr. Bernhisel's mail sacks a week earlier, Greeley made it clear that he was attacking the system, not the man who happened to be taking advantage of it in this instance.

sons of the president. After some unimportant conversation on general topics, I stated that I had come in quest of fuller knowledge respecting the doctrines and polity of the Mormon Church, and would like to ask some questions bearing directly on these, if there were no objection. President Young avowing his willingness to respond to all pertinent inquiries, the conversation proceeded substantially as follows:

H.G.—Am I to regard Mormonism (so-called) as a new religion, or as simply a new development of Christianity?

B.Y.—We hold that there can be no true Christian Church without a priesthood directly commissioned by, and in immediate communication with, the Son of God and Saviour of mankind. Such a church is that of the Latter-Day Saints, called by their enemies Mormons; we know no other that even pretends to have present and direct revelations of God's will.

H.G.—Then I am to understand that you regard all other churches professing to be Christian as the Church of Rome regards all churches not in communion with itself—as schismatic, heretical, and out of the way of salvation?

B.Y.—Yes, substantially.

H.G.—Apart from this, in what respect do your doctrines differ essentially from those of our Orthodox Protestant Churches—the Baptist or Methodist, for example?

B.Y.—We hold the doctrines of Christianity, as revealed in the Old and New Testaments—also in the Book of Mormon, which teaches the same cardinal truths and those only.

H.G.—Do you believe in the doctrine of the Trinity?

B.Y.—We do; but not exactly as it is held by other churches. We believe in the Father, the Son, and the Holy Ghost, as equal, but not identical—not as one person [being].* We believe in all the Bible teaches on this subject.

---

* I am quite sure that President Young used here the word "person" as I have it; but I am not aware that Christians of any denomination do regard the Father, Son and Holy Spirit, as one person.

178

H.G.—Do you believe in a personal devil—a distinct, conscious, spiritual being, whose nature and acts are essentially malignant and evil?

B.Y.—We do.

H.G.—Do you hold the doctrine of eternal punishment?

B.Y.—We do; though perhaps not exactly as other churches do. We believe it as the Bible teaches it.

H.G.—I understand that you regard baptism by immersion as essential?

B.Y.—We do.

H.G.—Do you practice infant baptism?

B.Y.—No.

H.G.—Do you make removal to these valleys obligatory on your converts?

B.Y.—They would consider themselves greatly aggrieved if they were not invited hither. We hold to such a gathering together of God's people, as the Bible foretells, and that this is the place, and now is the time appointed for its consummation.

H.G.—The predictions to which you refer have usually, I think, been understood to indicate Jerusalem (or Judea) as the place of such gathering.

B.Y.—Yes, for the Jews—not for others.

H.G.—What is the position of your church with respect to slavery?

B.Y.—We consider it of divine institution, and not to be abolished until the curse pronounced on Ham shall have been removed from his descendants.

H.G.—Are any slaves now held in this territory?

B.Y.—There are.

H.G.—Do your territorial laws uphold slavery?

B.Y.—Those laws are printed—you can read for yourself. If slaves are brought here by those who owned them in the states, we do not favor their escape from the service of those owners.

H.G.—Am I to infer that Utah, if admitted as a member of the Federal Union, will be a slave state?

H.G.—No; she will be a free state. Slavery here would prove useless and unprofitable. I regard it generally as a curse to the masters. I myself hire many laborers, and pay them fair wages; I could not afford to own them. I can do better than subject myself to an obligation to feed and clothe their families, to provide and care for them in sickness and health. Utah is not adapted to slave labor.

H.G.—Let me now be enlightened with regard more especially to your church polity: I understand that you require each member to pay over one-tenth of all he produces or earns to the church.

B.Y.—That is a requirement of our faith. There is no compulsion as to the payment. Each member acts in the premises according to his pleasure, under the dictates of his conscience.

H.G.—What is done with the proceeds of this tithing?

B.Y.—Part of it is devoted to building temples, and other places of worship; part to helping the poor and needy converts on their way to this country; and the largest portion to the support of the poor among the saints.

H.G.—Is none of it paid to bishops, and other dignitaries of the church?

B.Y.—Not one penny. No bishop, no elder, no deacon, nor other church officer, receives any compensation for his official services. A bishop is often required to put his hand into his own pocket, and provide therefrom for the poor of his charge; but he never receives anything for his services.

H.G.—How, then, do your ministers live?

B.Y.—By the labor of their own hands, like the first apostles. Every bishop, every elder, may be daily seen at work in the field or the shop, like his neighbors; every minister of the church has his proper calling, by which he earns the bread of his family; he who cannot, or will not, do the church's work for nothing is not wanted in her service; even our lawyers (pointing to General Ferguson and another present, who are the regular lawyers of the church) are paid nothing for their services; I am the only person in the church who has not a regular calling apart from the church's service, and I never received one farthing from her treasury; if I obtain anything from the tithing house, I am charged with, and pay for it, just as anyone else would; the clerks in the tithing store are paid like others clerks; but no one is ever paid for any service pertaining to the ministry. We think a man who cannot make his living aside from the ministry of Christ unsuited to that office. I am called rich, and consider myself worth two hunderd and fifty thousand dollars; but no dollar of it was ever paid me by the church, nor for any service as a minister of the everlasting Gospel. I lost nearly all I had when we were broken up in Missouri, and driven from that state. I was nearly stripped again, when Joseph Smith was murdered, and we were driven from Illinois; but nothing was ever made up to me by the church, nor by anyone. I believe I know how to acquire property, and how to take care of it.[3]

H.G.—Can you give me any rational explanation of the aversion and hatred with which your people are generally regarded by those among whom they have lived and with whom they have been brought directly in contact?

B.Y.—No other explanation than is afforded by the crucifixion of Christ and the kindred treatment of God's ministers, prophets and saints, in all ages.

H.G.—I know that a new sect is always decried and traduced—that it is hardly ever deemed respectable to belong to one—that the Baptists, Quakers, Methodists, Universa-

[3] In his dispatch (No. 23) on the army at Camp Floyd, Utah, Greeley gives an example of Young's business acumen.

lists, etc., have each in their turn been regarded in the infancy of their sect as the offscouring of the earth; yet I cannot remember that either of them were ever generally represented and regarded by the older sects of their early days as thieves, robbers, murderers.

B.Y.—If you will consult the contemporary Jewish account of the life and acts of Jesus Christ, you will find that he and his disciples were accused of every abominable deed and purpose—robbery and murder included. Such a work is still extant, and may be found by those who seek it.

H.G.—What do you say of the so-called Danites, or Destroying Angels, belonging to your church?

B.Y.—What do *you* say? I know of no such band, no such persons or organization. I hear of them only in the slanders of our enemies.

H.G.—With regard, then, to the grave question on which your doctrines and practices are avowedly at war with those of the Christian world—that of a plurality of wives—is the system of your church acceptable to the majority of its women?

B.Y.—They could not be more averse to it than I was when it was first revealed to us as the Divine will. I think they generally accept it, as I do, as the will of God.

H.G.—How general is polygamy among you?

B.Y.—I could not say. Some of those present (heads of the church) have each but one wife; others have more. Each determines what is his individual duty.

H.G.—What is the largest number of wives belonging to any one man?

B.Y.—I have fifteen; I know no one who has more; but some of those sealed to me are old ladies whom I regard rather as mothers than wives, but whom I have taken home to cherish and support.

H.G.—Does not the Apostle Paul say that a bishop should be "the husband of one wife"?

B.Y.—So we hold. We do not regard any but a married man as fitted for the office of bishop. But the apostle does not forbid a bishop having more wives than one.

H.G.—Does not Christ say that he who puts away his wife, or marries one whom another has put away, commits adultery!

B.Y.—Yes; and I hold that no man should ever put away his wife except for adultery—not always even for that. Such is *my* individual view of the matter. I do not say that wives have never been put away in our church, but that I do not approve of the practice.

H.G.—How do you regard what is commonly termed the Christian Sabbath?

B.Y.—As a divinely appointed day of rest. We enjoin all to rest from secular labor on that day. We would have no man enslaved to the Sabbath, but we enjoin all to respect and enjoy it.

Such is, as nearly as I can recollect, the substance of nearly two hours' conversation, wherein much was said incidentally that would not be worth reporting, even if I could remember and reproduce it, and wherein others bore a part; but as President Young is the first minister of the Mormon Church, and bore the principal part in the conversation, I have reported his answers alone, to my questions and observations. The others appeared uniformly to defer to his views, and to acquiesce fully in his responses and explanations. He spoke readily, not always with grammatical accuracy, but with no appearance of hesitation or reserve, and with no apparent desire to conceal anything, nor did he repel any of my questions as impertinent. He was very plainly dressed in thin summer clothing, and with no air of sanctimony or fanaticism. In appearance, he is a portly, frank, good-natured, rather thickset man of fifty-five, seeming to enjoy life, and to be in no particular hurry to get to heaven. His associates are plain men, evidently born and reared to a life of labor, and looking as little like crafty hypocrites or swindlers as any body of men I ever met. The absence of cant or snuffle from their manner was marked and general; yet I think I may fairly say that their Mormonism has not impoverished them—that they were generally poor men when they embraced it, and are now in very comfortable circumstances—as men averaging three or four wives apiece certainly need to be.

If I hazard any criticisms on Mormonism generally, I reserve them for a separate letter, being determined to make this a fair and full exposé of the doctrine and polity, in the very words of its prophet, so far as I can recall them. I do not believe President Young himself could present them in terms calculated to render them less obnoxious to the Gentile world than the above. But I have a right to add here, because I said it to the assembled chiefs at the close of the above colloquy, that the degradation (or, if you please, the restriction) of woman to the single office of child-bearing and its accessories, is an inevitable consequence of the system here paramount. I have not observed a sign in the streets, an advertisement in the journals, of this Mormon metropolis, whereby a woman proposes to do anything whatever. No Mormon has ever cited to me his wife's or any woman's opinion on any subject; no Mormon woman has been introduced or has spoken to me; and, though I have been asked to visit Mormons in their houses, no one has spoken of his wife (or wives) desiring to see me, or his desiring me to make her (or their) acquaintance, or voluntarily indicated the existence of such a being or beings. I will not attempt to report our talk on this subject; because, unlike what I have above given, it assumed somewhat the character of a disputation, and I could hardly give it impartially; but one remark made by President Young I think I can give accurately, and it may serve as a sample of all that was offered on that side. It was in these words, I think exactly: "If I did not consider myself competent to transact a certain business without taking my wife's or any woman's counsel with regard to it, I think I ought to let that business alone."* The spirit with regard to woman, of the entire Mormon, as of all other polygamic systems, is fairly displayed in this avowal. Let any such system become established and prevalent, and woman will soon be confined to the harem, and her appearance in the street with unveiled face will be accounted immodest. I joyfully trust that the genius of the nineteenth century tends to a solution of the problem of woman's sphere and destiny radically different from this.

21

THE MORMONS AND MORMONISM

Salt Lake City, July 18, 1859

Since my interview with Brigham Young, I have enjoyed opportunities for studying the Mormons in their social or festive and in their devotional assemblies. Of private social intercourse—that is, intercourse between family and family— I judge that there is comparatively little here; between Mormons and Gentiles or strangers, of course still less. Their religious services (in the tabernacle) are much like those that may be shared or witnessed in the churches of most of our popular sects; the music rather better than you

---

* Another feature of President Young's remarks on this topic strikes me on revision. He assumed as undeniable that, outside of the Mormon Church, married men usually keep mistresses—that incontinence is the general rule, and continence the rare exception. This assumption was habitual with the Mormons who, at various times, discussed with me the subject of polygamy.

will hear in an average worshiping assemblage in the states, the prayers pertinent and full of unction, the sermons adapted to tastes or needs different from mine. They seemed to me rambling, dogmatic, and ill-digested; in fact, Elder Orson Pratt, who preached last Sunday morning, prefaced his harangue by a statement that he had been hard at work on his farm throughout the week, and labored under consequent physical exhausion. Elder John Taylor (I believe he is one of the Twelve; at all events, he is a high dignitary in the church, and a man of decided natural ability) spoke likewise in the afternoon with little or no premeditation. Now, I believe that every preacher should be also a worker; I like to see one mowing or pitching hay in his shirtsleeves; and I hear with edification an unlettered but devout and earnest evangelist who, having worked a part of the week for the subsistence of his family, devotes the rest of it to preaching the gospel to small schoolhouse or wayside gatherings of hearers, simply for the good of their souls. Let him only be sure to talk good sense, and I will excuse some bad grammar. But when a preacher is to address a congregation of one to three thousand persons, like that which assembles twice each Sabbath in the Salt Lake City Tabernacle, I insist that a due regard for the economy of time requires that he should prepare himself, by study and reflection, if not by writing, to speak directly to the point. This mortal life is too short and precious to be wasted in listening to rambling, loose-jointed harangues, or even to those which severally consume an hour in the utterance, when they might be boiled down and clarified until they were brought within the compass of half an hour each. A thousand half hours, Reverend Sir!—have you ever pondered their value? Suppose your time to be worth ten times that of an average hearer; still, to take an extra half hour from a thousand hearers in order to save yourself ten or fifteen hours' labor in the

186

due and careful preparation of a sermon, is a scandalous waste, which I see not how to justify. Be entreated to repent and amend!

The two discourses to which I listened were each intensely and exclusively Mormon. That is, they assumed that the Mormons were God's peculiar, chosen, beloved people, and that all the rest of mankind are out of the ark of safety and floundering in heathen darkness. I am not edified by this sort of preaching. It reminds me forcibly of the Pharisee's prayer: "Lord, I thank thee that I am not as other men are—unjust, extortioners," etc. I do not think good men delight in this assumption of an exclusive patent for the grace of God; and I am quite sure it is not well adapted to the transformation of bad men into good. It is too well calculated to puff up its disciples with self-conceit and spiritual pride. That Jesus Christ is about to reappear on the earth in all the pomp and splendor of a mighty conqueror; that he will then proceed to take vengeance on his enemies (mankind in general, whether heathen or nominally Christians) and to glorify his elect (the Latter-Day Saints or Mormons) were treated by the Tabernacle preachers as propositions too self-evident to need demonstration. Having thus chastised his enemies and "gathered his elect from the four winds of heaven," the Saviour is to reign over them here on earth for a thousand years; at the end of which period, they are together to be transferred to heaven. Of course, I had heard the like of this before; but it always seems to me a very gross and wooden perversion of the magnificent imagery whereby the Bible foreshadows a great spiritual transformation. The spirit of the Mormon religion appears to me Judaic rather than Christian; and I am well assured that Heber C. Kimball, one of the great lights of the church, once said in conversation with a Gentile—"I *do* pray for my enemies: I pray that they may all go to hell." Neither from

187

the pulpit nor elsewhere have I heard from a Mormon one spontaneous, hearty recognition of the essential brotherhood of the human race—one generous prayer for the enlightenment and salvation of all mankind. On the other hand, I have been distinctly given to understand that my interlocutors expect to sit on thrones and to bear rule over multitudes in the approaching kingdom of God. In fact, one sincere, devout man has today assigned that to me as a reason for polygamy; he wants to qualify himself, by ruling a large and diversified family here, for bearing rule over his principality in the "new earth," that he knows to be at hand. I think he might far better devote a few years to pondering Christ's saying to this effect, "He who would be least in the kingdom of Heaven, the same shall be greatest."

I was undeceived with regard to the Book of Mormon. I had understood that it is now virtually discarded, or at least neglected, by the church in its services and ministrations. But Elder Pratt gave us a synopsis of its contents, and treated it throughout as of equal authority and importance with the Old and New Testaments. He did not read from it, however, but from Malachi, and quoted text after text from the prophets, which he cited as predictions of the writing and discovery of this book.

The congregation consisted, at either service, of some fifteen hundred to two thousand persons—more in the morning than the afternoon. A large majority of them (not including the elders and chief men, of whom a dozen or so were present) were evidently of European birth; I think a majority of the males were past the meridian of life. All gave earnest heed to the exercises throughout; in fact, I have seldom seen a more devout and intent assemblage. I had been told that the Mormons were remarkably ignorant, superstitious, and brutalized; but the aspect of these congregations did not sustain that assertion. Very few rural congregations would exhibit more heads evincing decided ability; and I doubt whether any assemblage, so largely European in its composition, would make a better appearance. Not that Europeans are less intellectual or comely than Americans; but our emigrants are mainly of the poorer classes; and poverty, privation, and rugged toil, plow hard, forbidding lines in the human countenance elsewhere than in Utah. Brigham Young was not present at either service.

Do I regard the great body of these Mormons as knaves and hypocrites? Assuredly not. I do not believe there was ever a religion whereof the great mass of the adherents were not honest and sincere. Hypocrites and knaves there are in all sects; it is quite possible that some of the magnates of the Mormon Church regard this so-called religion (with all others) as a contrivance for the enslavement and fleecing of the many, and the aggrandizement of the few; but I cannot believe that a sect, so considerable and so vigorous as the Mormon, was ever founded in conscious imposture, or built up on any other basis than that of earnest conviction. If the projector and two or three of his chief confederates are knaves, the great body of their followers were dupes.

Nor do I accept the current Gentile presumption that the Mormons are an organized banditti—a horde of robbers and assassins. Thieves and murderers mainly haunt the purlieus of great cities, or hide in caverns and forests adjacent to the great routes of travel. But when the Mormon leaders decided to set up their Zion in these parched mountain vales and canyon, the said valleys were utterly secluded and remote from all Gentile approach—away from any mail route or channel of emigration. That the Mormons wished to escape Gentile control, scrutiny, jurisprudence, is evident; that they meant to abuse their inaccessibility, to the detriment and plunder of wayfarers, is not credible.

Do I, then, discredit the tales of Mormon outrages and

crime—of the murder of the Parrishes, the Mountain Meadow massacre, etc. etc.—wherewith the general ear has recently been shocked? No, I do not. Some of these may have been fabricated by Gentile malice—others are doubtless exaggerated—but there is some basis of truth for the current Gentile conviction that the Mormons have robbed, maimed, and even killed persons in this territory, under circumstances which should subject the perpetrators to condign punishment, but that Mormon witnesses, grand jurors, petit jurors, and magistrates determinedly screen the guilty. I deeply regret the necessity of believing this; but the facts are incontestable. That a large party of emigrants—not less than eighty—from Arkansas to California were foully massacred at Mountain Meadows in September, 1857, more immediately by Indians, but under the direct inspiration and direction of the Mormon settlers in that vicinity—to whom, and not to the savages, the emigrants had surrendered, after a seige, on the strength of assurances that their lives at least should be spared—is established by evidence that cannot (I think) be invalidated—the evidence of conscience-smitten partakers in the crime, both Indian and ex-Mormon, and of children of the slaughtered emigrants, who were spared as too young to be dangerous even as witnesses, and of whom the great majority have been sent down to the states as unable to give testimony; but two boys are retained here as witnesses, who distinctly remember that their parents surrendered to white men, and that these white men at best did not attempt to prevent their perfidious massacre. These children, moreover, were all found in the possession of Mormons—not one of them in the hands of Indians; and, though the Mormons say they ransomed them from the hands of Indians, the children deny it, saying that they never lived with, nor were in the keeping of savages; and the Indians bear concurrent testimony. So in the Parrish case: the family had been Mormons, but had apostatized—and undertook to return to the states; they were warned that they would be killed if they persisted in that resolution; they did persist, and were killed. Of course, nobody will ever be convicted of their murder; but those who warned them of the fate on which they were rushing know why they were killed, and could discover, if they would, who killed them.

The vital fact in the case is just this: the great mass of these people, as a body, mean to be honest, just, and humane; but they are, before and above all things else, Latter-Day Saints, or Mormons. They devoutly believe that they are God's peculiar and especial people, doing His work, upbuilding His kingdom, and basking in the sunshine of His peculiar favor. Whoever obstructs or impedes them in this work, then, is God's enemy, who must be made to get out of the way of the establishment of Christ's kingdom on earth— made to do so by lawful and peaceful means if possible, but by any means that may ultimately be found necessary. The Parrishes were apostates; had they been allowed to pursue their journey to the states, they would have met many Saints coming up the road, whose minds they would have troubled if not poisoned; and they would have told stories after reaching their destination which would have deepened the general prejudice against the Saints; so the upbuilding and well-being of Christ's kingdom required that they should die. The Arkansas emigrants slaughtered at Mountain Meadows had in some way abused the Saints, or interposed obstacles to the progress of God's work, and they were consequently given over to destruction. Far be it from me to hint that one-fifth, one-tenth, one-twentieth, of the Mormons ever bore any part in these bloody deeds, or even know to this day that they were perpetrated. The great body of the Saints undoubtingly believe all the current imputations of Mormon homicide and outrage to be abominable calumnies.

191

Many of the highest dignitaries of the church may be included in this number. But there are men in the church who know that they are *not* calumnies—who know that Gentiles and apostates have been killed for the church's and for Christ's sake, and who firmly believe that they *ought* to have been. I grieve to say it, but I hold these more consistent and logical Mormons than their innocent and unsuspicious brethren. For if I were a Latter-Day Saint, undoubtingly believing all opposers of the Mormon Church to be God's enemies, obnoxious to His wrath and curse, and powerfully obstructing the rescue of souls from eternal perdition and torture, I should be strongly impelled to help put those opposers of God's purposes out of the way of sending any more immortal souls to everlasting fire. I should feel it my duty so to act, as a lover of God and man. And I confidently predict that not one Mormon who has killed a Gentile or apostate under a like view of his duty will ever be fairly convicted in this territory. No jury can be drawn here, unless in flagrant defiance of territorial laws, which is not mainly composed of Mormons; and no such jury will convict a Mormon of crime for any act done in behalf of God's kingdom—that is, of the Mormon Church.

I ask, then, the advocates of "popular sovereignty" in the territories to say what they propose to do in the premises. How do they intend to adapt their principle to the existing state of facts? They have superseded Brigham Young, with a full knowledge that at least nine-tenths of the people of Utah earnestly desired his retention as governor. They have sent hither a batch of judges, who would like to earn their salaries; but the Mormon legislature devotes its sessions principally to the work of crippling and fettering these judges, so that they shall remain here as mere dummies or be driven into resignation. Their juries are all drawn for them by Mormon officials, under regulations which virtually exclude all but Mormons from each panel; it is a violation of all the laws of Utah to cite in argument before any judge or jury here the decisions of any court—even the supreme court of the United States—but the courts of Utah; so that even the Dred Scott decision could not lawfully be cited here in a fugitive-slave case. In short, the federal judiciary, the federal executive, and the federal army, as now existing in Utah, are three transparent shams—three egregious farces; they are costing the treasury very large sums to no purpose; and the sooner the governor, marshal, judges, etc., resign, and the army is withdrawn, the better for all but a handful of contractors. "Popular sovereignty" has such full swing here that Brigham Young carries the territory in his breeches' pocket without a shadow of opposition; he governs without responsibility to either law or public opinion; for there is no real power here but that of "the church," and he is practically the church. The church is rich, and is hourly increasing in wealth; the church settles all civil controversies which elsewhere cause lawsuits; the church spends little or nothing, yet rules everything; while the federal government, though spending two or three millions per annum here, and keeping up a fussy parade of authority, is powerless and despised. If, then, we are to have "popular sovereignty" in the territories, let us have it pure and without shams. Let Brigham be reappointed governor; withdraw the present federal officeholders and army; open shorter and better roads to California through the country north of Bridger; and notify the emigrants that, if they choose to pass through Utah, they will do so at their own risk. Let the Mormons have the territory to themselves—it is worth very little to others, but reduce its area by cutting off Carson Valley on the one side, and making a Rocky Mountain territory on the other, and then let them go on their way rejoicing. I believe this is not only by far the cheapest but the safest and best mode of dealing with the difficulties already developed and daily developing here, unless the notion of "popular sovereignty" in the territories is to be utterly exploded and given up. "Popular sovereignty" in a territory is a contradiction in terms; but "popular sovereignty" in a territory, backed by a thousand sharp federal bayonets and a battery of flying artillery, is too monstrous a futility, too transparent a swindle, to be much longer upheld or tolerated.

22

SALT LAKE AND ITS ENVIRONS

Salt Lake City, July 18, 1859

A party of us visited the lake on Saturday. It is not visible from this city, though it must be from the mountains which rise directly north of it, and more remotely on all sides, but Antelope, Stansbury, and perhaps other islands in the lake, being mainly covered by high, rugged hills or mountains, are in plain sight from every part of the valley. The best of these islands is possessed by "the church" (Mormon) as a herd-ground, or ranch, for its numerous cattle, and is probably the best tract for that purpose in the whole territory. That portion of the lake between it and the valley is so shallow that cattle may, at most seasons, be safely driven over to the island; while it is so deep (between three and four feet) that none will stray back again, and it would be difficult and dangerous to steal cattle thence in the night, when that business is mainly carried on. So the church has a large and capital pasture, and her cattle multiply and wax fat at the least possible expense. The best canyon for wood near this city is likewise owned by the church—*how* owned,

I can't pretend to say—but whoever draws wood from it must deposit every third load in the church's* capacious yard. These are but specimens of the management whereby—though the Saints are generally poor, often quite poor, so that a Saint who has three wives can sometimes hardly afford to keep two beds—the church has a comfortable allowance of treasures laid up on earth. And her leading apostles and dignitaries also, by a curious coincidence, seem to be in thriving circumstances. It looks to me as though neither they nor the church could afford to have the world burnt up for a while yet.

Crossing, just west of the city, the Jordan (which drains the fresh waters of Lake Utah into Salt Lake, and is a large, sluggish creek), we are at once out of the reach of irrigation from the northern hills—the river intercepting all streams from that quarter—and are once more on a parched clay plain, covered mainly with our old acquaintances, sagebrush and greasewood; though there are wet, springy tracts, especially toward the southern mountains and near the lake, which produce rank, coarse grass. Yet this seeming desert has naturally a better soil than the hard, pebbly gravel on which the city stands, and which irrigation has converted into bounteous gardens and orchards. I rejoice to perceive that a dam over the Jordan is in progress, whereby a considerable section of the valley of that river (which valley is forty miles long, by an average of twenty broad) is to be irrigated. There are serious obstacles to the full success of this enterprise in the scarcity of timber and the inequality of the plain, which is gouged and cut up by numerous (now dry) watercourses; but, if this project is well engineered, it will double the productive capacity of this valley, and I

* On further inquiry, I learn that Brigham Young personally is the owner of this splendid placer; but, as he is practically the church, the correction was hardly worth making.

earnestly trust it may be. In the absence of judicious and systematic irrigation, there are far too many cattle and sheep on this great common, as the gaunt look of most of the cattle abundantly testifies. Water also is scarce and bad here; we tried several of the springs which are found at the bases of the southern mountains, and found them all brackish, while not a single stream flows from those mountains in the five or six miles that we skirted them, and I am told that they afford but one or two scanty rivulets through the whole extent of this valley. In the absence of irrigation, nothing is grown or attempted but wild grass; of the half-dozen cabins we have passed between the Jordan and the lake, not one had even the semblance of a garden, or of any cultivation whatever. A shrewd woman, who had lived seven years near the lake, assured me that it would do no good to attempt cultivation there; "too much alkali" was her reason. I learn that, on the city side of the Jordan, when irrigation was first introduced and cultivation attempted, the soil, whenever allowed to become dry, was covered, for the first year or two, with some whitish alkaline substance or compound; but this was soon washed out and washed off by the water, so that no alkali now exhibits itself, and this tract produces handsomely. Let the Jordan be so dammed, and its waters conducted into lateral canals that its whole valley may be amply irrigated, and there are few tracts of like area that will produce more generously, albeit, a majority of its acres now seem almost as sterile and hopeless as the Great American Desert.

That this lake should be salt is no anomaly. All large bodies of water into which streams discharge themselves, while they have severally no outlet, are or should be salt. If one such is fresh, that is an anomaly indeed. Lake Utah probably receives as much saline matter as Salt Lake, but she discharges it through the Jordan and remains herself fresh, while Salt Lake, having no issue save by evaporation, is probably the saltest body of water on earth. The ocean is comparatively fresh; even the Mediterranean is not half so salt. I am told that three barrels of this water yield a barrel of salt; that seems rather strong, yet its intense saltness, no one who has not had it in his eyes, his mouth, his nostrils, can realize. You can no more sink in it than in a claybank, but a very little of it in your lungs would suffice to strangle you. You make your way in from a hot, rocky beach over a chaos of volcanic basalt that is trying to the feet; but, at a depth of a yard or more, you have a fine sand bottom, and here the bathing is delightful.

The water is of a light green color for ten or twenty rods; then "deeply, darkly, beautifully blue." No fish can live in it; no frog abides it; few birds are ever seen dipping into it. The rugged mountains in and about it—just such scarped and seamed and gullied precipices as I have been describing ever since I reached Denver—have a little fir and cotton-wood or quaking asp in their deeper ravines or behind their taller cliffs, but look bare and desolate to the casual observer; and these cut the lake into sections and hide most of it from view. Probably, less than a third of it is visible from any single point. But this suffices.

LIFE IN UTAH

These Mormons are in the main an industrious, frugal, hard-working people. Few of them are habitual idlers; few live by professions or pursuits that require no physical exertion. They make work for but few lawyers—I know but four among them—their differences and disputes are usually settled in and by the church; they have no female outcasts, few doctors, and pay no salaries to their preachers—at least, the leaders say so. But a small portion of them use tea and coffee. Formerly they drank little or no liquor;

but, since the army came in last year, money and whisky have both been more abundant, and now they drink considerably. More than a thousand barrels of whisky have been sold in this city within the last year, at an average of not less than eight dollars per gallon, making the total cost to consumers over two hundred and fifty thousand dollars, whereof the Mormons have paid at least half. If they had thrown, instead, one hundred and fifty thousand dollars in hard cash into the deepest part of Salt Lake, it would have been far better for them. The appetite they are acquiring or renewing will cling to them after the army and its influx of cash shall have departed; and Saints who now drink a little will find themselves as thirsty as their valley, before they suspect that they care anything for liquor. As yet, I believe, they have few or no drunkards; but there is nothing more deceitful than the appetite for liquor. Utah has not a single export of any kind; the army now supplies her with cash; when that is gone, her people will see harder times. She ought to manufacture almost everything she consumes, or foreign debt will overwhelm her. Yet, up to this hour, her manufacturing energies have been most unhappily directed. Some two hundred thousand dollars was expended in preparations for iron-making at a place called Cedar City; but the ore, though rich, would not flux, and the enterprise had to be totally abandoned, leaving the capital a dead loss. Wood and flax can be grown here cheaply and abundantly; yet, owing to the troubles last year, no spinning and weaving machinery has yet been put in operation; I believe some is now coming up from St. Louis. An attempt to grow cotton is likely to prove a failure, as might have been predicted. The winters are long and cold here for the latitude, and the Saints must make cloth or shiver. I trust they will soon be able to clothe themselves.

Sugar is another necessary of life which they have had

198

bad luck with. They can grow the beet very well, but it is said to yield little or no sugar—because, it is supposed, of an excess of alkali in the soil. The sorghum has not yet been turned to much account, but it is to be. Common brown sugar sells here at sixty cents per pound; coffee about the same; in the newer settlements, they are of course still higher. All sorts of imported goods cost twice to six or eight times their prices in the states; even quack medicines (so-called) and yellow-covered novels are sold at double the prices borne on their labels or covers. Consider that the people came hither over a thousand miles mainly of desert, after reaching the Missouri, which was many hundreds if not thousands of miles from their former homes— that they generally reached these valleys in the fall, which afforded them excellent chances of starvation before they could raise a crop—that they have been constantly infested and begged or stolen from by the Indians whose game they killed or scared away, and who feel that they have a right to live here so long as there are cattle or crops to live on— that these valleys are lofty, narrow, and parched by intense drought from May to November—that implements and seeds are scarcely to be obtained short of a three months' journey, and then at an enormous cost—that they have had one year of virtual and costly hostilities with the federal government, in which very little could be done, and improvement was out of the question—and I am amazed that so much has been well done here in the way of building, tilling, fencing, planting trees, etc. Doubtless this city is far ahead of any rival, being the spiritual metropolis and the earliest settled; but I am assured that the valley of Utah Lake is better cultivated than this, though Provo, its county seat, is far behind this city, which, with its broad, regular streets, refreshed by rivulets of bright, sparkling, dancing water, and shaded by rows of young but thrifty trees, mainly locust and bitter cottonwood, is already more attractive to the eye than an average city of like size in the states. The houses (of adobe or merely sun-dried brick) are uniformly low and generally too small; but there is seldom more than one family to a dwelling, and rarely but one dwelling on a lot of an acre and a quarter. The gardens are well filled with peach, apple, and other fruit trees, whereof the peach already bears profusely, and the others begin to follow the example. Apricots and grapes are grown, though not yet abundant; so of strawberries. Plums are in profusion, and the mountain currants are large, abundant and very good. Many of the lots are fenced with cobblestones laid in clay mortar, which seems to stand very well. The wall of Brigham Young's garden and grounds is nine or ten feet high, three feet thick at the base, and cost some sixty dollars per rod. Undoubtedly, these people are steadily increasing in wealth and comfort.

Still the average life in Utah is a hard one. Many more days' faithful labor are required to support a family here than in Kansas, or in any of the states. The climate is severe and capricious—now intensely hot and dry, in winter cold and stormy; and, though cattle are usually allowed to shift for themselves in the valleys, they are apt to resent the insult by dying. Crickets and grasshoppers swarm in myriads, and often devour all before them. Wood is scarce and poor. Irrigation is laborious and expensive; as yet, it has not been found practicable to irrigate one-fourth of the arable land at all. Ultimately, the valleys will be generally irrigated, so far as water for the purpose can be obtained; but this will require very costly dams and canals. Frost is very destructive here; Indian corn rarely escapes it wholly, and wheat often suffers from it. Wheat, oats, corn, barley, rye are grown at about equal cost per bushel—two dollars may be taken as their average price; the wheat crop is usually heavy, though this year it threatens to be relatively light. I estimate that one hundred and fifty days' faithful labor in Kansas will produce as large an aggregate of the necessaries of life—food, clothing, fuel—as three hundred just such days' work in Utah. Hence, the adults here generally wear a toil-worn, anxious look, and many of them are older in frame than in years. I ardently hope it may not always be thus.

POLYGAMY

I do not believe the plural-wife system can long endure; yet almost every man with whom I converse on the subject seems intensely, fanatically devoted to it, deeming this the choicest of his earthly blessings. With the women, I am confident it is otherwise; and I watched their faces as Elder Taylor, at a social gathering on Saturday night, was ex-patiating humorously on this feature of the Mormon sys-tem, to the great delight of the men; but not one responsive smile did I see on the face of a woman. On the contrary, I thought they seemed generally to wish the subject passed over in silence. Fanaticism, and a belief that we are God's especial, exclusive favorites, will carry most of us a great way; but the natural instinct in every woman's breast must teach her that to be some man's third or fourth wife is to be no wife at all. I asked my next neighbor the name of a fair, young girl who sat some distance from us with a babe on her knee. "That is *one* of Judge Smith's ladies," was his quiet, matter-of-course answer. I need hardly say that no woman spoke publicly on that occasion—I believe none ever speaks in a Mormon assemblage—and I shall not ask any-one her private opinion of polygamy; but I think I can read an unfavorable one on many faces.

Yet polygamy is one main pillar of the Mormon Church. He who has two or more wives rarely apostatizes, as he could hardly remain here in safety and comfort as an apos-tate, and dare not take his wives elsewhere. I have heard of but a single instance in which a man with three wives renounced Mormonism and left for California, where he experienced no difficulty, "for", said my informant (a woman, no longer a Mormon), "he introduced his two younger wives (girls of nineteen and fourteen) as his daughters, and married them both off in the course of six weeks."

I am assured by Gentiles that there is a large business done here in *un*marrying as well as in marrying; some of them assure me that the church exacts a fee of ten dollars on the marriage of each wife after the first, but charges a still heavier fee for divorcing. I do not know that this is true, and I suspect my informants were no wiser in the premises than I am. But it certainly looks to me as though a rich dignitary in the church has a freer and fuller range for the selection of his sixth or eighth wife than a poor young man of ordinary standing has for choosing his first. And I infer that the more sharp-sighted young men will not always be content with this.

Since the foregoing was written, I have enjoyed opportunities for visiting Mormons, and studying Mormonism in the home of its votaries, and of discussing with them, in the freedom of social intercourse, what the outside world regards as the distinguishing feature of their faith and polity. In one instance, a veteran apostle of the faith, having first introduced to me a worthy matron of fifty-five or sixty—the wife of his youth, and the mother of his grown-up sons—as Mrs. T., soon after introduced a young and winning lady of perhaps twenty-five summers, in these words: "Here is another Mrs. T." This lady is a recent emigrant from our state, of more than average powers of mind and graces of person, who came here with her father, as a convert, a little over a year ago, and has been the sixth wife of Mr. T. since a few weeks after her arrival. (The intermediate four wives

202

of Elder T. live on a farm or farms some miles distant.)
The manner of the husband was perfectly unconstrained and
offhand throughout; but I could not well be mistaken in my
conviction that both ladies failed to conceal dissatisfaction
with their position in the eyes of their visitor, and of the
world. They seemed to feel that it needed vindication. Their
manner toward each other was most cordial and sisterly—
sincerely so, I doubt not—but this is by no means the rule.
A Gentile friend, whose duties require him to travel widely
over the territory, informs me that he has repeatedly stopped
with a bishop, some hundred miles south of this, whose two
wives he has never known to address each other, nor evince
the slightest cordiality, during the hours he has spent in
their society. The bishop's house consists of two rooms; and
when my informant stayed there with a Gentile friend, the
bishop being absent, one wife slept in the same apartment
with them rather than in that occupied by her double. I
presume that an extreme case, but the spirit which impels
it is not unusual. I met this evening a large party of young
people, consisting in nearly equal numbers of husbands and
wives; but no husband was attended by more than one wife,
and no gentleman admitted or implied, in our repeated and
animated discussions of polygamy, that *he* had more than
one wife. And I was again struck by the circumstance that
here, as heretofore, no woman indicated, by word or look,
her approval of any arguments in favor of polygamy. That
many women acquiesce in it as an ordinance of God, and have
been drilled into a mechanical assent of the logic by which
it is upheld, I believe; but that there is not a woman in Utah
who does not in her heart wish that God had *not* ordained it,
I am confident. And quite a number of the young men treat
it in conversation as a temporary or experimental arrangement, which is to be sustained or put aside as experience
shall demonstrate its utility or mischief. One old Mormon

farmer, with whom I discussed the matter privately, admitted that it was impossible for a poor working man to have a well-ordered, well-governed household where his children had two or more living mothers occupying the same ordinary dwelling. On the whole, I conclude that polygamy, as it was a graft on the original stock of Mormonism, will be outlived by the root—that there will be a new revelation, ere many years, whereby the saints will be admonished to love and cherish the wives they already have, but not to marry any more beyond the natural assignment of one wife to each husband.

I regret that I have found time and opportunity to visit but one of the nineteen common schools of this city. This was thinly attended, by children nearly all quite young, and of the most rudimentary attainments. Their phrenological developments were, in the average, bad; I say this with freedom, since I have stated that those of the adults, as I noted them in the Tabernacle, were good. But I am told that idiotic or malformed children are very rare, if not unknown here. The male saints emphasize the fact that a majority of the children born here are girls, holding it a proof that Providence smiles on their "peculiar institution"; I, on the contrary, maintain that such is the case in all polygamous countries, and proves simply a preponderance of vigor on the part of the mothers over that of the fathers wherever this result is noted. I presume that a majority anywhere of the children of old husbands by young wives are girls.

But again the wheels revolve, and my face must once more be turned westward. With the most hearty and grateful acknowledgements of the exceeding kindness and hospitality with which I have been treated here alike by Mormon and Gentile, and with barely a word of praise for the magnificent gardens I have been invited to visit—of which Brigham Young's is probably the most costly and eye-pleasing, but

I like Heber Kimball's the best—I bid adieu to Salt Lake City, the great mass of whose people, I am sure, have an unfeigned "zeal for God," though I must deem it "not according to knowledge." Long may they live to unlearn their errors, and enjoy the rich fruits of their industry, frugality, and sincere, though misguided piety!

Note. An inaccurate report of some casual remarks made by me at the social gathering, hereinbefore alluded to, having appeared in *The Valley Tan*, and been widely copied, I am impelled here to print these remarks more correctly; though, had nothing been already said on the subject, I should not have deemed them worth preservation.

The occasion was a meeting on Saturday evening, July 19th, in a public hall, under the *Deseret News* office, of the Deseret Typographical Association, at which I had expected to meet ten or twelve printers, Mormon and Gentile, but wherein I found myself face to face with some two hundred people, nearly half ladies. In response to a sentiment, in which the Art of Printing was honored, I spoke of the vast transformations which the world has witnessed since the auspicious invention of the art—the discovery of America—steam, and steamships—the steam printing press—the electric telegraph, etc., etc.—with the corresponding moral and intellectual growth of Christendom, the triumphs of religious liberty, the progress made toward a general recognition of the rights of man, and the true theory of government, etc., etc. Speeches were also made by Elder John Taylor, Elder Orson Hyde, and others, all devoted in good part to eulogiums on Mormonism, glances at the past history of their churches, denunciations of their enemies, etc., etc. I think fully two hours were devoted to these addresses. A pause ensuing, I rose, and said:

"The remarks of the friends who have addressed us, especially those which set forth the oppressions and outrages to which they have at sundry times and in different localities been subjected, remind me that I have not heard tonight, and I think I never heard, from the lips or the journals of any of your people, one word in reprehension of that gigantic national crime and scandal, American chattel slavery. You speak forcibly of the wrongs to which your feeble brethren have from time to time been subjected; but what are they all to the perpetual, the gigantic outrage involved in holding in abject bondage four millions of human beings? This obstinate silence, this seeming indifference on your part, reflects no credit on your faith and morals, and I trust they will not be persisted in."

The response to this appeal was made by Elder Taylor, in very nearly these words:

"The subject of slavery is one on which Mr. Greeley is known to be enthusiastic, as we are on the subject of our religion. We cannot help speaking of our religion at every opportunity, as he cannot help speaking of slavery. Those who do not relish this or that topic, must excuse its introduction." [I give the import, not the exact words of the Elder's remarks.]

At a later hour—as late as 11 o'clock, when many were impatient for adjournment to supper—one whose name I did not learn, rose and expressed a desire that I should make a speech, setting forth my views of woman's rights! A murmur of "Too late," "Not time," etc., being heard, I said:

"Mr. President, I can make the speech our friend requires in just one minute. I hold it the right of every woman to do any and every thing that she can do well, provided it ought to be done. If it ought not to be done at all, or if she cannot do it, then she has no right to do it; but if it ought to be done, and she can do it, then her right to do it is, to my mind, indisputable. And that is all that I have to say, now or ever, on the subject of woman's rights."

23

THE ARMY IN UTAH

Camp Floyd, Utah, July 21, 1859

Camp Floyd, forty miles south of Salt Lake City, is located on the west side of a dry valley, perhaps ten miles wide by thirty miles long, separated by high hills from Lake Utah, some fifteen to twenty miles distant on the northeast. This valley would be fertile were it not doomed to sterility by drought. A small stream takes its rise in copious springs at the foot of the western hills just north of the camp, but is soon drunk up by the thirsty plain. Water in this stream, and wood (low cedar) on the adjacent hills, probably dictated the selection of this site for a camp, though I believe a desire, if not a secret compact, to locate the troops as far as possible from the Mormon settlements had an influence in the premises. No Mormons live in this valley nor within sight of it, though all the roads leading from Salt Lake City, as well as from Provo and the other settlements around Lake Utah, are within a day's march, and may be said to be commanded by the camp. The soil is easily pulverized when dry, and keeps the entire area enveloped, during summer, in a dense cloud of dust, visible for miles in every direction. I saw it when eight miles away, as I came down

from Salt Lake City yesterday. We passed few houses on
the way; but a distillery and a brewery were among them.
We crossed the Jordan by fording, at a point seven or eight
miles from the lake, and twenty-five to thirty from Salt Lake
City. The stream is here swift and strong, but hardly thirty
inches deep, and not more than thirty yards wide. We passed
within sight of Provo, but several miles from it. We passed
one spring on the route, and two or three brooks running
from the high, steep mountains on the east. The drought
was intense, and seemed habitual in summer; there was no
cultivation nor industry of any sort on our road, save within
twenty miles of Salt Lake City.

The camp is formed of low and neat adobe houses, generally small. I presume there are three or four hundred of
them—enough, at all events, to make six or eight Kansas
Cities. Frogtown is a satellite, or suburb, whence grog and
other luxuries (including execrable whisky at about ten
dollars per gallon) are dispensed to thirsty soldiers who have
not already drunk up more than their pay amounts to. The
valley is covered with sagebrush and greasewood, as usual;
but the camp has been freed from these, and is mainly level
as a house floor. The adobes were made on the spot by Mexicans; the boards for roofs, finishing off, etc., supplied by
Brigham Young and his son-in-law, from the only canyon
opening into Salt Lake Valley which abounds in timber
(yellow pine, I believe) fit for sawing. The territorial
legislature (which is another name for the church) granted
this canyon to Brigham, who runs three saw mills therein,
at a clear profit of one hundred dollars or so per day. His
profit on the lumber supplied to the camp was probably
over fifty thousand dollars. The price was seventy dollars per
thousand feet, delivered. President Young assured me, with
evident self-complacency, that he did not need and would
not accept a dollar of salary from the church—he considered

208

himself able to make all the money he needed by business, as he had made the two hundred and fifty thousand dollars' worth of property he already possesses. With a legislature ever ready to grant him such perquisites as this lumber canyon, I should think he might. The total cost of this post to the government was about two hundred thousand dollars.

The army in Utah has numbered three thousand five hundred men—I believe its present strength is but about three thousand. It is mainly concentrated in this camp, though some small detachments are engaged in surveying or opening roads, guarding herds, etc., in different parts of the territory. I presume this is still the largest regular force ever concentrated upon the soil of our country in time of peace. It consists of the 5th, 7th and 10th regiments of infantry, a battalion of light artillery, and two or three companies of dragoons. I met, between Bridger and Ham's Fork, a considerable force of dragoons going down.

Let us briefly consider the history and position of this little army:

In the earlier half of 1857, it was concentrated in Kansas; late in that year, the several regiments composing it were severally put in march toward the Rocky Mountains. The Mormons soon full learned that this band was to be launched against them, and at once prepared to give it a warm reception; the army had no information on the subject, save general report. Detained in Kansas to give effect to Governor Walker's electioneering quackeries, it was at length sent on its way at a season too late to allow it to reach Salt Lake before winter. No commander was sent with it; General Harney was announced as its chief, but has not even yet joined it. It was thus dispatched on a long and difficult expedition, in detachments, without a chief, without orders, without any clear idea of its object or destination. Entering

Utah thus as no army, but as a number of separate, straggling detachments, none of which was ordered to protect the supply train, which followed one or two marches behind them, the soldiers had the mortification to learn, about the 1st of October, that those supply trains, without even an armed corporal's guard in their vicinity, had been surprised and burnt by a Mormon band, who thus in effect made war on the United States. Indignantly, but still without a leader and without definite orders, the army struggled on to Bridger, one hundred and thirteen miles from Salt Lake, which the Mormons abandoned on its approach. Bridger is many thousand feet above the sea level, and the ground was here so buried in snow that its gaunt animals died by hundreds, and the residue were unable to drag the baggage over the rivers and steep mountains which still separated it from Salt Lake. So the regiments halted, built huts to shelter themselves from the winter's inclemency, and lived through the snowy season as they might on a half allowance of beef from their lean, grisly animals, without salt.

Spring at length came; the order to march, long hoped and impatiently waited for, was given; they had been promised a warm reeption in the narrow defiles of Echo Canyon by Lieutenant-General Wells and his Mormon host, and they eagerly courted that reception. If General Wells were able, as he boasted, to send them to the right about, they would have nothing to do but to go. They had grown rusty from inaction, and stood ready to be polished, even by so rough an implement as General Wells. But news came that the whole affair had been somehow arranged—that Colonel Kane, Brigham Young, and Governor Cumming had fixed matters so that there would be no fighting—not even further train-burning. Yet the Mormons fled from Salt Lake City in anticipation of their entering it; they were somehow required to encamp as far from the Mormon settlements as possible;

210

and they have ever since been treated by the federal executive as though they had volunteered to come here in defiance of, rather than in obedience to, that executive's own orders.

Whether truly or falsely, this army, probably without an individual exception, undoubtingly believes the Mormons as a body to be traitors to the Union and its government, inflexibly intent on establishing here a power which shall be at first independent of, and ultimately dominant over, that of the United States. They believe that the ostentatious, defiant refusal of Brigham Young, in 1857, to surrender the territorial governorship, and his declaration that he would hold that post until God Almighty should tell him to give it up, were but the natural development of a polity which looks to the subjugation of all earthly kingdoms, states, empires, sovereignties, to a rule nominally theocratic, but practically autocratic, with Brigham Young or his designated successor as despot. They hold that the instinct of self-preservation, the spirit of that requirement of the Federal Constitution which enjoins that each state shall be guaranteed a Republican form of government, cry out against such a despotism, and demand its overthrow.

The army undoubtingly and universally believes that Mormonism is, at least on the part of the master spirits of the church, an organized, secret, treasonable conspiracy to extend the power, increase the wealth, and gratify the lecherous appetites of those leaders, who are using the forms and terms of religion to mask and shield systematic adultery, perjury, counterfeiting, robbery, treason, and even murder. It points to the wholesale massacre at Mountain Meadows, the murder of the Parrishes, and a hundred more such, as instances of Mormon assassination for the good of the church, the chastisement of its enemies, or the aggrandizement of its leading members—to the impossibility of bringing the perpetrators of these crimes to justice, to the territorial laws of Utah which empower Mormon functionaries to select the grand and petit jurors even for the United States courts, and impose qualifications which in effect secure the exclusion of all but Mormons from the jury box, and to the uniform refusal of those jurors to indict or convict those who have committed crimes in the interest of Mormonism,* as proof positive that all attempts to punish Mormon criminals by Mormon jurors and officers must ever prove abortive, and demands of the federal government that it shall devise and put in execution some remedy for this unbearable impunity to crime. It is uniformly believed in camp that not less than *seventy-five* distinct instances of murder by Mormons because of apostacy, or some other form of hostility to the church, or mainly for the sake of plunder, are known to the authorities here, and that there is no shadow of hope that one of the perpetrators will ever be brought to justice under the sway of Mormon "popular sovereignty" as now established in this territory. The army, therefore, turns an anxious eye to Washington, and strains its ear to hear what remedy is to be applied.

Manifestly, the recent responses from that quarter are not calculated to allay this anxiety. The official rebuke recently and publicly given to the federal judges here, for employing detachments of troops to arrest and hold securely Mormons accused of capital crime, elicits low mutterings of dissatisfaction from some, with a grave silence on the part of many whom discipline restrains from speaking. As the recent orders from Washington are understood here, no employment of federal troops to arrest or secure persons charged with or even convicted of crime is allowed, except where the civil power (intensely Mormon) shall have cer-

---

* Judge Cradlebaugh asserts that on the list of jurors recently imposed on him for the investigation at Provo of the Parrish and other murders, he knows there were not less than *nine* leading participants in those murders.

tified that the execution of process is resisted by a force
which it cannot overcome by means of a civil posse. How
opposite this is to the orders given and obeyed in the fugitive
slaves cases at Boston, etc., need hardly be indicated.

Very general, then, is the inquiry in the army, Why were
we sent here? and why are we kept here? What good can our
remaining do? What mischief can it prevent? A fettered,
suspected, watched, distrusted army—an army which must
do nothing—must not even be asked to do anything in any
probable contingency—what purpose does it subserve beyond enriching contractors and Mormon magnates at its
own cost and that of the federal treasury? Every article
eaten, drunk, worn, or in any manner bought by the soldiers,
costs three to ten times its value in the states; part of this
extra cost falls on the treasury, the residue on the troops
individually. Their position here is an irksome one; their
comforts few; home, family, friends are far away. If the
policy now pursued is to prevail, they cannot be needed in
this territory. Why, then, are they kept here? Brigham
Young will contract, and make money by contracting, to put
down all resistance to this policy at one-tenth the cost of
keeping the army here: why, then, not withdraw it?

I have not so bad an opinion of the Mormons as that entertained by the army. While I consider the Mormon religion,
so called, a delusion and a blight, I believe many of its devoted adherents, including most of those I have met, to be
pure-minded, well-meaning people; and I do not believe
that Mormons generally delight in plunder or murder,
though the testimony in the Mountain Meadows, Parrish,
and one or two other cases, is certainly staggering. But I
concur entirely in the conviction of the army, that there
is no use in its retention here under existing orders and circumstances, and that three or four companies of dragoons
would answer every purpose of this large and costly con-

centration of troops. The army would cost less almost anywhere else, and could not anywhere be less useful.

A suspicion that it is kept here to answer private pecuniary
ends is widely entertained. It is known that vast sums have
been made out of its transportation by favored contractors.
Take a single instance already quite notorious: twenty-two
cents per pound is paid for the transportation of all provisions, munitions, etc., from Leavenworth to this point.
The great contractors were allowed this for transporting
this year's supply of flour. By a little dexterous management
at Washington, they were next allowed to furnish the flour
here—Utah flour—being paid their twenty-two cents per
pound for transportation, in addition to the prime cost on
the Missouri. As Utah has a better soil for growing wheat
than almost anything else, they had no difficulty in subletting
this contract at seven cents per pound net, making a clear
profit of one hundred and seventy thousand dollars on the
contract, without risking a dollar, or lifting a finger. Of
course, I expect contractors to bargain for themselves, not
for the government, but somebody is well paid for taking
care of the public's interest in such matters. Has he done
his duty?

Again, pursuant to a recent order from Washington, the
Assistant Quartermaster-General here is now selling by
auction some two thousand mules—about two-thirds of all
the government owns in this territory. These mules cost one
hundred and seventy-five dollars each, and are worth today
one hundred and twenty-five to one hundred and fifty dollars. I attended the sales for an hour or so this forenoon; the
range of prices was from sixty to one hundred and fifteen
dollars; the average of the seven hundred already sold about
seventy-five dollars. Had these mules been taken to California,
and there properly advertised and sold, they would have
brought nearly cost; even at Leavenworth, they must have

sold for at least one hundred thousand dollars more than here, where there is practically no demand and no competition for such an immense herd; and after every Mormon who can raise a hundred dollars or over shall have supplied himself with a span of mules for half their value, one or two speculators will make as much as they please, while the dead loss to the people will be at least one hundred and fifty thousand dollars. Nobody here has recommended the sale of these mules; they were being herded, under the care of detachments of the army, at no cost but for herdsmen, and they could have been kept through next winter, in secluded mountain valleys, at a cost of about ten dollars per head; whereas the army can never move without purchasing an equal number; and they can neither be bought here nor brought here for two hundred thousand dollars more than these animals are now fetching. *Somebody's* interest is subserved by this sale; but it is certainly not that of the army nor of the people. The order is to sell seven hundred wagons as well; but these would not bring thirty dollars each, while they cost at least one hundred and thirty, and could not be replaced when wanted even for that, while the army cannot move without them, and keeping them costs absolutely nothing. Who issues such orders as this, and for whose benefit?

Look at another feature of this transaction. There is at this moment a large amount due to officers and soldiers of this army as pay, in sums of forty to five hundred dollars each. Many of those to whom this money is due would very much like to take mules in part payment, either to use while here to sell again, or to bear them and their baggage to California, or back to the Missouri, on the approaching expiration of their terms of enlistment. In many instances, two soldiers would doubtless club to buy a mule on which to pack their blankets, etc., whenever their time is out. Hundreds of mules would thus have been bought, and the proceeds of the sale considerably augmented, if the government, by its functionaries, had consented to receive its own honest debts in payment. But no! on some ridiculous pretense of ill-blood between the Pay and the Subsistence Bureau of the War Department, this is refused—it would be too much trouble to take certificates of soldier's pay actually due in payment for these mules; so the officers and soldiers must purchase of speculators at double price, or go without, and the mules be sold for far less than they would have brought, if those who must have them had been enabled to bid directly for them. Two or three speculators reap a harvest here at the sore cost of the soldiers and the treasury.

But it will be said that forage is dear in Utah. It would suffice to answer that idle mules obtain, save in winter, only grass growing on the public lands, which may as well be eaten in part by government mules as all by those of the Mormon squatters. But let us see how it costs so much. There have recently been received here thirty thousand bushels of corn from the states at a net cost, including transportation, of three hundred and forty thousand dollars, or over eleven dollars per bushel. No requisition was ever made for this corn, which could have been bought here, delivered, for two dollars per bushel, or sixty thousand dollars in all. The dead loss to the treasury on this corn is two hundred and eighty thousand dollars, even supposing that the service required it at all. *Somebody* makes a good thing of wagoning this corn from the Missouri at over ten dollars a bushel. Who believes that said somebody has not influential and thrifty connections inside of the War Department?

I will not pursue this exposition; Congress may.

Let me now give a sample of retrenchment in the public service in this quarter:

The mail from Missouri to Salt Lake has hitherto been carried weekly in good six-mule wagons, the contract time being twenty-two days. The importance of frequent and regular communication with headquarters, at least so long as a large army is retained here at a heavy extra cost, and because of some presumed public necessity, is evident. Yet the new Postmaster-General has cut down the mail service on this important central route from weekly to semi-monthly. But the contractors, who are obliged to run their stages weekly because of their passenger business, and because they have to keep their stock and pay their men, whether they work or play, find that they cannot carry the mail every other week so cheaply as they can every week. For instance, a mail from the states now often consists of twelve to sixteen heavy sacks (most of them filled with franked documents), weighing as many hundred pounds. Double this, and no six-mule team would draw it at the requisite pace, and no mail wagon stand the jerks and jolts of an unmade road. So they say, "Please let us carry the mail weekly, though you only pay us for carrying it semi-monthly." But no! this is strictly forbidden! The postmaster at Salt Lake has express written orders to refuse it, and of course he at St. Joseph also. And thus all this central region, embracing at least a dozen important military posts, and countless Indian agencies, is reduced to a semi-monthly mail service, though the contractor would gladly make it weekly at the same price!

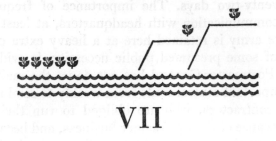

VII

SALT LAKE TO CALIFORNIA

Dispatches 24 & 25

Ten days of the hardest going yet endured, through the most desolate and forbidding country yet seen, now stood between Horace Greeley and his goal. The stagecoach kept going night and day for the last five of those ten days, averaging a hundred miles a day for the stretch. When finally it pulled up for an overnight stop at a comfortable, two-story station house some fifteen miles beyond Genoa at the foot of the Sierra Nevada, Greeley was so exhausted he slept but fitfully, despite a refreshing bath and a real bed. They were on the road again at dawn the next day, crossed Carson Pass, and started the long descent into the Sacramento Valley. Horace Greeley slept that night, August 1, 1859, in Placerville. He was in California at last.

218

24

FROM SALT LAKE TO CARSON VALLEY

Placerville, Cal., July 31, 1859

There are two emigrant trails from Salt Lake City to Carson Valley and the pass thence into California—the older and more favored starts northwest from the Mormon Zion, passes north and west of Salt Lake, crossing Weber and Bear Rivers near their mouths, with several small creeks, and gradually veering west and southwest so as to strike the headsprings of the Humboldt, which stream it follows more than three hundred miles to its "sink," within a hundred miles of the eastern base of the Sierra Nevada. The other route leaves the Mormon capital in a southwesterly direction, touches Lake Utah on the north, passes west of that Lake through Provo, and thence southerly through Fillmore, the nominal capital of the territory, and so down by Sevier River and Lake nearly to the southern boundary of Utah, whence it stretches west, nearly upon the southern rim of the Great Basin, on which are the Mountain Meadows, where a large emigrant party from Arkansas was so atrociously massacred in 1857. Thence this trail turns northwest to hit the sink of Carson River. (I can get no tolerable map of Utah, and the above may not be entirely correct, but is nearly so.) It will be seen that each of these routes must necessarily be very circuitous, and that almost, if not quite, half the territory lies between them. So, last year, Major Chorpening, the contractor for carrying the Salt Lake and California mail, resolved to seek a shorter route midway between them, which he partially succeeded in establishing. This route passes Camp Floyd, forty-three miles south of Salt Lake City, and thence strikes westsouthwest through the desert, so-called, which it penetrates for one hundred and fifty miles or more, thence turning northwest to reach and follow the original emigrant and mail route down the Humboldt. Even thus, it is somewhat shorter than any other traveled route from Salt Lake to Carson Valley, but still very tortuous, and at least one hundred and fifty miles longer than it should be. Capt. Simpson, of the U. S. Topographical Corps, has recently made his way quite through the desert, on a route which makes the distance only five hundred and sixty-one miles from Camp Floyd to Carson Valley, whereas it is six hundred and seventy by the present mail route, and further by any other. Capt. Simpson is now engaged in further surveys, whereby he hopes* to shorten the distance from Salt Lake City to Genoa, near the head of Carson Valley, to about five hundred and fifty miles; and two of Major Chorpening's superintendents are now examining the new portion of this route, intending to recommend a transfer of the mail to it should they deem it practicable for wagons, and not hopelessly destitute of grass and water. I trust they will find it passable; meantime, let me give some account of so much of it as I have traveled, as I am not aware that any is yet extant.

I left Camp Floyd in the mail wagon from Salt Lake City on the morning of Thursday, July 21st, pursuing a southwest course over a low mountain pass. Twenty miles on, we found a small brook making from the mountains south of us across a thirsty plain, which, I presume, soon drank it up. The vegetation was the same eternal sagebrush and greasewood, which I am tired of mentioning, but which, together or separately, cover two-thirds of all the vast re-

---

* These hopes have since been fully realized. The new direct central route is not only one hundred miles shorter, but is said to be better supplied with grass and water, than that I traveled.

gion between the Rocky Mountains and the Sierra Nevada. In places, the sagebrush, for miles in extent, is dead and withering, seemingly parched up by the all-pervading drought; the greasewood is either hardier or chooses its ground more judiciously, for it is rarely found dead by acres. There is some bunch grass on the sides of two or three mountains, but very little of aught that can be relied on to sustain human or animal life. The mountains and plains seem to divide the ground very fairly between them—the soil of both being mainly a white clay, while the former have that creased, gullied, washed-away appearance, which I have repeatedly noticed. Sometimes they are nearly perpendicular on one or more sides, like the buttes further east, but usually they can be ascended on any side, and seem to rise but one to three thousand feet above the plains at their bases. These plains appear from a distance to be level as so many tables; but, on attempting to cross them in a wagon, you find them creased and scored by innumerable watercourses, now dry, but showing that, in the wet season, water is most abundant here. In most instances, a gradual slope of a mile or two intervenes between the foot of a mountain and the adjacent plain or valley; this slope is apt to be intensely dry, sterile, and covered with dead or dying sagebrush. I judge these slopes to be composed of the rocky, gravelly material of the mountains, from which the lighter clay has been washed out and carried off. They often seem to be composed almost wholly of small bits of rock. The valleys or plains are from five to fifteen miles across, though they seem, in the clear, dry atmosphere of Utah, not half so much. These plains have an imperceptible slope to some point near their respective centers, where a wider watercourse runs toward some adjacent valley; in some cases, a marsh or naked space near the center indicates that the surplus water from the surrounding mountains forms here in winter and spring a petty, shallow lake, which the hot suns soon evaporate or the thirsty soil absorbs. The mountains are thinly belted or dotted with low, scrubby cedar, seldom ten feet high, and often nearly as far across the green top formed by three or four stalks or stems starting from a common root. The mountains seem to have no particular, or rather no general direction, some of the valleys being nearly or quite surrounded by them. Even in the wettest seasons, I cannot perceive that this region sends off any surplus water to Salt Lake or any other general reservoir. Such is the face of the country for some two hundred miles directly southwest of Camp Floyd.

We found a station, a change of horses, and something that was called dinner, on the little stream I have already mentioned, and halted here, twenty miles or more from Camp Floyd. In the afternoon, we came on, over a higher, rockier mountain pass and a far rougher road, to the next station— Simpson's Spring, neary fifty miles from Camp Floyd— where we halted for the night. I fear the hot suns of August will dry up this spring, while there is no other fit to drink for a weary distance south and west of this point.

The station keeper here gave me an incident which illustrates the character of the country. Some few days previously to our arrival, he ascertained that his oxen, eight in number, had gone off, two or three nights before, taking a southerly course; so he mounted a horse and followed their trail. He rode upon it one hundred miles without reaching water or overtaking the cattle, which had lain down but once since they started, and were still a day's journey ahead of him. If he continued the pursuit his horse must die of thirst, and then he too must perish; so he turned about and left his oxen to die in the desert or be found and eaten by savages. There was not a shadow of hope that he would ever see them again.

We had to drive the same team (mules, of course) all next day, making fifty miles; but we stopped to rest and feed them at a sub-station, only twenty miles from our starting point. It was about the forlornest spot I ever saw. Though at the foot of a low mountain, there was no water near it; that which was given our mules had been carted in a barrel from Simpson's Spring, aforesaid, and so must be for most of each year. An attempt to sink a well at this point had thus far proved a failure. The station keeper here lives entirely alone—that is, when the Indians will let him—seeing a friendly face but twice a week, when the mail stage passes one way or the other. He deeply regretted his lack of books and newspapers; we could only give him one of the latter. Why do not men who contract to run mails through such desolate regions comprehend that their own interest, if no nobler consideration, should impel them to supply their stations with good reading matter! I am quite sure that one hundred dollars spent by Major Chorpening in supplying two or three good journals to each station on his route, and in providing for their interchange from station to station, would save him more than one thousand dollars in keeping good men in his service, and in imbuing them with contentment and gratitude. So with other mail routes through regions like this.

We drove on that day thirty miles further, to Fish Springs Station, just before reaching which we passed one of the salt wells which are characteristic of this country, though not absolutely peculiar to it. This one is about six or eight feet in diameter, and perhaps an equal distance from the surface of the surrounding earth to that of the water, which has a whitish green aspect, is intensely salt, and said to be unfathomable, with a downward suction which a man could hardly or not at all resist. I had no desire to try, badly as I needed ablution.

Fish Springs forms quite a large pool at the north end of a low mountain range, and sends off a copious stream to be drunk up in the course of three or four miles by the thirsty clay of the plain. The water is brackish, and I think sulphurous, as that of a spring in the adjacent marsh near the station clearly is. There are many fish in the pool and stream, and they are said to be good. I should have liked to verify the assertion; and if they bite a hundredth part so freely as the mosquitoes do hereabout, it were an easy matter to afford the stage passengers here a change from their usual rations of pork, bread and coffee, which, when the flour, or the pork, or the coffee, happens to be out, as it sometimes is, renders the diet unsatisfactory, even to those who would seem to have been seasoned to the like by a passage across the Plains and the Rocky Mountains. Fish Springs is just fifty miles from living water on either side, and the stages have to run at least ten miles out of their course to strike it. There is some coarse grass here.

July 23d. We traveled this forenoon over a plain nearly surrounded by mountains. Said plain is very level to the eye, but the rapid traveler's sense of feeling contradicts this, for he finds it full of dry watercourses, which give him most uncomfortable jolts. Before noon, we came to the spot where the stage mules are turned out to feed and rest, by the side of a sink or depression in the plain, which is covered with coarse grass and reeds or bulrushes. By digging in the side of this sink, water has been easily obtained, but so sulphurous, and generally bad, as to be barely drinkable. Even the mules, I noticed, practice great moderation in the use of it. At one, we harnessed up, and were soon rising over a long mountain pass, hardly less than ten miles from the level plain to its summit, where a light thundershower—that is, a light rain with heavy thunder—overtook us. We drove rapidly down its western declivity and a little after 5 P.M. reached our next station in Pleasant Valley, a broad ravine, which descends to the southwest. Here we found water—bright, sweet, pure, sparkling, leaping water—the first water fit to drink that we had reached in a hundred miles; if Simpson's Spring ever dries up, the distance will then be at least a hundred and twenty. We were now across what is here technically known as the desert—that is to say, we had crossed the northeast corner of it. I believe it extends at least two hundred miles south from this point and is at least as far from east to west across its center. If Uncle Sam should ever sell that tract for one cent per acre, he will swindle the purchaser outrageously.

Let me endeavor, on quitting it, to give a clear idea of this desert, and thus of about half the land enclosed between the Rocky Mountains and the Sierra Nevada—the other half being mainly covered by mountains and the narrow ravines or canyons which separate them.

The plains or valleys of Utah, then, have generally a soil of white clay, sometimes rocky, at others streaked by sand or gravel, but usually pure clay, save as it is impregnated with some alkaline substance—usually saleratus, but in places niter; in others, salt or sulphur. Sometimes, but rarely, considerable areas of this alkali in a nearly pure state are exposed on the surface; in many places it covers the beds of shallow, dried-up lakes, and even streams, with a whitish incrustation; but it is more generally diffused through the soil, and thus impregnates the springs and streams. Irrigating a piece of ground, strongly imbued with alkali, will often bring an incrustation of it to the surface, after which no trouble from it is experienced in that place. I think the greater proportion of these plains or valleys —which could easily be cleared of their greasewood and sagebrush and plowed—would produce large crops of wheat, and of almost anything else, if they could be irrigated. But that can never be, unless by artesian wells. But little rain falls in summer, and that little is speedily evaporated from the hot earth, leaving the clay as thirsty as ever. I fear it is mainly doomed to perpetual barrenness.

The mountains which divide these plains exude very little water. Wherever a range is single—that is, with a broad valley each side of it—it is apt to be not more than one to three thousand feet high, and so to be early denuded of snow; its springs are few and generally feeble, and their waters are often dried up before trickling halfway down the sides of the mountain which gave them birth. If a spring is so copious, or so many are speedily combined, as to form a considerable stream, they may reach the plain, but only to be speedily drunk up by its scorched surface. Cultivation, therefore, save in a very few narrow spots, seems here impossible.

But wherever a chaos or jumble of mountains is presented —still more, where mountains rise behind mountains, range behind range, rank above rank, till the summits of the furthest that may be seen are flecked with snow—there the case is altered. Springs are there more abundant and more copious; the gradual melting of the snows swells the rivulets formed by the speedy meeting of their waters; and thus considerable brooks are formed and poured down upon the subjacent plains, as we observe in and around Salt Lake City, and north and west of Lake Utah. Thus are formed Bear and Weber Rivers; such, I believe, is the origin of the Humboldt. But such instances are far too rare in Utah. From the Jordan to the Humboldt is about three hundred and fifty miles by the route I traveled, and in all that distance the brooks and rills I crossed or saw, could they be collected into one channel, would barely form a decent millstream. I thence traveled down the south side of the Humboldt for two hundred and twenty-five miles, and in all that distance not more than two tributaries come in on that side, and their united currents would barely suffice to turn a grindstone. This desolation seems therefore irredeemable.

The mountains of Central Utah are less hopeless than the plains. Contrary to my former impression, they are fairly wooded; by which I mean that wood is procurable on them at almost any point. This wood is for the most part cedar, six to ten feet high, and from a foot downward in diameter near the ground. White pines of like size, and of equally scrubby character, are quite common in the western part of the mountains I traversed, and there is some balsam fir in the deeper canyons, which attains a diameter of fifteen to twenty inches, and a height of forty to sixty feet. Of this fir, several of the mail-station cabins are constructed; in Ruby Valley, they have one of red or Indian pine; but they are quite commonly built of stones and mud. One on the Humboldt is built of dwarf-willow canes or wattles—not one anywhere of cedar nor of the dwarfed white pine of this region. Neither could be made to answer.

But I must hurry on. At Pleasant Valley, we turned northwest up a broad ravine, and thenceforth held that general course to reach the Humboldt, instead of still making westsouthwest directly toward Carson Valley, as it is proposed hereafter to do if that be found practicable. For the next one hundred and forty miles or thereabouts, our trail led us mainly up one side of a mountain range and down the other, thence across a valley of some ten miles in width to the foot of another chain, and so on. As the train naturally runs up the deepest canyons and over the lowest passes, the ascent and descent are rarely abrupt for any considerable distance, and we seldom lacked water; but our route was the most devious imaginable—veering from northeast on one hand to south on the other. Sometimes, two or three hundred square miles were visible at a glance—the mountainsides half covered with cedar and pine, with some dwarf-willows and rose bushes often fringing their slender rivulets, but not a tree other than evergreen in sight. There is a large, pine-leaved shrub or small tree which a driver termed a mountain mahogany and a passenger called a red haw, growing sparingly among the evergreens on some mountain slopes, which seems about halfway between a thornbush and an untrimmed appletree, but nothing else deciduous above the size of the dwarf willow. Even the sagebrush and greasewood appear to be evergreens. Grass is here not abundant but unfailing, as it must be where water is perennial and wood in fair supply. The plains or valleys remain as further east, save that they are smaller and, because of the less scanty supply of water, more susceptible of improvement. At Shell Creek, forty-five miles from Pleasant Valley, where we spent our next night, there is a little garden—the first I had seen since Camp Floyd—and at Ruby Valley, fifty miles or so further on, the government has a farm in crop, intended for the benefit, and partly cultivated by the labor, of the neighboring Indians. The mail station also has its garden, and is cutting an abundance of hay. From this station, it is expected that the new cut off, saving one hundred miles or more in distance to Carson Valley, will be made, so soon as those now scrutinizing it shall have pronounced it practicable.

At Ruby, the stage usually stops for the night; but we had been six days making rather less than three hundred miles, and began to grow impatient. The driver had his own reasons for pushing on, and did so, over a road partly mountainous, rough and sideling; but, starting at 8 P.M., we had reached the next (Pine Valley) station, forty miles distant, before sunrise. Here we were detained three or four hours for mules —those we should have taken being astray—but at nine we started with a new driver, and were soon entangled in a pole bridge over a deep, miry stream—a drove of a thousand head of cattle (the first ever driven over this road) having recently passed, and torn the frail bridge to pieces. Our lead mules went down in a pile, but were got up and out and the wagon ran over, after a delay of an hour. We soon rose from Pine Valley by a long, irregular, generally moderate ascent, to a mountain divide, from which our trail took abruptly down the wildest and worst canyon I ever saw traversed by a carriage. It is in places barely wide enough at bottom for a wagon, and if two should meet here it is scarcely possible that they should pass. The length of this canyon is a mile and a half; the descent hardly less than two thousand feet; the side of the road next to the watercourse often far lower than the other; the roadbed is often made of sharp-edged fragments of broken rock, hard enough to stand on, harder still to hold back on. The heat in this canyon on a summer afternoon is intense, the sun being able to enter it while the wind is not. Two or three glorious springs afford partial consolation to the weary, thirsty traveler. I am confident no passenger ever rode down this rocky ladder; I trust that none will until a better road is made here, though a good road in such a gulch is scarcely possible. Fifteen miles further, across a plain and a lower range of hills, brought our mail wagon at last, about 7 P.M. of its seventh day from Salt Lake City, to:

THE HUMBOLDT

I am not going to describe the route down this river, as it is the old emigrant trail, repeatedly written about already. I only wish to record my opinion that the Humboldt, all things considered, is the meanest river of its length on earth. Rising in the Humboldt Mountains, hardly one hundred and fifty miles west of Salt Lake, it is at first a pure stream—or rather streams, for there are two main branches—but is soon corrupted by its alkaline surroundings, and its water, for at least the lower half of its course, is about the most detestable I ever tasted. I mainly chose to suffer thirst rather than drink it. Though three hundred and fifty miles in length, it is never more than a decent millstream; I presume it is the only river of equal length that never had a canoe launched upon its bosom. Its narrow bottom, or intervale, produces grass, but so coarse in structure, and so alkaline by impregnation, that no sensible man would let his stock eat it, if there were any alternative. Here, however, there is none. Cattle must eat this, or die—many of them eat it, and die. One of the most intelligent emigrants I conversed with on its banks informed me that he had all the grass for his stock mowed, as he had found by experience that his cattle, if grazed upon it, pulled up much of their grass by the roots, and these roots were far more alkaline than the stalks. I believe no tree of any size grows on this forlorn river from its forks to its mouth—I am sure I saw none while traversing the lower half of its course. Half a dozen specimens of a large, worthless shrub, known as buffalo bush or bullberry, with a prevalent fringe of willows about the proper size for a schoolma'am's use, comprise the entire timber of this delectable stream, whose gadflies, mosquitoes, gnats, etc., are so countless and so bloodthirsty as to allow cattle so unhappy as to be stationed on, or driven along this river, no chance to eat or sleep. Many have died this season of the bad water, that would have survived the water, but for these execrable insects, by which the atmosphere, at times, is darkened. It certainly is not a pleasure to ride, night and day, along such a stream, with the heat intense, the dust a constant cloud, and the roads all gullied, and ground into chuckholes; but then, who would stay in such a region one moment longer than he must?

I thought I had seen barrenness before—on the upper course of the Republican, on the North Platte, Green River, etc.—but I was green, if the regions washed by those streams were not. Here, on the Humboldt, famine sits enthroned, and waves his scepter over a dominion expressly made for him. On the above-named rivers, I regarded cottonwood with contempt; here, a belt, even the narrowest fringe, of cottonwood would make a comparative Eden. The sagebrush and greasewood, which cover the high, parched plain on either side of the river's bottom, seem thinly set, with broad spaces of naked, shining, glaring, blinding clay between them; the hills beyond, which bound the prospect, seem even more naked. Not a tree, and hardly a shrub, anywhere relieves their sterility; not a brook, save one small one, runs down between them to swell the scanty waters of the river. As the only considerable stream in the Great Basin that pursues a general east and west direction, the Humboldt may continue for years to be traveled; but I am sure no one ever left it without a sense of relief and thankfulness. There can never be any considerable settlement here.

After a course, at first west by south, then north by west, afterward southwest, and for the last fifty miles due south, the river falls into Lake Humboldt, a fine sheet of clear water, perhaps fifteen miles in length and forty in circumference. I tried to obtain an approximation to its depth, but could not, those who have stayed beside it longest assuring me that no boat had ever floated upon its waters—a statement which the destitution of wood in all this region renders credible. I am satisfied, however, that this lake is being slowly filled up from the gradual washing down, and washing in, of the hills which approach it on the east and south, and that time will make great changes in its configuration and the volume of its waters.

A stream, not so copious as the river, runs from the lake

on the south, and flows with a gentle, sluggish current into a large tule or reed marsh, which has no outlet, and is said to be but moderately salt. The lake water is accounted sweeter than that of the river. Here the Humboldt is said to *sink*, like the Carson, Truckee and Walker, which issue from the Sierra Nevada, and run eastwardly into the adjacent desert; but I suspect they are all drunk up by evaporation and by the thirsty sands which surround them. The Mississippi, if it ran across the Great Basin and kept clear of mountains, would be threatened by a similar fate.

We reached the Sink at 6:30 P.M. on Thursday, the 29th —scarcely two days from Gravelly Ford, where we struck the river, having in those two days traversed some two hundred and twenty miles of very bad and intensely hot, dusty road. At eight, we were ready to pass the desert—that is, the desolate plain which separates the Sink of the Humboldt from that of the Carson. But one of our fresh mules was sick and could not be replaced, which made our first drive a tedious one, and we contrived, by dexterous mismanagement, to get stuck in a bayou or backset of the Humboldt Sink, where we for a while seemed likely to spend the night. Our lead mules, having been mired and thrown down, would not pull; the sick wheeler could not. At length, by putting one of the leaders in his place, we made a start, and came through, finding the bottom firm and the water not deep, a yard either way from the place of our misadventure. By a little past midnight, we were at the halfway station, where a well of decent brackish water has been dug, and which a drove of four or five hundred mules reached about the time we did. They stopped here to rest, however, while we pushed on with a fresh team—for ten miles of the way, over as heavy a drag of sand as I ever endured, whereas most of this desert is a hard, alkaline clay. By 5 A.M., after riding four days and the intervening nights without rest, we drew up at the station near the sink of the Carson.

25

CARSON VALLEY—THE SIERRA NEVADA

Placerville, Cal., Aug. 1, 1859

Though the Carson sinks in or is absorbed by the same desert with the Humboldt, a glance at its worst estate suffices to convince the traveler that the former waters by far the more hopeful region. Large cottonwoods dot its banks very near its sink; and its valley, wherever moist, is easily rendered productive. You feel that you are once more in a land where the arm of industry need not be paralyzed by sterility, obstruction, and despair.

Still, the prevalence of drought is here a fearful fact. No rain in summer—that is, none that can be calculated on, none that amounts to anything—might well appall the cultivator accustomed to warm, refreshing showers throughout the growing season. We crossed, on our rapid ride up the Carson, a single high plain twenty-six miles long and from six to twelve wide, which drought alone dooms to sagebrush, sterility, and worthlessness. Two or three other plains or high intervales further up are nearly as scorched and barren. All these may be rendered most productive by irrigation, and here is the water at hand. If the new gold mines in this valley shall ultimately justify their present promise, a very large demand for vegetable food will speedily spring up here, which can only be satisfied by domestic production. The vast deserts eastward cannot meet it, the arable region about Salt Lake is at once too restricted and too distant; inland California is a dear country, and the transportation of bulky staples over the Sierra a costly operation. The time will ultimately come —it may or may not be in our day—when two or three great dams over the Carson will render the irrigation of these broad, arid plains on its banks perfectly feasible; and then this will be one of the most productive regions on earth.[1] The vegetable food of one million people can easily be grown here, while their cattle may be reared and fed in the mountain vales north and south of this valley. And when the best works shall have been constructed, and all the lights of science and experience brought to bear on the subject, it will be found that nearly everything that contributes to human or brute sustenance can be grown actually cheaper by the aid of irrigation than without it. As yet, we know little or nothing of the application of water to land and crops, and our ignorance causes deplorable waste and blundering. Every year henceforth will make us wiser on this head.

Twenty miles or so below Genoa, we passed Johntown, a Chinese settlement, whose people find employment in the recently discovered gold mines. These mines are some eight miles northward of Gold Canyon, and are reported immensely rich. Silver and copper are blended with gold in the same vein stone. A few are making money very fast here; but these few control all the available water, and it seems impossible to introduce more. If a supply can be obtained at all, it must be at enormous cost. I have vaguely heard of a patented process or processes for separating gold from other minerals or earths without the use of water; if there be any such process which is not a humbug, I urge the owner of the patent to haste to Carson Valley and there make his fortune. I assure him of an enthusiastic welcome.

Carson City, just above Johntown, though it has few houses as yet, aspires to be the emporium of the new gold region, and perhaps of the embryo state of Nevada; but Genoa, ten or fifteen miles further up, is the present emporium, though a village of but forty or fifty houses. Here a convention had been in session for a fortnight, and had com-

---

[1] This was another prophetic observation. Irrigation has played a major role in the economic development of this region.

pleted a constitution for the aforesaid embryo state of Nevada only the night before our arrival. We met some of the delegates bound homeward. Said state is to comprise the western half (very nearly) of Utah, with (I believe) a small strip of eastern California. California may object to this; but I trust Congress will organize at least the territory of Nevada at an early day. It is an established fact that a division of power between Mormons and Gentiles seldom works harmoniously; but in Utah there is no division—the Mormons have all. The people of Carson Valley, and of western Utah generally, are not Mormons; the legislation of Utah is unsuited and unacceptable to them; they desire to be set off, and I trust they soon may be. Though few in numbers as yet, they are rapidly increasing, and will soon possess all the elements of a state.

I had previously seen some beautiful valleys, but I place none of these ahead of Carson. I judge that portion of it already in good part under cultivation, about thirty miles long by ten to fifteen wide—an area destined to be largely increased, as I have already indicated. This valley, originally a grand meadow, the home of the deer and the antelope, is nearly inclosed by high mountains, down which, especially from the north and west, come innumerable rivulets, leaping and dancing on their way to form or join the Carson. Easily arrested and controlled, because of the extreme shallowness of their beds, these streams have been made to irrigate a large portion of the upper valley, producing an abundance of the sweetest grass, and insuring bounteous harvests also of vegetables, barley, oats, etc. Wheat seems to do fairly here; corn not so well; in fact, the nights are too cold for it, if the water were not. For this spring water, leaping suddenly down from its mountain sources, is too cold, too pure, to be well adapted to irrigation; could it be held back even a week, and exposed in shallow ponds or basins to the hot sunshine, it would be vastly more useful. When the whole river shall

235

have been made available, twenty to forty miles below, it will prove far more nutritious and fertilizing.

Genoa stands on the narrow bench or slope of hard granitic gravel, which intervenes betwixt the mountains and the valley, with half a dozen rivulets running through it, to fructify the fields and gardens below. Just behind it is the steep ascent of the mountain, its very soil formed of white, pulverized granite, gloriously covered with fragrant and graceful pines. As these steep aclivities are absolutely worthless for any other end than tree growing, I entreat the people of Genoa to take care of these woods, and not let their place be shorn of half its beauty, merely to save a mile or so in the hauling of fuel. I may never see this lovely valley again—it is hardly probable that I ever shall—but its beauty, its seclusion, its quiet, the brightness of its abundant rivulets, the grandeur of its inclosing mountains, the grace and emerald verdure of their vesture of pines, have graven themselves on my memory with a vividness and force which only he who has passed weary weeks on some great, shadeless, verdureless desert can fully realize.

We stopped but to dine in Genoa, then economized the residue of the daylight by pressing on fifteen miles to the point at which the California road enters the mountains by the side of the largest of the brooks which unite to form the Carson. Here we halted at a fair two-story house, the first one I had entered with the hope of resting in it since I left Salt Lake City. We had beds here—actual beds, and good ones—our first since Camp Floyd. Though our night was not a long one, for we were to start again by 4 A.M., I reckon good use was made of it by the four through passengers who had not lain down before since they left Shell Creek, five days ago, and nearly five hundred miles away. My own slumber was partial and broken, as it generally is; but the bath which preceded and prepared for it was a genuine refreshment, and

236

the sleep seemed quite sufficient. In fact, I felt that I could have gone without for another week, and experienced less discomfort than I did the first night that we rode, and the day after.

We were in motion again at the earliest dawn, for we had still about seventy-five miles of rugged mountain road to traverse before reaching this place. The Carson side of the road is not yet half made, while the half next to this place is in the main good. But in fact, the expense of a good highway up the eastern slope of the Sierra must be a heavy one. For that slope is here composed of granite—simple, naked rock—with scarcely a fraction of its surface thinly covered by soil. Of course, no trees but evergreens can live—a very few small quaking asps in the bottoms of the ravines scarcely form an exception—while almost every rood is covered by giant, glorious pines. I saw sugar and yellow pines at least eight feet in diameter and tall in proportion; I am assured that one was recently cut near this road which measured eight feet across at a height of eighty feet from the ground, and from which two hundred and forty thousand shingles were made. Besides these universal pines, there are giant cedars, balsam firs, and some redwood; after we crossed the summit, we found also oaks, which gradually increased in size and number as we descended. I think I saw oaks (the prevalent California species is much like our white oak) at least four feet through—in short, I never saw anything like so much nor so good timber in the course of any seventy-five miles' travel as I saw in crossing the Sierra Nevada. How greatly blest California is in this abundance, I need not say.

The road over this pass[2]—here claimed to be the lowest and most practicable of any over the Sierra Nevada—rises steadily for twelve or thirteen miles from our morning's starting point, then descends for two or three miles as

[2] Carson Pass, elevation 8,634 feet.

abruptly to the valley of a brook which runs north into Lake Bigler,[3] which in turn finds an outlet into Truckee River, whereby its waters are borne eastward into the desert and there dissipated. There is fine grass on Lake Bigler, and several hundred cows are kept there in summer, making butter for the California market. When snow falls, these cattle are driven down to the valley of the Sacramento, where the rains are now commencing, and they here live without hay till June, when they are taken back to the mountains again, where only is butter made from them. The business is very lucrative, the land costing nothing and being unfenced. Taking into account gold, timber, and grass, the Sierra Nevada is probably the richest and most productive mountain chain on earth.

From the valley aforesaid, we rose again for two miles, along a narrow road cut into the side of a mountain, with a precipitous declivity on the right. Then we began to descend once more, beside a rivulet which leaped and laughed on its way to the Pacific. The ascent from the Carson side is far shorter than the descent this way, Carson Valley being much higher than that of the Sacramento. But the road, even on this side, is, for most of the way, eaten into the side of a steep mountain, with a precipice of from five to fifteen hundred feet on one side and as steep an eminence on the other. Yet along this mere shelf, with hardly a place to each mile where two meeting wagons can pass, the mail stage was driven at the rate of ten miles an hour (in one instance eleven), or just as fast as four wild California horses, whom two men could scarcely harness, could draw it. Our driver was of course skillful; but had he met a wagon suddenly on rounding one of the sharp points or projections we were constantly passing, a fearful crash was unavoidable. Had his horses seen fit to run away (as they *did* run once, on the

[3] Lake Tahoe.

238

unhooking of a trace, but at a place where he had room to rein them out of the road on the upper side, and thus stop them), I know that he could not have held them, and we might have been pitched headlong down a precipice of a thousand feet, where all of the concern that could have been picked up afterward would not have been worth two bits per bushel. Yet at this breakneck rate we were driven for not less than four hours or forty miles, changing horses every ten or fifteen, and raising a cloud of dust through which it was difficult at times to see anything.[4] We crossed the south fork of the American River, eighteen miles above this point, rising two or three miles immediately after to the summit of the ridge south, and thenceforward the road, nearly to this city, descends steadily a beautifully inclined ridge, and, but for the dust, would be one of the finest drives on earth. And right glad was I to find myself once more among friends, surrounded by the comforts of civilization, and with a prospect of occasional rest. I cannot conscientiously recommend the route I have traveled to summer tourists in quest of pleasure, but it is a balm for many bruises to know that I am at last in CALIFORNIA.

[4] This first experience with California drivers was mild compared to the celebrated ride Greeley was soon to have in the coach driven by Hank Monk, from Folsom to Placerville. Made famous by Artemus Ward, the story is told in full in Don Seitz's biography of Greeley.

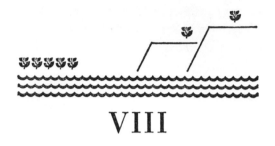

VIII

CALIFORNIA

Dispatches 26 through 32

Everything in California interested Greeley, but it was its agriculture—present and potential—that most excited him. He correctly predicted the state's great future in fruit, wine, and cattle. California had five needs, as Greeley saw it: more women, good farmers, land-title reform, more schools, and a transcontinental railroad.

For the return trip to New York Greeley had planned to take the Butterfield Overland Mail, the southern route, through Arizona and Texas. The record of the American West was to be denied Horace Greeley's account of that journey because of an affliction that even Horace Greeley's mule-tough constitution could not ignore—a bad case of boils. Injury, illness, thirst, all manner of discomfort and numbing fatigue, none of these had stopped him or even

240

delayed him long. But now he was forced to yield. "These pestilent boils!" he wrote in his last hour in San Francisco. "I have no choice but to return by way of the Isthmus, for I can wait no longer."

He was to write another dispatch at sea, and later in New York a capstone piece, a ringing call for early action on the transcontinental railroad, but Horace Greeley's overland journey was ended when the Golden Age *nosed out through the Golden Gate on September 5, 1859—four months lacking four days from the time he boarded the Erie train in New York—and steamed toward Panama. He arrived in New York on September 28, and, as the epilogue evinces, Reporter Greeley was soon once more Editor Greeley.*

26

CALIFORNIA MINES AND MINING

Sacramento, Aug. 7, 1859

I have spent the last week mainly among the mines and miners of El Dorado, Placer, and Nevada counties, in the heart of the gold-producing region. There may be richer diggings north or south; but I believe no other three counties lying together have yielded in the aggregate, or are now producing, so much gold as those I have named. Of course, I have not been within sight of more than a fraction of the mines or *placers* of these counties, while I have not carefully studied even one of them; and yet the little information I have been able to glean, in the intervals of traveling, friendly greeting, and occasional speech-making, may have some value for those whose ignorance on the subject is yet more dense than mine.

The three counties I have named lie near the center of the

state, at the base of the Sierra Nevada, between those mountains on the east and the valley of the Sacramento on the west. They are rugged in formation, being composed of innumerable hills (mainly spurs of the great chain), separated by narrow valleys, usually descending to the west, and gradually opening out into the broad, rich valley of the Sacramento. The three branches or forks of the American and those of the Yuba River come brawling down from the Sierra Nevada through very deep, narrow valleys or canyons, and unite respectively to run a very short course less rapidly ere they are lost in the Sacramento—the Yuba having previously formed a junction with the Feather. Bear River, Wolf Creek, Deer Creek, etc., are the names of still smaller streams, taking their rise among the foothills, and running a short course into some fork of the American or Yuba, their scanty waters, with a good portion of those of the rivers aforesaid, being mainly drawn off into canals or "ditches," as they are inaccurately termed, by which the needful fluid is supplied to the miners.

THE CANALS

These canals are a striking characteristic of the entire mining region. As you traverse a wild and broken district, perhaps miles from any human habitation or sign of present husbandry, they intersect your dusty, indifferent road, or are carried in flumes supported by a framework of timber twenty to sixty feet over your head. Some of these flumes or open aqueducts are carried across valleys each a mile or more in width; I have seen two of them thus crossing side by side. The canals range from ten to sixty or eighty miles in length, and are filled by damming the streams wherefrom they are severally fed, and taking out their water in a wide trench, which runs along the side of one bank, gradually gaining comparative altitude as the stream by its side falls lower and lower in its canyon, until it is at length on the crest of the headland or mountain promontory which projects into the plain, and may be conducted down either side of it in any direction deemed desirable. Several of these canals have cost nearly or quite half a million dollars each, having been enlarged and improved from year to year, as circumstances dictated and means could be obtained. One of them, originally constructed in defiance of sanguine prophecies of failure, returned to its owners the entire cost of its construction within three months from the date of its completion. Then it was found necessary to enlarge and every way improve it, and every dollar of its net earnings for the next four years was devoted to its perfection. In some instances, the projectors exhausted their own means and then resorted to borrowing on mortgage at California rates of interest; I learn without surprise that nearly or quite every such experiment resulted in absolute bankruptcy and a change of owners. Of late, the solvent and prosperous companies have turned their attention to damming the outlets of the little lakes which fill the hollows of the Sierra, in order to hold back the superabundant waters of the spring months for use in summer and autumn. This course is doubly beneficient, in that it diminishes the danger from floods to which this city is specially subject, but which is also serious in all the valleys or canyons of the mining region wherein there is anything that water can injure. I judge that the cost and present cash value of these mining canals throughout California must be many millions of dollars, paying in the average a fair income, while their supply of water is at this season, and from July to November, utterly inadequate. Water is sold by them by the cubic inch—a stream four inches deep and six wide, for instance, being twenty-four inches, for which, at fifty cents per inch, twelve dollars per day must be paid by the taker. A head of six inches—that is, six inches' depth of water in the flume above the top of the aperture through which the water escapes into the miners' private ditch or flume—is usually allowed. The price per day ranges from twenty cents to a dollar per inch, though I think it now seldom reaches the higher figure, which was once common. Were the supply twice as copious as it is, I presume it would all be required; if the price were somewhat lowered by the increase, I am sure it would be. Many works are now standing idle solely for want of water.

THE MINES

Go where you will, in the mining region, you are seldom a mile distant from past or present diggings. Speaking generally, every ravine, gully, or watercourse has been prospected; each has, at some point, been dug open to the bedrock, and the overlaying earth or gravel run through a "rocker," "tom," or "sluice," in the hope of making it yield the shining dust. Many of these watercourses have been deeply and widely dug up for miles in extent. If any are left entirely undisturbed, the presumption is strong that the subjacent rock is so near the surface that gold has had no chance to deposit itself thereon. In some instances, basins or depressions in the rock have been gradually filled up with earth—probably auriferous—through thousands of years, and the gold which might otherwise have been strewn down the valley for miles is here collected, so that it would be sheer waste to mine throughout those miles. But the more general opinion seems to be that gold is diffused throughout the soil of the entire mining region, especially upon, and just above the surface of, the bedrock, though only in certain localities is it sufficiently abundant to justify efforts to extract it. I find no one seeming to cherish any apprehensions that California will cease to produce gold abundantly, at least within the next quarter of a century. On the contrary, the current belief seems to be that the influx of population will in time so reduce the wages of labor, or the progress of invention and discovery so increase its efficiency, that extensive districts will ultimately be mined with profit, which are now necessarily avoided. If the amount of available water were doubled, with a considerable reduction of price, the gold product of California would thereupon be increased several millions per annum. At present, mining enterprises of considerable promise and indefinite magnitude remain in abeyance, simply because the price of labor, the rate of interest, and other elements of the cost of mining, are deemed too high to justify their prosecution.

MODES OF MINING

In the course of a week's travel through a portion of the mining district, I did not see a single miner engaged with pick and pan in prospecting. Higher up in the mountains, or further to the north, I might have found such. Nor do I remember having seen white men, save, perhaps, in a single instance, engaged in digging and washing the gravel or earth in the bed of any watercourse, whether river, creek, or dry gulch. But Chinese bands, of six to twelve, were often hard at work in these watercourses—Bear River, the south fork of the Yuba, etc.—digging, and washing with rocker, sluice, and a sort of wheel-and-flume arrangement, which I did not get the hang of.

The Chinese are hardly[1] used here. In the first place, they are taxed four dollars each per month for the naked privilege of mining at all. Next, they are not allowed to mine anywhere but in diggings which white men have worked out and abandoned, or which no white man considers worth working.

[1] Meaning ill-used, not scarcely used. Greeley was no more sentimental about the Chinese than he was about the Indians but in both cases he saw them as human beings, a viewpoint shared by few in the West in those days.

245

Thirdly, if these rejected diggings happen, in Chinese hands, to prove better than their reputation, and to begin yielding liberally, a mob of white sovereigns soon drive the Chinese out of them, neck and heels. "John" does not seem to be a very bad fellow, but he is treated worse than though he were. He is not malignant nor sanguinary, and seldom harms any but his own tribe. But he is thoroughly sensual, and intent on the fullest gratification of his carnal appetites, and on nothing else. He eats and drinks the best he can get, and as much as he can hold; but he is never so devoid of self-respect as to be seen drunk in a public place; even for an opium debauch, he secludes himself where none but a friendly eye can reach him. His "particular wanity" in the eating line is rice, whereof he will have the best only, if the best is to be had; he likes a fat chicken also, and will pay his last dollar for one, rather than go without. Lacking the dollar, it is charged that he will rob hen roosts; at all events, hen roosts are sometimes robbed, and "John" has to bear the blame. He is popularly held to spend nothing, but carry all his gains out of the country and home to his native land —a charge disproved by the fact that he is an inveterate gambler, an opium smoker, a habitual rum drinker, and a devotee of every sensual vice. But he is weak in body, and not allowed to vote, so it is safe to trample on him; he does not write English, and so cannot tell the story of his wrongs; he has no family here (the few Chinese women brought to this country being utterly shameless and abandoned), so that he forms no domestic ties, and enjoys no social standing. Even the wretched Indians of California repel with scorn the suggestion that there is any kinship between their race and the Chinese. "John" has traits which I can neither praise nor justify; yet I suspect that, if other men's faults were punished as severely as his, a good many Californians would be less comfortable than they are.

As to quartz-mining—or the reduction to powder of the vein stone wherein gold is contained, and the extraction of the gold from the powder, by means of water, quicksilver, etc. —I judge that the time has not even yet arrived for its profitable prosecution. There are conspicuous instances of its success, that of the concern known as Allison's Ranche, in Grass Valley, for example—but I am confident that fully three out of every four quartz-mining enterprises have proved failures, or have at best achieved no positive success. The current estimates of the yield of gold by quartz rock are grossly exaggerated. I judge that the average yield of gold by quartz vein stone is less than twenty dollars per ton— barely one cent per pound—and that this yield will not pay the average cost of sinking shafts, running drifts or adits, pumping out water, raising ore (and an immense aggregate of dead rock with it), crushing it and extracting the gold, in a country where common labor costs two and a half to three dollars per day. At forty dollars per ton of vein stone, quartz mining might pay, but where one vein yields forty dollars per ton, there are many which yield less than twenty dollars. There are some instances of profitable quartz-mining by men on the spot who thoroughly understand the business; but I have not heard of an instance in which money has been invested in quartz-mining, by persons out of California, who have not lost every farthing of it.

I think the most popular form of mining at present is that of sinking or drifting into hills which have a stratum of gravel at or near their base, directly overlying the bedrock. Many of these hills would seem to have been piled, in some far-off, antediluvian period, upon a bed or basin of solid granite, which often hollows or dips toward its center like a saucer. If, then, a tunnel can be run in through the "rim rock" or side of this saucer so happily as to strike the level of the bottom, thereby draining off the water, and affording

247

the utmost facility for extracting the gold-bearing gravel, the fortune of the operator may be made by one lucky, or better than lucky, operation. In a few instances, these subterranean gravel basins would seem to have formed parts of the beds of ancient rivers, and so to be extraordinarily rich in the precious dust. In some cases, the "pay dirt" is hauled by steam up an inclined plane, or even raised perpendicularly by windlass; but it is easier to extract it by a horizontal drift or tunnel, wherever possible. Many mines of this order are worked night and day on the "three-shift" plan, and are paying very handsomely.

But the newest, most efficient, most uniformly profitable mode of operation is that termed *hydraulic mining*—that is, the washing down and washing away of large deposits of auriferous earth by means of a current of water so directed as to fall on the right spot, or (better still) projected through a hose and pipe with the force generated by a heavy fall. The former of these methods is exhibited in perfection at Nevada, the latter at North San Juan, as, doubtless, at many other places. At North San Juan, near the middle fork of the Yuba, streams at least three inches in diameter, and probably containing twenty measured inches of water, are directed against the remaining half of a high hill, which they strike with such force that boulders of the size of cannon-balls are started from their beds and hurled five to ten feet into the air. By this process, one man will wash away a bank of earth sooner than a hundred men could do it by old-fashioned sluicing. I believe earth yielding a bare cent's worth of gold to the pan may be profitably washed by this process, paying a reasonable price for the water. As much as one hundred dollars per day is profitably paid for the water thrown through one pipe. The stream thus thrown will knock a man as lifeless as though it were a grapeshot. As the bank, over a hundred feet high, is undermined by this battery, it frequently caves from the top downward, reaching and burying the careless operator. Three men have been thus killed at San Juan within the last month, until at length greater caution is exercised, and the operator stands twice as far away as he formerly did. Very long sluices—as long as may be—conduct the discharged water away; and I am told that it is no matter how thick with earth the water may run, provided the sluice be long enough. It is of course so arranged as to present riffles, crevices, etc., to arrest the gold at first borne along by the turbid flood. I believe there are companies operating by this method whose gross receipts from a single sluice have reached a thousand dollars per day.

One of the novelties (to me) of this region is the presence of soft granite—putty granite, if I may coin a name for it. Unlike most soft rocks, this seems not to harden by exposure to the atmosphere. It is found at various depths, and I know no way of accounting for it. It seems to me that one-fourth of the granite I saw at the base of recent excavations appeared soft as cheese. Is not this peculiar to California?

Mining is a necessary art, but it does not tend to beautify the face of nature. On the contrary, earth distorted into all manner of ungainly heaps and ridges, hills half torn or washed away, and the residue left in as repulsive shape as can well be conceived, roads intersected and often turned to mire by ditches, watercourses torn up and gouged out, and rivers, once pure as crystal, now dense and opaque with pulverized rock—such is the spectacle presented throughout the mining region. Not a stream of any size is allowed to escape the pollution—even the bountiful and naturally pure Sacramento is yellow with it, and flows turbid and uninviting to the Pacific. (The people of this city have to drink it, nevertheless.) Despite the intense heat and drought always prevalent at this season, the country is full of springs, which are bright and clear as need be; but wherever three or four of these

249

have joined to form a little rill, some gold-seeker is sharp on their track, converting them into liquid mud. California, in giving up her hoarded wealth, surrenders much of her beauty also.

Worse still is the general devastation of timber.[2] The whole mining region appears to have been excellently timbered—so much of it as I have traversed was eminently so. Yellow, pitch, and sugar (white) pine (and what is here called pitch pine is a large, tall, and graceful tree), white, black, and live oak, with stately cedars, once overspread the whole country, not densely, as in eastern forests, but with reasonable spaces between the noble trunks—the oaks often presenting the general appearance of a thrifty apple orchard, undergrown with grass and bushes. But timber is wanted for flumes, for sluices, for drifts or tunnels, for dwellings, for running steam engines, etc., and, as most of the land has no owner, everybody cuts and slashes as if he cared for nobody but himself, and no time but today. Patriarchal oaks are cut down merely to convert their limbs into fuel, leaving the trunks to rot; noble pines are pitched this way and that, merely to take a log or two from the butt for sawing or splitting, leaving the residue a cumberer of the ground; trees fit for the noblest uses are made to subserve the paltriest, merely because they are handy, and it is nobody's business to preserve them. There was timber enough here ten years ago to satisfy every legitimate need for a century; yet ten years more will not elapse before the miners will be sending far up into the mountains at a heavy cost for logs that might still have been abundant at their doors, had the timber of this region been husbanded as it ought. Remonstrance were idle, but I must be permitted to deplore.

[2] Wanton destruction of timber was painful to Greeley. His love of trees is revealed again and again throughout the journal. He was a true conservationist, years ahead of his time.

27

CALIFORNIA—THE YOSEMITE

Bear Valley, Cal., Aug. 14, 1859

I left Sacramento on Monday morning last, traveling by stage to Stockton, forty-eight miles nearly due south, crossing the Mokelumne, and keeping first the Sacramento and then the San Joaquin a few miles on our right, and Mount Diablo conspicuous still further west. We traversed a level, fertile plain, sparsely wooded near the rivers—a plain which should be, but is not yet, densely peopled, and very productive. There are some fine orchard gardens near the cities, and might well be many; but a good part of the intermediate country is uninclosed, and the residue mainly devoted to large ranches (or loose and slovenly cattle husbandry), and in less degree to the growing of small grain—wheat and barley. The stubble indicates good crops, but there is not a sufficient area devoted to them. Uncertainty of land titles—that paramount curse of California—is assigned as the cause of this inadequacy of cultivation, which I trust is not to continue.

Stockton is situated on a bayou of the San Joaquin, at the head of regular steamboat navigation on that river, which makes it the third or fourth city of California, with fifteen thousand inhabitants, and an extensive carrying trade. The better dwellings are in good part surrounded by fine gardens, well filled with delicious fruit. In some of them, the primitive, wide-spreading oaks have been preserved, giving them an aspect of beauty and coolness most grateful to the traveler recently arrived from the plains. Stockton has the State Insane Asylum, and a very interesting commencement of a cabinet of natural history; better still, she has an artesian well one thousand feet deep, bored at a cost of ten thousand dollars, and pouring forth a copious and unfailing stream, some feet above the surface of the earth. Deep as it is, it penetrates only successive strata of what appears to be alluvial deposit, never touching bedrock. Artesian wells are becoming common in California, and I trust are yet to play an important part in the development and extension not only of her agricultural but also of her mining industry, now crippled (especially in the south) by the general dearth of water. I have a suspicion that all the water hitherto obtained by canals or ditches, so expensively constructed, could have been procured far cheaper by digging artesian wells, which, however multiplied, could hardly fail, at the foot of the Sierra Nevada, to strike copious fountains at no unreasonable depth.

I left Stockton next morning in a carriage with a friend who proposed to go through to Bear Valley (seventy-five miles) before sleeping—a feat which I doubted the ability of any span of livery horses to accomplish. My doubt was misplaced. Good horses, an early start, careful, considerate driving, frequent watering, and the dry, bracing air of California, carried us through by a little after 10 P.M., and our team would readily have gone ten miles further had we required it. I judge that sixty miles of just such roads would have been as hard a drive in any state east of the Rocky Mountains.

Our general course this day was east by south, passing mainly over moderately undulating prairie of very unequal but generally indifferent fertility, and crossing successively, at intervals of about twenty miles, the small rivers Stanislaus, Tuolumne, and Merced, all flowing from the mountains westward into the San Joaquin, and all rendered turbid by the mining operations in progress on their banks or in their beds. The Stanislaus runs through a belt of rather light and thin oak, some two or three miles wide; the others have a few scattering oaks and that is all. There is considerable husbandry—mainly of the ranching order, near Stockton and along the rivers aforesaid, but very little industry of any kind on the naked prairies between them, and not a drop of running water, except, perhaps, a spring or two under some of the low hills which have a tolerably steep side respectively. There are a very few deep holes in some of the winter watercourses at which cattle still find drink, though of a bad quality. One settler from Massachusetts, who lives mainly by cattle-growing, informed us that he came around Cape Horn eight or ten years since, has now about ninety head of cattle, which are fast increasing, and intends to erect a windmill this winter, by whose aid he will be able to have a good garden at once, and a fine fruit orchard within a few years. (Windmills located over wells or other reservoirs of water, which they raise for use in irrigation, are very common in Stockton, and are rapidly going up throughout middle California.) He has to go seven miles for his fuel, fencing stuff, etc., on the Stanislaus. His nearest neighbors, on the road we traveled, are some five to ten miles distant, but I believe he has nearer. He is doubtless richer here than in Massachusetts, but I cannot realize that his family are happier or more favorably situated for mental and moral improvement, there being no school within reach, and the children depending for instruction on their New England mother alone. But *their* children will not have New England mothers—and what then? I fear this cattle-ranching, with long intervals between the ranches, is destined to half-barbarize many thousands of the next generation, whom schools can scarcely reach, and to whom "the sound of the church-going bell" will be a stranger. Most of the agriculturists of this region, however, came here from Missouri, Arkansas, or Texas—many of them from Missouri or Arkansas by way of Texas—and do not seem to regard common schools as essential to civilized life.

We crossed the Merced sixty miles from Stockton (all these rivers are crossed by toll bridges, or ferries—charges, one dollar each per wagon) just before sunset; and now our road became rugged and bad, as we rose the first of the foothills of the Sierra. Thus far we had feen few traces of mining, save the muddy-colored waters of the rivers; but seven miles further brought us to Quartzburg, in the center of a nearly washed-out valley of gold-bearing gravel; and thence our way led seven miles further, over a far higher foothill, into Bear Valley, where we found friends and grateful rest. The next day I devoted to an examination of Colonel Frémont's mines and works, of which I may speak hereafter, but must now hurry on to the Yosemite.

I left Bear Valley, two hours later than was fit, at 6 A.M., on Thursday, resolved to push through to my immediate destination that night. My friend[1] had preceded me betimes to Mariposa, twelve miles on our way, to complete preparations for the trip; but we were unluckily delayed here again by misapprehensions and the pre-engagement of animals for attendance on a camp meeting, so that it was high noon when we reached the end of the wagon road, twelve miles below Mariposa, where the saddle is the only resource, while it is still nearly forty miles (many of them steep ones) to the Yosemite Fall. Everyone assured us that to get through that day was impossible; yet I had no more time to give to the journey, and must try. My friend is a good rider, while I can barely ride at all, not having spent five hours on horseback, save in my visit to the Kansas gold mines, within the last thirty years. But the two gentlemen from Mariposa who accompanied and guided us knew all about the journey that we didn't—which is saying a great deal—so we pressed bouyantly, confidently on.

Hussey's steam sawmill, where we mounted (or rather

[1] Later identified as a man from San Francisco but never named.

I did, for the rest had done so before), marks pretty fairly the division between the oaks of the lower and the firs of the higher elevations, though the two of course melt into each other. As we rose gradually but steadily, the white soon faded out, then the black, and last the live oak, though the genuineness of this last is disputed, while the yellow, pitch, and sugar pines, cedars, and balsam firs became more numerous and stately, till they at length had the ground almost wholly to themselves, save that the manzanito and other shrubs (mostly evergreens also) clustered on nearly every opening among the trees. There is little or no precipice or bare rock for miles, and we rose along the southern face of the ridge overlooking the Chowchilla Valley, until we seemed to have half California spread out before us like a map. Our range of vision extended south to the tule lake, or immense morass, in which the San Joaquin has its source, and west to the Coast Range, which alone barred the Pacific Ocean from our view. Still rising, we wound gradually around the peak of our first mountain through a slight depression or pass, and soon looked off upon the valley of the South Fork of the Merced, which opened for miles north and east of us. On this side, the descent is far steeper, and we traversed for miles a mere trace along the side of the mountain, where a misstep must have landed us at least a thousand feet below. In time, this too was left behind, and we descended fitfully and tortuously the east end of the mountain to the South Fork, whereon, sixteen miles from Hussey's and but five from the Big Trees of Mariposa, we halted for rest and food. Before six, we were again in the saddle, crossing the fork and winding up over another mountain northward, with a precipitous descent of at least two thousand feet beside us for a mile or so. A steep ascent of half a mile carried us over the divide, whence we descended very rapidly to Alder Creek, at the northern base. Following up this creek over a succession of steep pitches, interleaved with more level patches, we bade adieu to daylight at Grizzly Flat, a spot noted for encounters with the monarch of our American forests, and thence crossed a ridge to Summit Meadows, a succession of mainly narrow grassy levels, which wind in and out among the promontories of more or less shattered granite which make down from the mountain peaks on either side, but pursue a generally eastward direction to pour their tiny tribute into the Great Chasm. Our route led us six or eight times across these meadows—which were often so boggy as to require a very nice choice of footing—and, intermediately, across the generally wooded promontories which deflected the probably continuous meadow into what seemed to us many, until we stood at length, about 10 P.M., on the brink of the awful abyss, and halted a moment to tighten girths and take breath for the descent.

And here let me renew my tribute to the marvelous bounty and beauty of the forests of this whole mountain region. The Sierra Nevadas lack the glorious glaciers, the frequent rains, the rich verdure, the abundant cataracts of the Alps; but they far surpass them—they surpass any other mountains I ever saw—in the wealth and grace of their trees. Look down from almost any of their peaks, and your range of vision is filled, bounded, satisfied, by what might be termed a tempest-tossed sea of evergreens, filling every upland valley, covering every hillside, crowning every peak but the highest, with their unfading luxuriance. That I saw during this day's travel many hundreds of pines eight feet in diameter, with cedars at least six feet, I am confident; and there were miles after miles of such and smaller trees of like genus standing as thick as they could grow. Steep mountainsides, allowing them to grow, rank above rank, without obstructing each other's sunshine, seem peculiarly favorable to the production of these serviceable giants. But the Summit Meadows are peculiar in their heavy fringe of balsam fir of all sizes, from those barely one foot high to those hardly less than two hundred, their branches surrounding them in collars, their extremities gracefully bent down by the weight of winter snows, making them here, I am confident, the most beautiful trees on earth. The dry promontories which separate these meadows are also covered with a species of spruce, which is only less graceful than the fir aforesaid. I never before enjoyed such a tree-feast as on this wearing, difficult ride.

Descent into the Yosemite is only practicable at three points—one near the head of the valley, where a small stream makes in from the direction of the main ridge of the Sierra, down which there is a trail from the vicinity of Water River, Utah—a trail practicable, I believe, for men on foot only. The other two lead in near the outlet, from Mariposa and Coulterville respectively, on opposite banks of the Merced, and are practicable for sure-footed mules or horses. We, of course, made our descent by the Mariposa trail, on the south side of the little river which here escapes from the famous valley by a canyon which water alone can safely, if at all, traverse, being shut in by lofty precipices, and broken by successive falls.

My friends insisted that I should look over the brink into the profound abyss before clambering down its side; but I, apprehending giddiness, and feeling the need of steady nerves, firmly declined. So we formed line again, and moved on.

The night was clear and bright, as all summer nights in this region are; the atmosphere cool, but not really cold; the moon had risen before seven o'clock, and was shedding so much light as to bother us in our forest path, where the shadow of a standing pine looked exceedingly like the substance of a fallen one, and many semblances were unreal and misleading. It was often hard to realize that the dark, narrow current-like passage to the left was our trail, and not the winding, broader, moonlighted opening on the right. The safest course was to give your horse a free rein, and trust to his sagacity, or self-love for keeping the trail. As we descended by zigzags the north face[2] of the all but perpendicular mountain, our moonlight soon left us, or was present only by reflection from the opposite cliff. Soon, the trail became at once so steep, so rough, and so tortuous, that we all dismounted; but my attempt at walking proved a miserable failure. I had been riding with a bad Mexican stirrup, which barely admitted the toes of my left foot; and continual pressure on these had sprained and swelled them, so that walking was positive torture. I persevered in the attempt, till my companions insisted on my remounting, and thus floundering slowly to the bottom. By steady effort, we descended the three miles (four thousand feet perpendicular) in two hours, and stood at night by the rushing, roaring waters of the Merced.

That first full, deliberate gaze up the opposite height! Can I ever forget it? The valley is here scarcely half a mile wide, while its northern wall of mainly naked, perpendicular granite is at least four thousand feet high—probably more.[3] But the modicum of moonlight that fell into this awful gorge gave to that precipice a vagueness of outline, an indefinite vastness, a ghostly and weird spirituality. Had the mountain spoken to me in audible voice, or began to lean over with the purpose of burying me beneath its crushing mass, I should hardly have been surprised. Its whiteness, thrown into bold relief by the patches of trees or shrubs which fringed or flecked it wherever a few handfuls of its moss,

[2] Greeley either meant the north-*facing* side or mistakenly said "north" when he meant "south." Having approached from the south, the party of necessity went down that side.

[3] He was probably looking up the face of El Capitan.

slowly decomposed to earth, could contrive to hold on, continually suggested the presence of snow, which suggestion, with difficulty refuted, was at once renewed. And, looking up the valley, we saw just such mountain precipices, barely separated by intervening watercourses (mainly dry at this season) of inconsiderable depth, and only receding sufficiently to make room for a very narrow meadow inclosing the river, to the furthest limit of vision.

We discussed the propriety of camping directly at the foot of the pass, but decided against it, because of the inadequacy of the grass at this point for our tired, hungry beasts, and resolved to push on to the nearest of the two houses in the valley, which was said to be four miles distant. To my dying day, I shall remember that weary, interminable ride up the valley. We had been on foot since daylight; it was now past midnight; all were nearly used up, and I in torture from over twelve hours' steady riding on the hardest trotting horse in America. Yet we pressed on, and on, through clumps of trees, and bits of forest, and patches of meadow, and over hillocks of mountain debris, mainly granite boulders of every size, often nearly as round as cannonballs, forming all but perpendicular banks to the capricious torrent that brought them hither—those stupendous precipices on either side glaring down upon us all the while. How many times our heavy eyes—I mean those of my San Francisco friend and my own—were lighted up by visions of that intensely desired cabin—visions which seemed distinct and unmistakable, but, which, alas! a nearer view proved to be made up of moonlight and shadow, rock and trees, into which they faded one after another. It seemed at length that we should never reach the cabin; and my wavering mind recalled elfish German stories of the Wild Huntsman, and of men who, having accepted invitations to a midnight chase, found on their return that said chase had been prolonged till all their relatives and friends were dead, and no one could be induced to recognize or recollect them. Gladly could I have thrown myself recklessly from the saddle, and lain where I fell till morning, but this would never answer, and we kept steadily on.

Time and the hour wear out the longest day.

At length the *real* cabin—one made of posts and beams and whipsawed boards, instead of rock, and shadow, and moonshine—was reached, and we all eagerly dismounted, turning out our weary steeds into abundant grass, and stirring up the astonished landlord, who had never before received guests at that unseemingly hour. (It was after 1 A.M.) He made us welcome, however, to his best accommodations, which would have found us lenient critics even had they been worse; and I crept into my rude but clean bed so soon as possible, while the rest awaited the preparation of some refreshment for the inner man. There was never a dainty that could have tempted me to eat at that hour. I am told that none ever before traveled from Bear Valley to the Yosemite in one day—I am confident no green horns ever did. The distance can hardly exceed thirty miles by an air-line; but only a bird could traverse that line, while, by way of Mariposa and the South Fork, it must be fully sixty miles, with a rise and fall of not less than twenty thousand feet.

The *fall* of the Yosemite, so called, is a humbug. It is not the Merced River that makes this fall, but a mere tributary trout brook, which pitches in from the north[4] by a barely once-broken descent of two thousand six hundred feet, while the Merced enters the valley at its eastern extremity, over falls of six hundred and two hundred and fifty feet. But a river thrice as large as the Merced, at this season, would be

---

[4] Again, Greeley probably has his directions confused. He is undoubtedly referring here to Bridal Veil Falls, which is on the south wall of the canyon.

utterly dwarfed by all the other accessories of this prodigious chasm. Only a Mississippi or a Niagara could be adequate to their exactions. I readily concede that a hundred times the present amount of water may roll down the Yosemite Fall in the months of May and June, when the snows are melting from the central ranges of the Sierra Nevada, which bound this abyss on the east; but this would not add a fraction to the wonder of this vivid exemplification of the divine power and majesty. At present, the little stream that leaps down the Yosemite, and is all but shattered to mist by the amazing descent, looks like a tapeline let down from the cloud-capped height to measure the depth of the abyss. The Yosemite Valley (or Gorge) is the most unique and majestic of nature's marvels, but the Yosemite Fall is of little account. Were it absent, the valley would not be perceptibly less worthy of a fatiguing visit.

We traversed the valley from end to end next day, but an accumulation of details on such a subject only serve to confuse and blunt the observer's powers of perception and appreciation. Perhaps the visitor who should be content with a long look into the abyss from the most convenient height, without braving the toil of a descent, would be wiser than all of us; and yet that first glance upward from the foot will long haunt me as more impressive than any look downward from the summit could be.

I shall not multiply details, nor waste paper in noting all the foolish names which foolish people have given to different peaks or turrets. Just think of two giant stone towers, or pillars, which rise a thousand feet above the towering cliff which form their base, being styled the Two Sisters! Could anything be more maladroit and lackadaisical? The Dome[5] is a high, round, naked peak, which rises between the Merced

[5] Perhaps the same that is now called Half Dome, a refinement that probably would not have impressed Greeley any more favorably.

and its little tributary from the inmost recesses of the Sierra Nevada already instanced, and which towers to an altitude of over five thousand feet above the waters at its base. Picture to yourself a perpendicular wall of bare granite nearly or quite one mile high! Yet there are some dozen or score of peaks in all, ranging from three thousand to five thousand feet above the valley, and a biscuit tossed from any of them would strike very near its base, and its fragments go bounding and falling still further. I certainly miss here the glaciers of Chamonix, but I know no single wonder of nature on earth which can claim a superiority over the Yosemite. Just dream yourself for one hour in a chasm nearly ten miles long, with egress, save for birds and water, but at three points, up the face of precipices from three thousand to four thousand feet high, the chasm scarcely more than a mile wide at any point, and tapering to a mere gorge, or canyon, at either end, with walls of mainly naked and perpendicular white granite, from three thousand to five thousand feet high, so that looking up to the sky from it is like looking out of an unfathomable profound—and you will have some conception of the Yosemite.

We dined at two o'clock, and then rode leisurely down the valley, gazing by daylight at the wonders we had previously passed in the night. The spectacle was immense, but I still think the moonlight view the more impressive.

Our faithful beasts climbed the steep acclivity at a little more than the rate of a mile per hour, so that we had still an hour or two of sunshine before us as we stood at last on the summit. I took a last long look into and up the valley, with the sun still lighting up the greater portion of the opposite cliffs, and then turned my horse's head westward. We reached, at 10:30 P.M., the ranch on the South Fork, kept by a solitary man, who has no neighbor nearer than sixteen miles, and there halted for the night.

28

CALIFORNIA—THE BIG TREES

Steamboat Cornelia, on the
San Joaquin, Aug. 15, 1859

On reaching Clark's ranch, we were so happy as to meet the Reverend O. C. Wheeler, secretary of the State Agricultural Society, and his associates on the visiting committee of that society, now on a tour of official observation through various districts of the state. We had agreed at Sacramento to make the trip to the Yosemite together, but some mishap had detained them fourteen miles back of Bear Valley during the night of Wednesday last, and when at length they reached Mariposa, my party had been some hours on our way, while not a horse nor mule could be hired that day, to replace their jaded nags, whose immediate proceeding on so rough a trip was out of the question. So they halted, perforce, till next morning, and were only going up to the Yosemite when we were coming down, as aforesaid.

But they had just returned to Clark's from the big trees of Mariposa, having visited those of Calaveras two or three days before. The general impression seems to be that the Calaveras trees are the larger and finer; but Mr. Wheeler, having just visited each, was very decided in his preference for those of Mariposa, and I understood all his associates to concur in that verdict. They found the Calaveras trees in far better condition, in the charge of a keeper, and approached by a road over which a light carriage may readily be driven up to the very trees themselves. These are no light advantages; but they assured us that, on the other hand, the Mariposa trees are considerably more numerous (some six hundred against two hundred and fifty), and are really larger

263

and finer specimens of their kind. Mr. Wheeler found by careful measurement of the diameter of one of these trees one hundred feet above the ground to be twenty feet, while its first limb, which put off at that height, had a diameter of six feet. Just think of a twig six feet through at that elevation! He obtained these results by measuring the tree's shadow, which I need hardly remark was probably narrower than the tree itself. He had several tapeline measurements of Mariposa trees over one hundred feet in circumference; but one of the Calaveras trees is claimed to be, I think, nearly one-fourth larger than this. No matter—those of either county are big enough.

We went up to the Mariposa trees early next morning. The trail crosses a meadow of most luxuriant wild grass, then strikes eastward up the hills, and rises almost steadily, but in the main not steeply, for five miles, when it enters and ends in a slight depression or valley, nearly on the top of this particular mountain, where the big trees have been quietly nestled for I dare not say how many thousand years. That they were of very substantial size when David danced before the ark, when Solomon laid the foundations of the Temple, when Theseus ruled in Athens, when Aeneas fled from the burning wreck of vanquished Troy, when Sesostris led his victorious Egyptians into the heart of Asia, I have no manner of doubt.

The big trees, of course, do not stand alone. I apprehend that they could not stand at present, in view of the very moderate depth at which they are anchored to the earth. Had they stood on an unsheltered mountaintop, or even an exposed hillside, they would doubtless have been prostrated, as I presume thousands like them were prostrated, by the hurricanes of centuries before Christ's advent. But the locality of these, though probably two thousand five hundred feet above the South Merced, and some four thousand five hundred above the sea, is sheltered and tranquil, though several of these trees have manifestly fallen within the present century. Unquestionably, they are past their prime, though to none more than to them is applicable the complimentary characterization of "a green old age."

Let me try to give as clear an idea of these forest mastodons as I can, though I know that will be but a poor one.

In measuring trees, it is so easy to exaggerate by running your line around the roots rather than the real body, that I place little dependence on the reported and recorded measurements of parties under no obligations to preserve a judicial impartiality. But I believe a fair measurement of the largest trees standing in this grove would make them not less than ninety feet in circumference, and over thirty in diameter, at a height of six feet from their respective bases, and that several of them have an altitude of more than three hundred feet. I believe the one that was last uprooted measures a little over three hundred.

But these relics of a more bounteous and magnificent world seem destined to speedy extinction. I deem them generally enfeebled by age and the racking and wrenching of their roots by the blasts that sweep through their tops. These malign influences they might withstand for ages, however, were it not for the damage they have already sustained, and are in danger of hereafter sustaining, through the devastating agency of fire. For these glorious evergreen forests, though the ground beneath them is but thinly covered with inflammable matter, are yet subject to be overrun every second or third year by forest conflagrations. For the earth, to a depth of several feet, even, is dry as an ash heap, from July to October, and the hills are so steep that fire ascends them with wonderful facility. And thus the big trees are scarred, and gouged, and hollowed out at the root and upward, as the effects of successive fires, one of which, originating far southward, ran through this locality so late as last autumn, burning one of the forest kings so that it has since fallen, half destroying another already prostrate, through the hollow of which two horsemen (not G. P. R. James's, I trust) were accustomed to ride abreast for a distance of fully one hundred feet, and doing serious damage to very many others. If the village of Mariposa, the county, or the state of California, does not immediately provide for the safety of these trees, I shall deeply deplore the infatuation, and believe that these giants might have been more happily located.

The big trees are usually accounted redwood, but bear a strong resemblance to the cedar family, so that my intelligent guide plausibly insisted that they are identical in species with their probable contemporaries, the famous cedars of Lebanon. The larger cedars in their vicinity bear a decided resemblance to the smallest of them; and yet there are quite obvious differences between them. The cedar's limbs are by far the more numerous, and come far down the trunk; they are also relatively smaller. The cedar's bark is the more deeply creased up and down the trunk, while the foliage of the big trees is nearer allied to that of certain pines than to the cedar's. The bark of the big trees is very thick—in some instances, over two feet—and is of a dry, light quality, resembling cork: hence the fatal facility of damage by running fires. The wood of the big trees is of a light red color, seeming devoid alike of sap and resin, and to burn about as freely while the tree lives as a year or more after its death. Unless in the cedars of Lebanon, I suspect these mammoths of the vegetable world have no counterparts out of California.

They are of course not all of extraordinary size, yet I cannot remember one that would girth so little as twenty feet at a height of two yards from the earth's surface, which is the proper point for horizontal measurement. Hardly one is entirely free from the marks of fire at its root, while several have been burned at least half through, and are so hollowed by fire that a tree eight feet in diameter would probably find ample room in the cavity. And, while many are still hale and thrifty, I did not perceive a single young one coming forward to take the place of the decaying patriarchs. I believe these trees now bear* no seed cone or nut, whatever they may have done in Scipio's or in Alexander's time, and there is no known means of propagating their kind; and I deeply regret that there is not, though starting a tree that would come to its maturity in not less than four thousand years would seem rather slow business to the fast age in which it is our fortune to live.[1] Possibly, the big trees are a relic of some bygone world—some past geologic period—contemporaries of the gigantic, luxuriant ferns whereof our mineral coal is the residuum. I am sure they will be more prized and treasured a thousand years hence than now, should they, by extreme care and caution, be preserved so long, and that thousands will then visit them, over smooth and spacious roads, for every one who now toils over the rugged bridlepath by which I reached them. Meantime, it is a comfort to know that the vandals who bored down with pump augers the largest of the Calaveras trees, in order to make their fortunes by exhibiting a section of its bark at the east, have been heavy losers by their villainous speculation.

We left the big trees a little after 10 A.M., returned to Clark's and fed, and then struck for Mariposa, where we arrived a little before 6 P.M.—I alone so covered with boils,

---

* I am assured that this was a mistake, and that young trees of this species, propagated from seed cones, are now growing in several nurseries. I am sure I saw no cones on any of the giants, though they were in season; and I still suspect that the seeds from which young trees have been started, grew on the younger and smaller trees of the species, not on the mammoths.

[1] With the steam engine and the telegraph in mind, Greeley could say this in perfect sincerity.

caused immediately by horseback exercise, as to make riding in any way a torture. My friend who had taken me up to Hussey's in his carriage was promptly on hand on my return, though he had been a hundred times assured that I could not possibly be back at the time appointed. We had a gathering and a talk at Mariposa in the evening, and I then rode over to Bear Valley, which we reached a little before midnight. Next evening, we ran down so far as the Tuolumne on our return, and today came on to Stockton, where we took the steamboat for San Francisco, which we hope to reach a little after midnight.

COLONEL FRÉMONT'S MINES

I have already stated that I spent most of Wednesday in an examination, under Colonel Frémont's guidance, of the mines he is working in Bear Valley, and of the mills in which he reduces the rock and separates the gold. I usually observe carefully the rule which enjoins reserve, when addressing the public, respecting matters of purely personal and private concern; but there are circumstances in the case of Col. F. which seem to justify a departure from the general usage. Chosen three or four years since the standard bearer of a new political organization in an exciting contest, and exposed, because of that choice, to a torrent of personal defamation which not merely impeached his integrity as a man and his fidelity as a public servant, but sought to divest him at once of his name, his religious faith, and even of his native land, I believe there are many thousands who cherish for Colonel Frémont a personal regard and affection which render them profoundly solicitous with respect to his good or evil fortune.[2] It is for this class only that I write the following:

The public are generally aware that Colonel Frémont

---

[2] It was to be expected that Greeley should visit Colonel Frémont and that he should write sympathetically of him. As one of the founders of

purchased from a Mexican at an early day a large tract or grant of wild mountain land lying among the foothills of the Sierra Nevada, called by the Mexicans, La Mariposa (the butterfly), after a wildflower known to abound here. It is known also that this tract was, some years after, discovered or presumed to be rich in gold—the first piece of rich vein stone having been taken out by the proprietor's own hand. It is further known that all manner of difficulties and obstructions were interposed to defeat the confirmation of the grant under which Colonel Frémont holds his title, and that a protracted and most expensive litigation was thus forced upon him. Meantime, the property was wholly unproductive—that is, to its owner—and the most inviting portions of it were clutched by squatters, who claimed, as they still claim, a right to dig its soil into utterly worthless chasms and heaps in quest of gold, to cut down its timber and feed off its grass at their own discretion, leaving to the fortunate owner only the privilege of paying the taxes, which, under the management of public affairs by officers politically and personally hostile to him, have been swelled to no less than sixteen thousand dollars per annum—his taxes, remember, on an estate which everybody used or wasted as they saw fit, and which was yielding him no income whatever. For the feeble efforts at quartz-mining made in his behalf in his years of absence—in the absence, too, of all successful experience in such mining—only served to involve him still more deeply in debt, which was further swelled by unfortunate agencies and business connections, until the aggregate of his liabilities on account of his property can hardly have fallen short of half a million dollars.

Such were the circumstances, under which he determined,

---

the Republican Party, to which he had given its name in an editorial published June 24, 1854, Greeley was a friend and admirer of "the Pathfinder," the first Republican candidate for President. Frémont was defeated in the campaign of 1856 by James D. Buchanan.

in 1857, to return to his California estate, and here, surrounded by his family, devote all his time and energies to its improvement and renovation. In the spirit of that determination he has since lived and labored, rising with the lark, and striving to obtain a complete knowledge and master of the entire business, taking more and more labor and responsibility on his own shoulders as he felt himself able to bear them, until he is now manager, chief engineer, cashier, accountant, and at the head of every other department but that of law, for which he finds it necessary still to rely on professional aid. And his mines are at length becoming productive and profitable. His first (steam) mill, near his dwelling, runs eight stamps night and day; his second (water) mill, three miles distant, on the Merced, at the north end of his estate, runs twelve stamps, also constantly; and the two are producing gold at the rate of at least two hundred and fifty thousand dollars per annum, at an absolute cost, I am confident, of not more than one hundred and fifty thousand dollars. Of course he needs all the profits, if not more, to extend and perfect his works, having already a much larger water mill nearly ready to go into operation beside that on the Merced, in which he expects, I believe, to run fifty-six stamps, and he hopes to have one hundred in all running before the close of 1860. With that number, I presume, he would be able, by giving his constant personal attention to the business, aided by faithful and capable assistants, to realize a net profit of at least ten thousand dollars per week, which would very soon clear him of debt and leave him unincumbered in the ownership of perhaps the finest mining property in the world.

Still, the Spanish proverb, "It takes a mine to work a mine," is exemplified in his case, as in others. A large additional investment is needed to render his property as productive as it might be. For instance: he has just contracted for the transportation of thirty thousand tons of vein stone from his great mine to his mill in the Merced (barely a mile and a half downhill) for sixty thousand dollars. One half of this sum would construct a railroad from the heart of the mine down to the floor of the mill, and take down this amount of rock, leaving the railroad and thirty thousand clear gain. But he must have the rock at once, while the railroad would require time, and a heavy outlay of ready cash. A Rothschild would build the road forthwith, and save forty thousand dollars; but Col. F., not being yet a Rothschild, whatever he may in time become, must bide his time.

His great vein, though not the richest, is probably the most capacious of any in California. Its thickness varies from eight to thirty-eight feet—I believe it is in one place sixty feet wide. It is, in fact, a cliff or pyramid of gold-bearing quartz inclosed in a mountain of slate—a mountain deeply gashed and seamed in various directions by the water-courses which run down it to the Merced. These ravines, this river, aided by proper engineering, obviate all the usually heavy, often ruinous, expense of pumping; the mine, properly opened, will not only clear itself of water, but the vein stone may be easily run out on inclined tram roads, instead of being hoisted to the surface through shafts by an enormous outlay of power. Then the width of the vein obviates all necessity for dead-work, save in sinking shafts and running up adits; the principal work is rather quarrying than mining, and there can be no apprehension that the vein will give out or grow poor, because it has already been tested at its various outcrops to a depth of fifteen hundred feet, and is richer at the bottom than near the top, where it has mainly been worked to this time. I have no doubt that there are ten millions of dollars in this mine above water level—that is, the level of the Merced—and that, though the yield of gold thus far has fallen rather below twenty dollars per ton, it may, even at that rate, be mined at a net profit of at least one-fourth of the gross product. Col. F. is confident that his present works do not separate half the gold contained in the rock, and that, by the use of the new amalgamators he is about to apply, he will double his weekly product without any increase of cost. This conviction is founded on chemical experiments and tests, which seem to leave no doubt of the fact that the additional gold is in the rock; but whether the means of extracting it have yet been discovered, remains to be seen. At all events, I feel sure that the productiveness of these works will increase much faster than their expenses, so long as Colonel Frémont shall devote himself to their management so entirely as he is now doing. In the hands of agents and attorneys, they would probably become again what they once were, and what all quartz-mining works, managed at second-hand, have been.

29

CALIFORNIA PHYSICALLY CONSIDERED

San José, Cal., Aug. 27, 1859

The state of California may be roughly characterized as two ranges of mountains—a large and a small one—with a great valley between them, and a narrow, irregular counterpart separating the smaller from the Pacific Ocean. If we add to these a small strip of arid, but fertile coast and a broad sandy desert behind it, lying southwest of California proper, and likely one day to be politically severed from it, we have a sufficiently accurate outline of the topography of the Golden State.

Such a region, stretching from north latitude 32° 30′ up to latitude 42°, and rising from the Pacific Ocean up to perpetually snow-covered peaks fifteen thousand feet high, can hardly be said to have a climate. Aside from the Alpine crests of the Sierra, and the sultry deserts below the Mohave and Santa Barbara, California embodies almost every gradation of climate, from the semi-arctic to the semi-tropical. There are green, fertile valleys in the Sierra which only begin to be well grassed when the herbage of the great valley is drying up, and from which the cattle are driven by snows as early as the first of October—long before grass begins to start afresh on the banks of the Sacramento. There are other valleys upon and near the seacoast, wherein frost and snow are strangers, rarely seen, and vanishing with the night that gave them being. Generally, however, we may say of the state that it has a mild, dry, breezy, healthy climate, better than that of Italy, in that the sultry, scorching blasts from African deserts have here no counterpart. Save in the higher mountains, or in the extreme northeast, snow never lies, the earth never freezes, and winter is but a milder, greener, longer spring, throughout which cattle pick up their own living far more easily and safely than in summer.

The climate of the valleys may be said to be created, as that of the mountains is modified, by the influence of the Pacific Ocean. Sea breezes from the southwest in winter, from the northwest in summer, maintain an equilibrium of temperature amazing to New Englanders. San Francisco—situated on the great bay formed by the passage of the blended waters of the Sacramento and the San Joaquin—the former draining the western slope of the Sierra Nevada from the north, as the latter does from the south—is thus, as it were, in the throat of the bellows through which the damp gales from the Pacific are constantly rushing to cool the parched slopes, or warm the snow-clad heights of the interior. I presume there was never a day without a breeze at San Francisco—generally, a pretty stiff one. The sea breeze is always damp, often chilly, and rolls up clouds which hide the sun for a part, at least, of most days. Though ice seldom forms, and snow never lies in her streets, San Francisco must be regarded as a cold place by most of her visitors and unacclimated summer denizens. I presume a hot day was never known there, and no night in which a pair of good woolen blankets were not esteemed a shelter and a comfort by all but extremely hot-blooded people. Thick flannels and warm woollen outer garments are worn throughout the year by all who have, or can get them. In short, San Francisco is in climate what London would be with her summer rains transformed into stiff and almost constant breezes.

The soil of California is almost uniformly good. The valleys and ravines rejoice in a generous depth of dark, vegetable mould, usually mingled with, or resting on clay, while the less precipitous hillsides are covered by a light reddish clayey loam of good quality, asking only adequate moisture to render it amply productive. Bring a stream of water almost anywhere, save on the naked granite, and you incite a luxuriant vegetation.

Yet the traveler who first looks down on the valleys and lower hillsides of California in mid-summer is generally disappointed by the all but universal deadness. Some hardy weeds, a little sour, coarse grass along the few still living watercourses, some small, far-between gardens and orchards rendered green and thrifty by irrigation, form striking exceptions to the general paralysis of all the less inspiring manifestations of vegetable life. High up in the mountains, he has found green valleys whereon the snow doubtless lingered till late in June, leaving the soil saturated like a wet sponge for a month later; and there are swampy meadows whereon the coarse grass grows thick to a height of several feet; while beds of delicate flowering plants, sheltered by the tall forests, maintain their vitality on the mountain slopes till late in August; but he passes out of the region of evergreens into that of oaks as he descends to a level of some three thousand feet above the ocean, and green valleys, luxuriant meadows, and mountain glades of flowering plants, still living, salute him no longer. The oaks gradually become sparse and scattered; their dark foliage contrasts strongly with the dun, dead herbage beneath and between them; as he descends to the plains, the oaks vanish or become like angels' visits, while a broad expanse of dried-up pasture range vies with occasional strips of wheat or barley stubble in evincing the protracted fierceness of the summer drought. His vision sweeps over miles after miles of stubble and range whereon no sign of vegetable life—not even a green weed—is presented; he sees seven-eighths of the watercourses absolutely, intensely dry, while the residue are reduced from rivers to scanty brooks, from brooks to tiny rivulets, and he murmurs to himself, "Is this the American Italy? It looks more like a Sahara or Gobi."

Yet this, like most hasty judgments, is a very unsound one. These slopes, these vales, now so dead and cheerless, are but resting from their annual and ever successful efforts to contribute bountifully to the sustenance and comfort of man. Summer is their season of torpor, as winter is ours. Dead as these wheatfields now appear, the stubble is thick and stout, and its indications are more than justified by the harvest they have this year yielded. *The California State Register* gives the following as the officially returned wheat yield of the state for the last three years:

Years	Total Acres in Wheat	Total Product
1856	171,869	3,879,032
1857	164,642	3,205,484
1858	186,464	3,568,669

Giving as the aggregate of three years' growth of wheat, 10,653,185 bushels from 522,975 acres, or more than twenty bushels per acre. I am confident that the aggregate yield of the Atlantic states for those same three years did not exceed ten bushels per seeded acre. The average yield of barley throughout the state, according to these returns, is about twenty-five bushels, and of oats something over thirty bushels, per seeded acre. I know the majority will say, "These are but moderate crops"; and so they may be, if compared with what might be grown, and in particular instances are grown, but if compared with the actual average yield of small grain throughout the Atlantic states, they are large indeed.

California—though very little of her soil produces good crops of* Indian corn, owing to the coolness of her summer nights and the want of seasonable rains—now grows her own bread, and may easily grow far more. Estimating her population at half a million, her last year's crop exceeded seven bushels per head, which is an ample allowance; and this year's crop is still better, with a larger area sown.

But, while only 756,734 acres in all of the soil of the state were cultivated last year (which still shows an increase on any former year), there were 1,159,813 acres of inclosed land—with, of course, a much larger area of uninclosed—devoted to grazing. Cattle-growing was the chief employment of the Californians of other days; and cattle-growing, next after mining, is the chief business of the Californians of 1859. There are comparatively few farms yet established, while ranches abound on every side. A corral into which to drive his wild herd when use or security is in question, and a field or two in which to pasture his

* Yet the returns of 1858 give a yield of 620,323 bushels from 12,978 acres, or forty-eight bushels per acre where grown. But it can only be grown to profit in limited localities.

276

milch cows and working cattle, are often all of the ranch that is inclosed; the herd is simply branded with the owner's mark and turned out to range where they will, being looked after occasionally by a mounted ranchero, whose horse is trained to dexterity in running among or around them. Stables for horses I have seen; but such a thing as an honest, straight-out barn has not blessed my eyes in connection with any farm since I left civilized Kansas —if even there. A Californian would as soon think of cutting hay for the sustenance of his family as for that of his herd. In fact, winter is, after spring, his cattle's best season— that in which they can best take care of themselves with regard to food. From August to November is their hardest time. But the herbage which rendered the hills and plains one vast flower garden in spring is, though dead and dry as tinder, still nutritious; its myriad flowers have given place to seeds which have the qualities of grain; and, if the range be broad enough, cattle, which have nought to do but forage, contrive to eke out a pretty fair living. But it were absurd to suppose that a single crop of dead herbage can afford, acre for acre, equal nourishment with the constantly renewed grasses of an eastern pasture; and many herds suffer from want of consideration of this fact. As ranches are multiplied and herds increased, a change of system becomes inevitable. The cattle-grower must fence off a portion of his range and sow it to Indian corn, to sorghum, to turnips, beets, and carrots, wherewith to supply the deficiency of his summer and fall feed. Then he can keep a much larger herd than is now profitable if possible, and may double his annual product of cheese or butter. At present, I judge this product to be smaller per cow or per acre in California than in almost any other state, except what is made in the high valleys of the Sierra Nevada.

Fruit, however, is destined to be the ultimate glory of

California. Nowhere else on earth is it produced so readily or so bountifully. Such pears, peaches, apricots, nectarines, etc., as load the trees of this valley, and of nearly every valley in the state which has had any chance to produce them, would stagger the faith of nine-tenths of my readers. Peach trees only six years set, which have borne four large burdens of fruit while growing luxuriantly each year, are quite common. Apple trees, but three years set, yet showing at least a bushel of large, fair fruit, are abundant. I have seen peach trees four or five years from the states which have all the fruit they can stagger under, yet have grown three feet of new wood over this load during the current season. Dwarf pears, just stuck into the black loam, and nowise fertilized or cultivated, but covered with fruit the year after they were set, and thenceforward bearing larger and larger yields with each succeeding summer, are seen in almost every tolerably cared-for fruit patch. I cannot discover an instance in which any fruit tree, having borne largely one year, consults its dignity or its ease by standing still or growing wood only the next year, as is common our way. I have seen greengages and other plum trees so thickly set with fruit that I am sure the plums would far outweigh the trees, leaves and all. And not one borer, curculio, caterpillar, appleworm, or other nuisance of that large and undelightful family, apears to be known in all this region. Under a hundred fruit trees, you will not see one bulb which has prematurely fallen—a victim to this destructive brood.[1]

Of grapes, it is hardly yet time to speak so sanguinely as many do; for years will be required to render certain their exemption from the diseases and the devastators known to other lands of the vine. But it is certain that some kinds of grapes have been grown around the old Jesuit Missions for generations, with little care and much success; while it

[1] The insects arrived in due time.

does not appear that the more delicate varieties recently introduced are less thrifty or more subject to attack than their Spanish predecessors, and vineyards are being multiplied and expanded in almost every farming neighborhood; single vines and patches of choice varieties are shooting up in almost every garden throughout the mining regions; and there can be little doubt that California is already better supplied with the grape than any other state of the Union. That she is destined soon to become largely and profitably engaged in the manufacture and exportation of wine is a current belief here, which I am at once unable and disinclined to controvert.

That California is richest of all the American states in timber, as well as in minerals, I consider certain, though the forests of Oregon are doubtless stately and vast. Even the Coast Range between this valley and Santa Cruz on the southwest is covered by magnificent redwood—some of the trees sixteen feet through, and fifty in circumference. In soil, I cannot consider her equal to Illinois, Iowa, Kansas, or Minnesota, though the ready markets afforded by her mines to her farms probably render this one of the most inviting states to the enterprising, energetic husbandman. But it must be considered that not half the soil of California can ever be deemed arable; the larger area being covered by mountains, ravines, deserts, etc. In fact, when one-fourth of the entire state shall have been plowed and reduced to tillage, I judge that the residue might better be left to grow timber and grass. Steep, rocky hillsides, on which no rain falls from June to November, can never be tilled to much profit.

This persistent summer drought is not an unmixed evil. It is a guaranty against many insects, and against rust, even in the heaviest grain. Grain and hay are got in at far less cost and in much better average condition here than they can be where the summers are not cloudless and rainless. Weeds are far less persistent and pestilent here than at the east; while the air is so uniformly dry and bracing, and the days so generally tempered by a fresh breeze, that the human frame maintains its elasticity in spite of severe and continued exertion. I was never before in a region where so much could be accomplished to the hand in summer as just here.

And yet—and yet—my early prejudices in favor of a refreshing shower occasionally are not fully overcome. I dislike to look for miles across so rich and beautiful a valley as this of San José, and see paralysis and death the rule, greenness and life the exception. I dislike to see cattle picking at the dry, brown herbage, and can't help thinking they would like a field of sweet, green clover, or thick blue grass, a good deal better. This may be a mistake on my part; but, if so, it is one that does credit to their discernment and taste. And I like to see a garden planted in well-grounded reliance on the rains of heaven—not dependent for its very existence on the "saki," or artificial brook, which I am always glad to see flowing into a field, no matter on which side of the Rocky Mountains. I believe firmly in irrigation; but I prefer land that there is some credit in irrigating, to that which must be irrigated, or it might better have lain unplowed and unsown.

Of course it is understood that irrigation is exceptional, even here. All the grains are grown here without irrigation; but the small grains are hurried up quite sharply by drought, and in some instances blighted by it, and, at best, are doubtless much lighter than they would be with a good, soaking rain early in June, while Indian corn, and most roots and vegetables, are only, in favored localities, grown to perfection without artificial watering. Hence, it is supposed that every garden throughout the state, save a part of those near the coast, and within the immediate influence of the damp sea breeze, must have its stream of water, or it comes to nothing, and various devices are employed to procure the needful fluid. Of these, I like artesian wells far best; and they are already numerous, especially in this valley. But ordinary wells, surmounted by windmills, which press every casual breeze into the service, and are often pumping up a good stream of water while the owner and all hands are asleep, are much more common, and are found to answer very well; while some keep their little gardens in fair condition by simply drawing water, bucket after bucket, in the old, hard way. In the valleys, and perhaps on the hillsides as well, it is generally held that the vine requires no irrigation, after being set two years; and the better opinion seems to be that fruit trees, after two years' watering, do better without. I have not yet satisfied myself as to the feasibility of superseding irrigation by deep plowing, though my strong conviction is that every orchard and garden should be thoroughly dug up and pulverized, to a depth of three, if not four feet; and that those so treated would thereafter need little, if any, artificial watering. I hope to learn further on this point.

Let me close this too long letter with a grateful acknowledgement to an emigrant—M. Sheals, I read his name—who found my trunk by the Three Crossings of Sweetwater (not in the stream, as I supposed it was) and brought it along over three hundred miles to Salt Lake City, where he delivered it to the California Stage Company, which forwarded it to me. Mr. Sheals writes that he found it in, or beside, the road, broken open; but, as I do not miss any papers of consequence, I presume nothing of much value to me was taken from it. How it came in the road—the half mile between the station, whence we started that morning, and the place where I missed it, having been twice ridden over in quest of it within half an hour after its loss—I have not yet been able to conjecture, and I will thank whoever can, to shed even a ray of light on the subject. If Mr. Sheals will favor me with his address, he will add sensibly to the debt I already owe him.

30

CALIFORNIA—HER RESOURCES

Marysville, Cal., Sept. 2, 1859

Since my last, I have traversed the rich valley of San José, looking through some of its choicer gardens and orchards, and stopping at Santa Clara, Warm Spring, Old Mission, San Leandro (county seat of Alameda), and Oakland, returning to San Francisco, and coming thence by steamboat to Sacramento and by a much smaller boat up to this city, which I reached last evening, in season to listen to the annual address, by Mr. Rhodes of Oroville, at the agricultural fair, and to break my own voice for a time in attempting to follow him in some offhand remarks. The edifice erected by the public spirit of Marysville for the fairs which are to be held here annually, and at which all northern California is invited to compete for very liberal premiums, is quite spacious and admirably adapted to all its purposes except that of public speaking; and herein is collected the finest show of fruits and vegetables I ever saw at anything but a state fair. Indian corn not less than twenty feet high; squashes like brass kettles, and watermelons of the size of buckets, are but average samples of the wonderful productiveness of the Sacramento and Yuba valleys, while the peaches, plums, pears, grapes, apples, etc., could hardly be surpassed anywhere. The show of animals is not extensive, but is very fine in the departments of horses and horned cattle, though lamentably meager in every other respect. The most interesting feature of this show was its young stock—calves and colts scarcely more than a year old, equal in weight and size, while far superior in form and symmetry, to average horses and bulls of ripe maturity. With generous fare and usage, I am confident that steers and heifers two years old in California will equal in size and development those a year older in our northern states, and that California colts of three years will be fully equal to eastern colts of like blood and breeding a good year older— an immense advantage to the breeder on the Pacific. I am reliably assured that steers a year old, never fed but on wild grass, and never sheltered, have here dressed six hundred pounds of fine beef. Undoubtedly, California is one of the cheapest and best stock-growing countries in the world— and will be, after these great, slovenly ranches shall have been broken up into neat, modest farms, and when the cattle shall be fed at least three months in each year on roots, hay and sorghum, or other green fodder.

Marysville is the chief town of northern California, and disputes the claim of Stockton to rank third among the cities of the state. Unlike Stockton, it is quite compactly built, mainly of brick. Its population is probably a little over fifteen thousand; and it expects to be soon connected by railroad with Sacramento and San Francisco, which will give a new and strong impulse to its already rapid growth. Located at the junction of the Yuba and Feather Rivers, just above their union with the Sacramento, and at the head of steamboat navigation in the direction of the northern mines, it needs but the railroad connections aforesaid to render it a formidable rival to Sacramento herself. The census of 1870 will probably find its population exceeding fifty thousand.[1]

[1] Marysville's 1960 population was 9,553.

The valleys of the rivers first named are exceedingly deep and fertile, and their productiveness in this vicinity almost surpasses belief. I visited in the suburbs this morning, gardens, vineyards, orchards, of rarely equaled fruitfulness. The orchard of Mr. Briggs, for example, covers a hundred and sixty acres, all in young fruit, probably one-half peaches. He has had a squad of thirty or forty men picking and boxing peaches for the last month, yet his fruit by the cartload ripens and rots ungathered. The wagons which convey it to the mines have their regular stations and relays of horses like mail stages, and are thus pulled sixty miles up rough mountain passes, per day, where twenty-five miles would be a heavy day's work for any one team. But he is not sending to the mines only, but by steamboat to Sacramento and San Francisco as well. His sales last year, I am told, amounted to $90,000; his net income was not less than $40,000. And this was realized mainly from peaches, apricots and nectarines; his apples and pears have barely begun to bear; his cherries will yield their first crop next year. There are of course heavier fruit-growers in California than Mr. Briggs, but he may be taken as a fair sample of the class. Their sales will doubtless be made at lower and still lower prices; they are now a little higher than those realized for similar fruit grown in New Jersey; they were once many times higher than now, but, though their prices steadily decrease, their incomes do not, because their harvests continued to be augmented by at least twenty-five per cent per annum.

Let me give one other instance of successful fruit-growing in another district: Mr. Fallon, the mayor of San José, has a fine garden, in which are some ten or twelve old pear trees—relics of the Spanish era and of the Jesuit missions. The trees being thrifty but the fruit indifferent, Mr. F. had them pretty thoroughly grafted with the Bartlett variety, and the *second* year thereafter gathered, from one tree, one thousand pounds of Bartlett pears, which he sold for two hundred dollars, or twenty cents per pound. The other trees similarly treated bore him six to seven hundred pounds each of that large, delicious fruit, which he sold at the same price. And, every year since, these trees have borne large yields of these capital pears. I dare not hope for equal success in the East,[2] but surely the expedient of grafting fine, large varieties on our now worthless pears, at the same time bounteously enriching the soil beneath them, ought to be more generally adopted than it has yet been.

Just a word now on grain. California is still a young state, whose industry and enterprise are largely devoted to mining; yet she grows the bread of her half a million well-fed inhabitants on less than a fortieth part of her arable soil, and will this year have some to spare. I am confident her wheat crop of 1859 is over four millions of bushels, and I think it exceeds twenty-five bushels for each acre sown. Today, its price in San Francisco is below a dollar per bushel, and it is not likely to rise very soon. Though grown, harvested and threshed by the help of labor which costs her farmers from thirty to forty dollars per month, beside board, it is still mainly grown at a profit; and so of a very large breadth of barley, grown here instead of oats as food for working horses and cattle. Though wheat is probably the fullest, I judge that barley is the surest of any grain crop grown in the state. It has never failed to any serious extent.

Indian corn is not extensively grown; only the Russian River and one or two other small valleys are generally supposed well adapted to it. And yet, I never saw larger nor better corn growing than stands today right here on the

[2] He refers to his beloved farm at Chappaqua, some thirty miles north of New York City, where the Greeleys lived for twenty years. His neighbors irreverently called it "Greeley's bog," but he rejoiced in every acre of it.

Yuba—not a few acres merely, but hundreds of acres in a body. I judge that nearly all the intervales throughout the state would produce good corn, if well treated. On the hillsides, irrigation may be necessary, but not in the valleys. None has been resorted to here; yet the yield of shelled grain will range between seventy-five and a hundred bushels per acre. And this is no solitary instance. Back of Oakland, across the bay from San Francisco, Mr. Hobart, a good farmer from Massachusetts, showed me acres of heavy corn which he planted last May, after the rains had ceased and the dry season fairly set in, since which no hoe nor plow has been put into the field; yet the soil remains light and porous, while there are very few weeds. Not one drop of water has been applied to this farm; yet here are not only corn, but potatoes, beets, etc., with any number of young fruit trees, all green and thriving, by virtue of subsoiling and repeated plowings last spring. The ground (sward) was broken up early in the winter, and cross-plowed whenever weeds showed their heads, until planting time; and this discipline, aided by the drought, has prevented their starting during the summer. Such thorough preparation for a crop costs something; but, this once made, the crop needs here only to be planted and harvested. Such farming pays.

The fig tree grows in these valleys side by side with the apple; ripe figs are now gathered daily from nearly all the old Mexican gardens. The olive grows finely in Southern California, and I believe the orange and lemon as well. But the grape bids fair to become a staple throughout the state. Almost every farmer, who feels sure of his foothold on the land he cultivates, either has his vineyard already planted, or is preparing to plant one, while most of those who have planted are extending from year to year. I have looked through many of these vineyards, without finding one that is not thrifty—one that, if two years planted, is not now loaded with fruit. The profusion and weight of the clusters is marvelous to the fresh beholder. I will not attempt to give figures, but it is my deliberate judgment that grapes may be grown here as cheaply as wheat or corn, pound for pound, and that wine will ultimately be made here at a cost per gallon not exceeding that of whisky in Illinois or Ohio. Wine will, doubtless, constitute a heavy export of California within a very few years. So, I think, will choice timber, should the wages of labor even fall here so as to approximate our Eastern standards. At present, I estimate the average cost of labor in California at just about double the rates paid for such labor in the Middle States, which, with wheat and beef at New York prices, or lower, or clothing little higher in a climate which requires little fuel, ought to make the condition of the effective worker here a very fair one. Such I consider it to be, while I am assured by practical men that a fall of even twenty-five per cent in wages would incite a large and prompt extension of mining, farming, etc., affording employment to additional thousands of laborers. Should fair, average day labor ever fall here to a dollar per day, I think the demand for it in mining would very speedily be doubled, and soon quadrupled. I do not imply that such reduction is either desirable or probable, but I can see why the owners of large estates or of mining claims should strongly desire an ample and incessant immigration. This is plain enough; while it is not so obvious, though I deem it equally true, that an immigration of one hundred thousand effective workers per annum, would be readily absorbed by California, and would add steadily and immensely to her prosperity and wealth.

Yet I cannot conclude this survey without alluding once more to the deplorable confusion and uncertainty of land titles, which has been, and still is the master scourge of this state. The vicious Spanish-Mexican system of granting lands by the mere will of some provincial governor or municipal chief without limitation as to area, or precise delineation of boundaries, here develops and matures its most pernicious fruits. Your title may be ever so good, and yet your farm be taken from under you by a new·survey, proving that said title does not cover your tract, or covers it but partially. Hence, many refuse or neglect to improve the lands they occupy, lest some title adverse to theirs be established, and they legally ousted, or compelled to pay heavily for their own improvements. And, in addition to the genuine Spanish or Mexican grants, which the government and courts must confirm and uphold, there are fictitious and fraudulent grants—some of them only trumped up to be bought off, and often operating to create anarchy, and protract litigation between settlers and the real owners. Then there are, doubtless, squatters, who refuse to recognize and respect valid titles, and waste in futile litigation the money that might make the lands they occupy indisputably their own. I blame no party exclusively, while I entreat the state and federal governments and courts to do their utmost to settle the titles to lands in this state beyond controversy, at the earliest possible day. Were the titles to lands in California today as clear as in Ohio or Iowa, nothing could check the impetus with which California would bound forward in a career of unparalleled thrift and growth. It were far better for the state and her people that those titles were wrongly settled, than that they should remain as now. I met today an intelligent farmer, who has had three different farms in this state, and has lost them successively by adjudication adverse to his title. I would earnestly implore grantees and squatters to avoid litigation wherever that is possible, and arrest it as soon as possible, eschewing appeals, save in flagrant cases, and meeting each other halfway in settlement as often as may be. The present cost of litigation, enormous as it is, is among the lesser evil consequences of this general anarchy as to land titles.

Should these ever be settled, it will probably be found advisable to legislate for the speedy breaking up and distribution of the great estates now held under good titles by a few individuals. There will never be good common schools on, nor about these great domains, which will mainly be inhabited by needy and thriftless tenants, or dependents of the landlords. An annual tax of a few cents per acre, the proceeds to be devoted to the erection of schoolhouses, and the opening of roads through these princely estates, would go far to effect the desired end. But, whether by this, or by some other means, the beneficent end of making the cultivators of the soil their own landlords must somehow be attained—the sooner the better, so that it be done justly and legally. In the course of several hundred miles's travel through the best settled portions of this state, I remember having seen but two schoolhouses outside of the cities and villages, while the churches are still more uniformly restricted to the centers of population. Whenever the land titles shall have been settled, and the arable lands have become legally and fairly the property of their cultivators, all this will be speedily and happily changed.

I believe, too, that the time is at hand when some modification of the present mining laws will be demanded and conceded. Hitherto, the operators with pick and pan have been masters of the state, and have ruled it, like other aristocracies, with a sharp eye to their own supposed interests. To dig up a man's fenced garden, or dig down his house, in quest of gold, is the legal privilege of any miner who does not even pretend to have any rights in the premises but such as the presumed existence of gold thereon gives him. Of course, the law contemplates payment for damages sustained; but suppose the digger is pecuniarily irresponsible, and digs down your house without finding any more gold than he spends in the quest, what are you to do about it? Such laws, I trust, cannot stand. I am sure they should not.

31

CALIFORNIA—SUMMING UP

San Francisco, Sept. 4–5, 1859

The entire area of this state is officially estimated as containing a fraction less than one hundred millions of acres, but, as this total includes bays as well as lakes, rivers, etc., the actual extent of unsubmerged land can hardly exceed ninety millions of acres, or rather more than nine times the area of New Hampshire or Vermont—perhaps twice the area of the state of New York. It is only a guess on my part, but one founded on considerable travel and observation, which makes not more than one-third of this extent—say thirty millions[1] of acres—properly arable; the residue being either ruggedly mountainous, hopelessly desert, or absorbed in the tule marshes which line the San Joaquin and perhaps some other rivers. The arable thirty millions of acres—nearly the area of all New England, except Maine—are scarely equaled in capacity of production by any like area on earth. They embrace the best vinelands on this continent, to an extent of many millions of acres—an area capable of producing all the wine and all the raisins annually consumed on the globe. All the fruits of the temperate zone are grown here in great luxuriance and perfection, together with the fig, olive, etc., to which the lemon and orange may be added

[1] In his *Recollections of a Busy Life*, published in 1868, Greeley reduces this estimate to twenty millions of acres.

in the south. No other land on earth produces wheat, rye, and barley so largely with so little labor as the great majority of these thirty million acres; a portion of them are well adapted also to Indian corn. To stock-growing in an easy, slovenly, reckless way, this mild climate and fertile soil also lend themselves readily; yet I must believe that many more acres are required here to graze a thousand head of cattle than in New York or Kentucky, and that the capacities of California to furnish beef and milk in this poor fashion have been taxed very nearly to the utmost. Doubtless, four, six, or even ten times the present number of cattle will be fed here at some future day, but not wholly on the spontaneous growth of the valleys and hillsides. Nay, I hear already that, as the wild oats and natural grasses are closely fed year after year, so as to preclude their seeding or prevent the seed falling to the earth and germinating, they gradually die out, and are supplanted by coarse, worthless weeds. Evidently—and I rejoice over the fact—the day of ranches, or broad unfenced domains over which the cattle of the owner range at will, protected only by his brand from indiscriminate appropriation, is passing away forever. And it is high time. Though the range is yet many acres per head, and the feed ample for the greater part of the year, yet the cows of California give less milk today than a like number kept for milk on any other portion of the globe. The dry grass and stubble on which they subsist keep them in fair flesh, but furnish a scanty overplus for butter and cheese. Good butter is worth fifty cents and over per pound, and has generally at this season a white, insipid look, like that made in winter at the East. Cheese commands twenty-five cents per pound, and is seldom seen on hotel or private tables. Yet the production, though meager, is rapidly increasing, the little valleys opening directly on the Pacific, and thus kept green by its fogs and damp winds, in spite of the six months' absence of rain, yielding it most abundantly. A cheese weighing seven hundred and fifty pounds, the product of a single dairy, is now here, on its way to the State Fair at Sacramento; the large store in which I saw it is full, from basement to attic, of California-made cheese. Yet California does not nearly supply her own wants, whether of cheese or butter, and never will until her dairymen shall deem it profitable to shelter their stock in winter and supply them with green fodder in later summer and fall. Whenever they shall generally devote one-quarter of their lands to growing Chilian clover, sowed corn, beets, parsnips and carrots, wherewith to feed their cows from August to February, they will make twice or thrice their present product of butter and cheese, and prove theirs one of the best dairy regions on earth. But habits, especially bad ones, are stubborn things, and they will only come to this wisdom by degrees.

Whether California would be a better country if it had rain in summer, I have already somewhat considered. That it would be more inviting and attractive in aspects, especially to those unaccustomed to such sterility through the latter half of each year, cannot be doubted. With such rain, its natural pasturage would suffice for twice its present number of cattle, while cultivation could be extended far up into the mountains, on lands now deemed arable only when irrigated. Yet, on the other hand, these dry summers have their advantages. By their aid, the most bountiful harvests of hay and grain are secured in the best order, and by means of the least possible labor. Weeds are not half so inveterate and troublesome here as in rainy countries. A given amount of labor accomplishes for more in any direction than at the East. The wise man may start on a journey, of business or pleasure, without consulting his barometer, and the fool without looking into his almanac. Nobody, save in winter or early spring, ever casts an apprehensive look at the skies; it may be cloudy or foggy, as it often is, but you know it cannot rain till next November, and lay your plans accordingly. I have passed large fields of standing wheat that have been dead ripe for at least a month; they will shell some when cut, but the grain will be bright and plump as ever. All through the grain region, you see wheat that has been threshed and sacked, and piled up in the open field where it grew, to await the farmer's convenience in taking it to market; and it may lie so for months without damage, unless from squirrels or gophers. Wheat is sown throughout the winter, though the earlier sown is the surer. Plowing commences with the rains, and sowing should follow as closely as may be. Very decent crops of "volunteer" grain are often grown, by simply harrowing in the seed shelled out and lost in the process of harvesting—sometimes even though the harrowing is omitted. But the ground squirrels are apt to intercept this process by filling the grainfields with their holes, and eating up all the scattered grain and a good deal more. They are a great pest in many localities, and strychnine is freely and effectively employed to diminish their numbers.

THE MOUNTAINS AND MINES

I have estimated that barely one-third of the total area of unsubmerged California is perfectly arable: but it would be a great mistake to suppose the residue worthless. At least thirty millions of acres more are covered by rugged hills and mountains, mainly timbered—much of the timber being large and of the best quality. Yellow, pitch and sugar pine— the pitch pine being scarcely akin to its stunted and scrubby New England namesake, but a tall and valuable tree—the sugar being nearly identical with our white pine, save that its sap is saccharine—white cedar, redwood, spruce, balsam fir—all these averaging at least twice the size of the trees in any forest I ever saw elsewhere, while the balsam is just the most shapely and graceful tree on earth—such are the forests which cover all but the snowy peaks of the mountains of California. Trees six to eight feet in diameter are as common in the Sierra Nevada, and I hear in the coast range also, as those three to four feet in diameter are (or were) in the pine forests of New York and New England. Consider that these giants look down on the gold mines wherein a very large proportion of the most active population of this state must for ages be employed, while the agricultural districts lie just below them, and even the seaboard cities are but a day's ride further, and the value of these forests becomes apparent. The day is not distant—there are those living who will see it—when what is now California will have a population of three to six millions;[2] then eligible timberlands in the Sierra will be worth more per acre than would now be paid for farms in the richest valleys near San Francisco.

The timber of the lower hills and plains is generally oak—short-bodied, wide-spreading, and of poor quality, save for fuel, being brush (easily broken, like clay pipestem), and not durable. The more common variety looks like the white oak found in New England pastures, but resembles it in looks only. Live oak is next in abundance, and also a poor article. It has a smooth, dark bark, a short, crooked trunk, a profusion of good-for-nothing limbs, and small, deep green leaves, which defy the frosts of winter. The trunk is often barked by vandals for tanning, leaving the tree standing alive, but certain to die. Black and rock oak are found

[2] California passed the three-million mark between 1910 (2,377,549) and 1920 (3,426,861). It is doubtful that even Greeley would have been prepared to believe what happened after 1920: a doubling of population in the next twenty years and a two and a half times increase of *that* in the next twenty years—nearly sixteen million in 1960.

in some of the mountain valleys, and seem to be of fair quality. Large cottonwood and sycamore line some of the streams, but very sparingly. Her evergreens are the pride of California.

The gold mines are generally found among the foothills of the Sierra, or in the beds of the streams which traverse those hills. In many instances, hills now tower where rivers once ran—how long since, who may tell? Trees in a state of semi-petrifaction are dug out from under hundreds of feet of solid earth, which seems to have lain undistrubed for thousands of years. The beds of ancient lakes are covered by rugged heights; and, these beds being often auriferous, it is one of the arts of the miner to know just where to tunnel through the "rim rock" so as to strike what was the bottom of the lake, and thus extract its gold as cheaply as may be. Washing the beds of modern streams, which was the earliest and most profitable field of mining adventure, is now nearly at an end, or turned over to the Chinese, who are willing to work hard and steadily for much less than will satisfy the aspirations of a Yankee. There are still some creek beds that will pay in winter, when water is abundant, that remain to be washed out; but, in the main, river-mining is at its last gasp. Very few dams are being or have recently been constructed to turn rivers from their beds and permit those beds to be sluiced out; and I doubt that this special department of mining ever paid its aggregate cost. The expense is serious; the product often moderate, and subject to many contingencies. Henceforth, dams will be constructed mainly to feed the canals or "ditches" whereby water is supplied to works that must otherwise be abandoned. Of these ditches, *The State Register* for 1859, has a list of several hundreds in number, amounting in the aggregate to five thousand seven hundred and twenty six miles of artificial watercourses constructed wholly for mining purposes, at a total cost of $13,-

575,400, or about twice that of the original Erie Canal. The largest of these ditches is that of the Eureka Canal Company, leading water from the north fork of the Cosumnes River to Diamond Springs, two hundred and ninety miles, at a cost of eighty thousand dollars; but there are many far more expensive and important, being far larger and carried over a more difficult country. At the head of these stand the Mokelumne Hill Canal, in Calaveras County, only sixty miles long, but costing six hundred thousand dollars; the Columbia and Stanislaus, in Tuolumne County, eighty miles long, which also cost six hundred thousand dollars; and the South Yuba Canal, in Nevada County, costing five hundred thousand dollars. Many larger enterprises than even these have been projected, but not yet carried out, because capitalists cannot be found willing to supply the needful cash. Thus, in Mariposa alone it has been estimated that an annual rental of ten millions of dollars would be paid for water, could enough of it be had at living rates. I merely guess that it could not be paid many years.

I do not suppose that the gold mines of California will ever be thoroughly worked out—certainly not in the next thousand years; yet I do not anticipate any considerable increase in their annual production, because I deem fifty millions of dollars per annum as much as can be taken out at a profit, under existing circumstances. The early miners of California reaped what nature had been quietly sowing through countless thousands of years. Through the action of frost and fire, growth and decay, air and water, she had been slowly wearing down the primitive rocks in which the gold was originally deposited, washing away the lighter matter, and concentrating the gold thus gleaned from cubic miles of stubborn quartz and granite into a few cubic feet of earth at the bottom of her watercourses. Many a miner has thus taken out in a day gold which could not in weeks have been extracted from the rock where it first grew. Even the hills, in which it is now mainly found, can be washed down at one dollar or less per cubic yard, by the best hydraulic appliances. But when the miner is brought face to face with the rough granite, which he must drill, and blast, and tunnel for all the gold he gets, the case is gravely altered. He may make money here; he sometimes does; but I am sure that, up to this hour, not one quartz-mining enterprise in every four has paid its bare expenses, and, though there will be brilliant exceptions, I am confident that quartz-mining, as a whole, will not pay for many years to come. Either labor must be cheaper, or the process of quartz-mining far more economical and efficient, or the yield per ton much greater, before one undeniably auriferous quartz vein in ten will pay the cost of working it. And, while I presume improvements will, from time to time, be made, I hear doubtingly the talk of sanguine inventors and operators of doubling the product of gold by this or that new amalgamator, or other device. So many of these contrivances have proved futile, or of little worth, that I wait. Chemical tests indicate that a portion of the gold actually contained in the vein stone (especially if a sulphuret) is now obtained by the crushing and washing process; but how soon, or by what process, this proportion may be essentially increased, I do not know—who does? And, until it shall be, I must consider quartz-mining, with labor at the present rates, the poorest business now prosecuted in California. A few, who have struck pockets rather than veins of peculiarly rich quartz, are making a good thing of it, and their luck is in every one's mouth; but of the hundreds who drive up long adits through dead rock, or sink costly shafts to strike a vein at the best point, and find it, after all, too poor to pay for working, little is said or thought, till they drop into the gulf of acknowledged bankruptcy, and pass away. I believe fewer quartz veins are being worked today than were some years ago; I think fewer still will be worked a year hence, and thenceforward, until cheaper labor, or more effective processes, shall have rendered quartz-mining a very different business. And, until such change is effected, I apprehend that the annual gold product of California will not be essentially augmented.

POPULATION—EDUCATION—MORALS

The total population of Upper California (our California, in contradistinction to the peninsula still held by Mexico) was estimated, on the 1st of January, 1849, at twenty-six thousand; viz: natives of the country (not including Indians) thirteen thousand; United States Americans, eight thousand; Europeans, five thousand. The aborigines were estimated, in 1856, by Colonel Henley, superintendent of Indian affairs, at sixty-five thousand. I deem this a gross exaggeration. Six Indian reservations have been officially established in different sections of the state, on which all the Indians have been gathered that could be; and these amount to barely seventeen thousand two hundred and five, according to the official returns, which, being the basis of requisitions on the government, are certain not to fall below the truth. I do not believe there are so many more Indians in the state; and, whatever may be the number, it is steadily and rapidly diminishing. These Indians are generally idle and depraved, while the white men who come in contact with them are often rascals and ruffians, who hold that Indians have "no rights that white men are bound to respect." By these, the poor savages are intruded upon, hunted, abused, robbed, outraged, until they are themselves driven to acts of violence, when a "war" ensues, and they are butchered without mercy. If an honest census of the various tribes and bands be taken in 1860, their number will not be found to much exceed thirty thousand, which 1870 will find reduced to ten thousand. The native or

Spanish Californians are already reduced in number since 1849, and are now mainly confined to the southern agricultural counties. I have not seen half a dozen of them in a month's travel through the heart of the state.

The census of 1850 made the total population of California (Indians not counted) ninety-two thousand five hundred and ninety-seven; but there were some counties from which no returns were received, which, it was estimated, would increase the aggregate to one hundred and seventeen thousand five hundred and thirty-eight. Only two years thereafter, a state census was taken, which increased the number to two hundred and sixty-four thousand four hundred and thirty-five— it having more than doubled (by immigration) in two years. Of this number, only twenty-two thousand one hundred and ninety-three were females—less than one-tenth of the whole —while the great majority were men in the vigorous prime of life. The state of public morals among a population so disproportioned, in a land far removed from the restraining influences of home and kindred, were better imagined than described.

Today, the total population of the golden state (excluding Indians) is probably not less than half a million; the census of 1860 will doubtless give a still larger aggregate.[3] Of these, I judge some fifty thousand are Chinese, with about an equal number of Europeans or Mexicans, not including those who, by treaty or naturalization, have become American citizens. Of the half million, probably seventy-five thousand are under eighteen years of age, while perhaps an equal number are women and girls over eighteen, though I fear not. This would leave three hundred and fifty thousand men, including boys over eighteen, nearly all in the prime of life

[3] He overestimated considerably. California's population in 1860 was 379,994.

—vigorous, active, enterprising, and industrious. There are idlers, and drones, here as elsewhere, but there probably was never before a community of half a million people capable of doing so much good work in a year as this population of California. The facts that they mine gold to the extent of fifty millions of dollars annually, while growing four millions of bushels of wheat, five millions of bushels of barley, with large amounts of other grains and an ample supply of vegetables and fruits for home consumption, would go far toward establishing the fact.

But the industry of California produces important results which are not exhibited above. No part of the union is making more rapid strides in building, fencing, opening farms, setting fruit trees, breeding stock, etc. The number of grapevines alone was increased from 1,540,134 in 1856 to 3,954,-548 last year (of which 1,650,000 were in the southern county of Los Angeles alone). The aggregate will be carried this year above 6,000,000. Los Angeles in 1857 produced 350,000 gallons of wine. Probably no other market on earth is so well supplied with fruit throughout the year as that of San Francisco—a city hardly yet ten years old. Strawberries are abundant here today, and are in season from April to December. Raspberries are ripe in May, and are now plentiful and perfect. Peaches are fresh from June to November. Grapes come in July, and are sold till December. All these and other fruits require preparation and outlay before they begin to make returns. The orchards and vineyards of California have cost millions of dollars, which are destined to return to their proprietors with interest in the course of a few years. As yet, there are probably more apple trees in the state than there have been gathered bushels of apples up to this day.

The following are the latest school statistics of the state that I have been able to find:

Year	Com. Schools	Teachers	*Pupils
1853	53	56	11,242
1856	313	417	30,019
1857	367	486	36,222

Next after the deficiency of women shown to exist in the population of California, this "beggarly account" of schools is the darkest shade in the picture. I believe I have seen but *two* schoolhouses outside of cities or considerable villages in the course of my travels through the state. And, so long as ranches, of five hundred to many thousand acres each, stand in place of small, neat, well-cultivated farms, this deficiency, though it may be modified, will continue.

I have visited several of the common schools of San Francisco, and found them admirable in their appointments, under intelligent and vigilant supervision, and in a high state of efficiency. There may somewhere be better-managed seminaries than the high school, but I never entered their doors. Most of the smaller cities are taking hold of the subject in the right spirit, but under many disadvantages. Youth are too often kept away from school to earn money which their parents could do without, and many parents wait till they have improved their circumstances essentially before they think of educating their children. I was told in Marysville that many of the pupils of fourteen years and upward, in her schools, were just learning to read. There ought to be two thousand good common schools in operation this winter in California; but I fear there will not be six hundred. I entreat the early and earnest attention of her better citizens to her lamentable lack of schools. In no way can her energy

* This number of pupils was not in actual attendance in the schools, but is a return of all the children between four and eighteen years living in the cities or towns which had organized schools. The number who actually attended school for even a part of a term was of course much smaller.

and wealth be better employed than in multiplying and improving them.

I have endeavored so to arrange the facts embodied in my letters from this state as to furnish an answer to this question. I will here only sum up my conclusions:

1. California has still a great need of virtuous, educated, energetic women. One hundred thousand more of these would find homes and be useful here. Certainly, I would advise no woman to pitch into such a community devoid of the protection of relatives or trusted friends; but women who can teach, manage a dairy, keep house, etc., and do not fancy any useful work degrading, are still greatly needed here. House servants command twenty to thirty dollars per month; capable female workers in other capacities are paid in proportion. For a resolute, capable young woman, who has a married sister or trusted friend here, and who is not detained elsewhere by strong natural ties, I believe, there is no better country than this.

Good farmers, who have considerable means, but especially those who understand the dairy business, and have families who can and will tender them efficient help in it, can also do well here. The naked facts that, while wheat now sells for one dollar per bushel, butter brings fifty and cheese twenty-five cents per pound, are enough to show that dairy farming is profitable. The best grazing country is found along the coast, but it is all good for those who understand it, and are willing to grow feed for a part of each year. Bees do far better here than elsewhere, are worth one hundred dollars per hive, and good property at that. Fruit-growing is still profitable; vine-growing will always be. I believe a young, energetic, intelligent farmer, with a good wife and two thousand dollars or over, can do as well in California as elsewhere, in spite of the horrible confusion of land titles.

Buy no tract of which the title is at all doubtful, unless you can buy all the conflicting claims, but pay higher for good land well located, and as to the ownership of which there is no dispute. Such may at all times be found; if settlers were willing to pay for this rather than buy uncertainties at lower rates, it would be far better for them.

I do not think it advisable for young men, or any others, to come here expecting to "make their pile," and return to the East. The chances for doing this, always doubtful, have nearly ceased to exist. No more merchants or clerks are wanted; and of those who come hereafter, nine-tenths will go back disappointed and impoverished, or stay here paupers. Goods are sold in California at as reasonable rates, all things considered, as in New England or New York, and there are quite sellers enough. The chances for big strikes in the mines are few, and greenhorns cannot share them. Mining is reduced to a business, and one, at best, no better, in the average, than other business. The men who dig the gold carry away but a small share of it. Better leave the chances of gold-digging to those who understand it.

As to labor for wages, it is generally well paid here—say from twenty-five to forty dollars per month, beside board, and for mechanics still higher. But employment is precarious, whether in the cities, or the mines, while the farmers are shy of hiring at high wages when wheat brings but one dollar per bushel. I cannot consider it worth any man's while to risk the price of a passage hither for the chance of getting employment by the month. The experiment will usually cost all it comes to. If you come to California at all, come to stay; and nowhere else will you find a little money more desirable than here. Even one thousand dollars, well applied, may, with resolute industry and frugality, place you soon on the high road to independence.

But the steamship's shrill pipe gives warning that I must be up and away. I had ardently hoped and expected to return by the Butterfield Overland Mail, via Los Angeles, Fort Yuma, Tucson, El Paso, etc., but this was not to be. These pestilent boils, which are the scourge of many overland comers to California, forbid it. I have no choice but to return by way of the Isthmus, for I can wait no longer. And so, as the good steamer *Golden Age* swings from her moorings, I wave to my many and generous friends in California—whose number I trust my visit has not tended to diminish—a fervent and hearty adieu!

32

CALIFORNIA—FINAL GLEANINGS

Steamship Golden Age,
Pacific Ocean, Sept. 9, 1859

Though my overland journey is ended, some facts gathered in its last stages remain to be noted. They relate exclusively to the moral and intellectual well-being and prospects of the golden state.

RELIGION

The last *State Register* gives a tabular view of religious denominations, making two hundred and sixteen Christian, and five Jewish congregations in the state, with two hundred and eighty-nine Christian, and three Hebrew clergymen. Of the Christian, one hundred and thirty-three—nearly one-half —are Methodists, and seventy-one—nearly one-fourth—are Roman Catholics. I hear from different quarters that the Methodists and Catholics manifest generally far more energy and vitality than the other churches. The Catholics enjoy certain marked advantages over all others. Theirs is the church of the old Californians—that is, of the Spanish-Mexican population without exception—also a part of the Indians. The

Catholic inhabitants are estimated to exceed one hundred thousand. But the old church is strong in position and wealth, as well as numbers. Much of the most valuable land in the state was long since conceded by Spanish or Mexican officials to the Catholic missions; and, though a good deal of this has been clutched by squatters, a very valuable property still remains. Santa Clara College,[1] near San José, is probably the best literary institution in the state, and attracts many sons of non-Catholic parents, though a Catholic seminary. It has by far the largest theological library to be found on this coast. Oakland College, opposite San Francisco, is a young, but thriving seminary, under orthodox direction. There is to be a San Francisco University, I believe, but is not yet. Whatever colleges of a high grade may be established in the state, for many years will owe their existence to religion.

As yet, the great majority of the non-Catholic Californians have no habit of attendance on religious worship—no proclaimed attachment to any church whatever. Estimating their number (not including Chinese or Indians) at three hundred and fifty thousand, I judge that less than one-tenth of them statedly attend church, or make any religious profession. I simply state the facts as they appear to me, without drawing therefrom any deduction beyond this: an unsettled, homeless population rarely or never build churches, or habitually frequent them.

THE PRESS

There are between ninety and one hundred periodicals published in California.[2] Thirty-one of the forty-five counties

[1] Founded 1851. Oakland College no longer exists. The date listed for the founding of The University of San Francisco is 1855, suggesting either that Greeley did not know of it or that it was founded under a different name.

[2] In 1960 California had 850 newspapers (143 of them dailies) and 526 other publications, according to *N. W. Ayer & Son's Directory of Newspapers and Periodicals.*

have each one or more journals. Of these, twenty are issued daily—six of them of the Buchanan-Lecompton stripe in politics, three anti-Lecompton, and only one (*The San Francisco Times*) decidedly Republican. The remainder are independent—most of them with strong anti-Lecompton proclivities. At the head of these stands *The Sacramento Union* (daily and weekly), which, by means of extensive and systematic reporting, presents the fullest and fairest account of whatever is said or done in California of any journal, and which has, very naturally, the largest and widest circulation. Next in importance and influence stands *The Alta California*, the oldest paper in the state, and I believe the first ever issued in San Francisco. *The Bulletin* is the only evening paper issued in that city, and is distinguished for the fullness of its correspondence. *The California Farmer*, by Colonel Warren, is the pioneer work in its line, and has hardly been exceeded in usefulness to California by any other. I trust it has a long and prosperous career before it.

Of the weekly newspapers issued in the state, twenty-five support Lecompton democracy, fourteen are anti-Lecompton, only two or three Republican, the residue independent—several of them with strong and outspoken anti-Lecompton tendencies. It will thus be seen that the influence of the local press leans strongly to the side of whatever may for the time being be commended as regular democracy. No state is more intensely scourged by office-seeking than California, offices being here numerous and salaries and pickings very fat; hence each county has its powerful junto of office-seekers who understand (if little else) that the way to their goal lies through "sticking to the party," right or wrong—in fact, if it be wrong, the merit of sticking to it is, in the party sense, so much greater, and the reward is likely to be larger. Intelligent as a majority of the people of this state are known to be, it is still deplorably true that the great mass of the facts which impelled and necessitated the Republican movement and organization have never been made known through their journals—not even through those of the independent order. To this hour, California, otherwise well informed, imagines that there was no serious struggle in Kansas—or if there was, that one side was about as much in fault as the other—that Kansas was invaded, her people driven from the polls, her ballot boxes stuffed, and the verdict of her settlers falsified (if at all) as much by Republicans (whence?) as by the Missouri border ruffians! One Democrat with whom I discussed the matter supposed they came over from Iowa! Had the independent press done its simple duty in the premises, such monstrous fabrications could neither be credited nor profitably coined. But I rejoice in the hope that the break on Lecompton insures a more ample and truthful presentment of the current history of the great struggle hereafter. I trust that the people of this state are not much longer to be held in the leading strings of slavery and sham-democracy.

Of the ninety-odd periodicals in California, three are printed in the French language, two in Spanish, one in German, and at least one in Chinese. (Whoever would subscribe to *The Chinese News* should address its editor, Hung Tai, at Sacramento.) Six are devoted to religion, two to agriculture, nine or ten to literature, mining, medicine, etc. About one-third of the whole number are issued from San Francisco alone.

SAN FRANCISCO

The city of San Francisco is built along the eastern base and up the side of a row of high sand hills, which stretch southwardly from the Golden Gate, between the Pacific Ocean on the west and the bay of San Francisco on the east. The city has been built out into the bay some fifty to a hundred rods by carting in sand from the eastern slope of the hills, which are thus left more abrupt than they originally were. The compactly built district seems rather more than two miles north and south, by somewhat less east and west. I judge that the city is destined to expand in the main southwardly, or along the bay, avoiding the steep ascent toward the west. The county covers 26,000 acres, of which one-half will probably be covered in time by buildings or country seats. I estimate the present population at about 80,000.* It seems not to have increased very rapidly for some years past, and this is as it should be. San Francisco has the largest trade of any city on the Pacific; but as yet she is the emporium of California and Oregon only. A railroad communication with the Atlantic states would make her the New York of this mighty ocean—the focus of the trade of all America west of the Andes and Rocky Mountains, and of Polynesia as well, with an active and increasing Australian commerce. Without an interoceanic railroad, she must grow slowly, because the elements of her trade have been measured and their limits nearly reached. The gold product of this region has for years averaged about fifty millions per anum, and is not likely soon to rise much above that amount. That sum does not require, and will not create, a larger mart than San Francisco now is. The horrible anarchy of land titles forbids any rapid expansion of agricultural industry hereabouts; but if it were to expand, where is its market? Wheat is cheaper here today than in New York or Liverpool; yet whither can any considerable amount of it be exported at a profit? I do not know.

With an efficient protective tariff, San Francisco would become, what she ought now to be, a great manufacturing center—the united Manchester and Birmingham of the South Seas. She ought to make half the wares she now merely buys and sell. Under our present tariff, with the high

---

* The S. F. Directory for 1859 makes it 78,083, including 3,150 Chinese and 1,605 Africans.

rates of labor prevailing in this state, this cannot be. She is evidently destined to become a great city, but not yet.

Some of the elements of greatness she certainly has—a spacious, secure, magnificent harbor, with easy access to the ocean, and a noble river-communication inland; a temperate and equable climate—one very favorable to the highest efficiency in industry, though I do not deem it a pleasant one; an inexhaustible supply of the finest timber close at hand; the richest mines of the precious metals; and a fertile, beautiful, but not unlimited agricultural region filling up the interval between her and those mines, and stretching hundreds of miles north and south. She has a population rarely surpassed in intelligence, enterprise, and energy. Add to these a railroad and telegraph to the Atlantic, and she could hardly fail to grow in population, trade, industry, and wealth, with a rapidity for which there have been few precedents.

San Francisco has some fine buildings, but is not a well-built city—as, indeed, how could she be? She is hardly yet ten years old, has been three or four times in good part laid in ashes, and is the work mainly of men of moderate means, who have paid higher for the labor they required than was ever paid elsewhere for putting so much wood, stone, brick and mortar into habitations or stores. Her growth for the first five years of her existence was very rapid; but Pottsville,[3] Chicago, Liverpool have also had rapid growths, and St. Louis is now expanding faster than this city has done since 1852. Cities are created and enlarged by the wants of populations outside of their own limits; San Francisco will take another start when she shall have become beneficent if not indispensable to a much larger radius than that now buying and selling mainly through her. In the hope that the time for this is not far distant, I bid her God speed.

[3] Pottsville's rapid growth did not continue. In 1950 this Pennsylvania city had a population of 23,640 and in 1960, of 21,659.

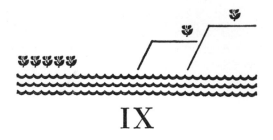

IX

EPILOGUE: "Men and Brethren!"

Dispatch 33

A RAILROAD TO THE PACIFIC

New York, Oct. 20, 1859

I propose in this letter to present such considerations as seem to me pertinent and feasible, in favor of the speedy construction of a railroad, connecting at some point our Eastern network of railways with the waters of the Pacific Ocean.

Let facts be submitted to, and pondered by, considerate, reflecting men. There are thousands of usually intelligent citizens who have decided that a Pacific railroad is a humbug—the fantasy of demagogues and visionaries—without having ever given an hour's earnest consideration to the facts in the case. Let me have a patient hearing while I set forth some of the more material of those facts: and first, in answer to the question, *Is there a national need of a railroad from the Missouri to the Pacific?* Let us study the records.

The number of passengers arriving at, and departing from San Francisco by water, so far as we have official returns of them, is as follows:

Years	Arrivals	Departures
1849	91,415	No returns.
1850	36,462	No returns.
1851	27,182	No returns.
1852	66,988	22,946
1853	33,232	30,001
1854	47,531	23,508
1855	29,198	22,898
1856	28,119	22,747
1857	22,990	16,902
TOTAL	381,107	139,002

Of course, these were not all from the Atlantic slope, via the Isthmus, or Nicaragua; but the great mass of them were. Probably most of those brought by small vessels from the Pacific ports were not reported to, or recorded at the custom-house at all. There were some immigrants to California who did not land at San Francisco, though the great mass undoubtedly did. Then there was a heavy, though capricious overland emigration. Governor Bigler stated the number in 1854 alone at sixty-one thousand four hundred and sixty-two; and there was a very large migration across the Plains in 1852. In 1857, the number was estimated at twelve thousand five hundred. This year, my estimate of the number, founded on personal observation, is thirty thousand; but others make it forty thousand to sixty thousand. There was, also, a very considerable emigrant movement across the

Plains in an easterly direction. So far, I have taken no account of the emigration to and travel from Oregon and Washington. I know I am within bounds in estimating the number who have passed from the Atlantic slope to California and Oregon or Washington at an average of fifty thousand, while the average number who have annually returned thence cannot have fallen below thirty thousand.

Can there be any doubt that nine-tenths of these would have traveled by railroad, had such a road stretched from the Missouri or Mississippi to the Pacific, the fare being moderate, and the passage made within ten days? I estimate that twice to thrice the number who actually did go to California would have gone, had there been such a means of conveyance, and that the present Anglo-American population of the Pacific slope would have been little less than two millions—say, California, one million five hundred thousand; Oregon, three hundred thousand; Washington, one hundred thousand; Sonora and Mexican California, one hundred thousand.

Now as to the gold crop of California:

The customhouse returns of San Francisco show the following shipments of gold from that city:

Year	Amount	Year	Amount
1849	$ 4,921,250	1853	$57,331,024
1850	27,676,346	1854	51,328,653
1851	42,582,695	1855	43,080,211
1852	46,586,134	1856	48,887,543
		1857	$48,592,743

The returns for the last two years and the first three-quarters of the present are not before me, but they are known to have varied little from the rate of fifty millions of dollars per annum, making the total amount entered at the customhouse of San Francisco, as shipped at that port up to this date, rather over five hundred millions of dollars. How many more millions have been brought away in the trunks or belts of returning emigrants, or mercantile passengers, I will not attempt to guess, but the amount is certainly large. On my recent trip homeward, one of the steerage passengers was currently reported as having thirty thousand dollars in gold in his carpetbag, which he kept in his hands or under his head; others were said to have their thousands each, to a very large aggregate amount. Manifestly, the export of gold from California, the current produce of her mines, has exceeded fifty millions of dollars per annum, while a considerable amount is retained in the country.

Now all this gold is sent away to pay for goods—many of them very costly in proportion to their bulk and weight —silks and other dear textile fabrics; jewelry; rare wines; expensive wares; drugs, spices, etc. Experience has amply proved that all such products take the quickest rather than the cheapest route. I believe that twenty million dollars of costly or perishable merchandise would annually seek California overland if there were a continuous line of railway from the Atlantic to the Pacific seaboard; and that this amount would steadily and rapidly increase. When the Erie Railroad earns over three million dollars per annum by freight, it certainly must be moderate to hope that ten million dollars would be paid as freight on all the merchandise sent from this side to the Pacific by railroad, and that the larger share of this freight must be earned by and paid to the Pacific road.

Now let us see how far the government would necessarily patronize such a road:

The Post Office Department is now paying at least one million and a quarter for the conveyance of mails between the Atlantic and Gulf states and California, and was recently paying one million and a half. For this, it gets a semi-monthly mail by way of the Isthmus (six thousand miles, or more than double the distance direct), and a semi-weekly mail by the Butterfield route (also very circuitous), which carries letters only. There are two or three slow mails on other routes, but they cannot be said to add anything of moment to the facilities enjoyed by California and the older states for the interchange of messages or ideas.

As to military transportation, I cannot say what is its amount, nor how far a single line of railway could reduce its proper cost. I believe, however, that the government is now paying at least six millions of dollars for the transportation of men, munitions and provisions to our various military posts between Kansas proper and California, and that fully half of this would necessarily be saved and earned by a railroad to the Pacific.

Utah is now receiving accessions of population (mainly from Europe) over the Plains, though very much of their household stuff has to be sacrificed to the exigencies of the long, hard, tedious journey in wagons drawn by weary, thirsty, famishing cattle. Her people generally live poorly, yet they have to eat and drink, while most of them like to smoke or chew also. At present, most of them abstain from the use of tea, coffee, etc., because these are very dear, while the Saints are mostly poor. If there were a good railroad through Utah from Missouri to California, I believe the Saints would patronize it to the amount of at least half a million per annum, and that this amount would rapidly grow to one million. It would of course not stop there. The Rocky Mountain gold mines are no longer a matter of speculation. They just as surely exist as we live; and I believe they are destined to increase in importance and productiveness. I advise no man to dig gold or start for Pike's Peak. I presume ten of those who go thither will come back ragged and penniless, for every one that they make rich. I expect to hear many times yet that the Kansas gold mines are a humburg—that they have exploded—that everyone has left or is leaving them, etc., etc.—and I expect further to hear of new discoveries in this direction or in that, and to record the receipts of millions thence in each of the years from 1861 to 1871 inclusive. Meantime, those who prospect or mine there must live—a point to which eating is rather essential in that keen mountain air. Everything that can be eaten or drunk is selling in the Kansas mines at far more than California prices. A railroad from the Missouri to the heads of the Platte or Arkansas would reduce, in those mines, the average cost of food at least half, and would thereby diminish sensibly the cost, and increase the profit of digging gold. If one hundred thousand persons can manage to live in the Rocky Mountain gold region as it stands, three hundred thousand could do better there with a railroad up from the Missouri. And that number, if located there, could not supply less than three million dollars per annum of travel and transportation to a Pacific railroad.

Let us sum up, now, and see what elements of support for such a railroad may be presumed to already exist:

I. Fifty thousand passengers from the Missouri to California and thirty thousand the other way, half first-class at $100, and the residue, second-class at $50 each. Total passage money $ 6,000,000

II. Fifty millions of gold brought from California, now paying 1¼ per cent freight and insurance, if charged 1 per cent for conveyance over the railroad, would pay   500,000

III. Freight on merchandise sent overland to California, say $20,000,000 worth, paying at least $5,000,000 freight, of

	which the Pacific road could not receive less than	3,000,000
IV.	Conveyance of troops, with freight on arms, munitions, and provisions forwarded to the various military posts between the Missouri and California	3,000,000
V.	Conveyance of a daily mail each way in ten days between the Missouri and California, at least	1,000,000
VI.	Freight and passage for the Mormons	500,000
VII.	Ditto for the Kansas and Rocky Mountain gold region	3,000,000
	Total yearly earnings of the road	$17,000,000

In this statement, I have made no account whatever of India, China, Australia, Polynesia, etc., as taking this road in their way to and from either shore of the Atlantic. I do not doubt that they would make some use of it at first, and more and more annually thereafter; but this is not a resource to be relied on. I count on no transportation of aught but passengers and gold from California eastward, though I am sure that much grain would flow thence into the *placers* and settlements of the Great Basin, especially the rich mines newly discovered in Carson Valley. I know that California would soon begin to send wines, fruits, etc., eastward, and that her wool, hides, etc., would soon follow in their path. I can have no doubt that a railroad from the Missouri to the Pacific would earn seventeen millions of dollars the year after its completion, and that its income would increase thenceforth at the rate of at least one million per annum for ten or fifteen years.

Let us now consider the political or national necessity and use for a railroad from the Missouri to the Pacific:

1. The federal government is now paying some twenty-five millions per annum for military service, mainly west of the Mississippi. Nearly half of this heavy sum is paid for

transportation in its various shapes—for the conveyance of provisions, munitions, etc., to the army in Utah, and to the various posts scattered through the Indian country; for horses, mules, and wagons, required to facilitate the conveyance of soldiers, arms, munitions, and baggage from post to post, etc., etc. Every regiment employed in the Indian country, or on the Pacific, costs the treasury at least one thousand dollars per man per annum, of which I estimate that nearly half would be saved by a Pacific railroad. Certainly, the saving from this source could not fall short of five millions per annum.

2. But the efficacy, the power of an armed force, in the defense and protection of a vast empire, depend less on its numbers than on its mobility—on the facility with which it can be conveyed to the point at which it may at any time be wanted. For instance, our government has now some six to eight thousand regulars scattered over Nebraska, Kansas, New Mexico, Northern Texas, Utah, California, Oregon, and Washington. These six or eight thousand are not as efficient at two thousand would be, if it were in the power of the government instantly to transfer those two thousand, by a mere order, to the point at which they might at any time be wanted. A Pacific railroad would not, indeed, fully effect this; but it would go far toward it.

3. Suppose our little army, now largely concentrated in Utah, were urgently needed to repel some sudden danger, whether on the Pacific or the Atlantic coast: It would be a good three months' work to provide the needful animals, and remove that force to either seaboard. But with a Pacific railroad, the whole might be in New York, Charleston, New Orleans, or San Francisco within a fortnight after the order was dispatched by telegraph from the War Department, at Washington. The value of this facility of movement can hardly be overestimated.

4. At present, the regiments employed on the Pacific are

317

almost or quite wholly raised and recruited in the Atlantic states. Their removal thence to their destination costs largely, heavily, in direct expense, and in that time which is money. Suppose a regiment to cost half a million per annum, and that six months are now consumed in sending it from Baltimore to Puget's Sound, while one month would suffice with a Pacific railroad. In addition to the saving on the present cost of its transportation, the saving in the time of that regiment would be two hundred thousand dollars directly, and practically much more, as a part of the cost of recruiting, drilling, etc., now lost in the tedious transportaion, would be saved by the accelerated movement.

5. In case of war with any great maritime power, in the absence of a Pacific railroad, we should be compelled either to surrender the Pacific states to subjugation and spoliation, or maintain a double armament at enormous cost. Our army on this side of the Rocky Mountains would be utterly ineffective as against an expedition launched against the Pacific coast, and vice versa. But, with a Pacific railroad, and the telegraph which would inevitably accompany it, it would be morally impossible that an expedition directed against either seaboard should not be anticipated in its arrival by the concentration, to oppose its landing, of our soldiers, drawn from every part of the country. Our government, in aiding the construction of such a road, would inevitably stipulate for its use—exclusive, if required—in times of public peril, and would thus be enabled to transfer fifty thousand men from either coast to the other in the course of twenty or thirty days.

6. We have already expended some scores of millions of dollars on fortifications, and are urgently required to expend as many more. Especially on the Pacific is their construction pressingly demanded. I do not decide how fast nor how far this demand may or should be responded to; but I do say that a Pacific railroad, whereby the riflemen of the mountains

could be brought to the Pacific within three days, and those of the Missouri within ten, would afford more security to San Francisco than ever so many gigantic and costly fortifications.

But enough on this head.

The social, moral, and intellectual blessings of a Pacific railroad can hardly be glanced at within the limits of an article. Suffice it for the present that I merely suggest them:

1. Our mails are now carried to and from California by steamships, via Panama, in twenty to thirty days, starting once a fortnight. The average time of transit from writers throughout the Atlantic states to their correspondents on the Pacific exceeds thirty days. With a Pacific railroad, this would be reduced to ten, for the letters written in Illinois or Michigan would reach their destinations in the mining counties of California quicker than letters sent from New York or Philadelphia would reach San Francisco. With a daily mail by railroad from each of our Atlantic cities to and from California, it is hardly possible that the amount of both letters and printed matter transmitted, and consequently of postage, should not be speedily quadrupled.

2. The first need of California today is a large influx of intelligent, capable, virtuous women. With a railroad to the Pacific, avoiding the miseries and perils of six thousand miles of ocean transportation, and making the transit a pleasant and interesting overland journey of ten days, at a reduced cost, the migration of this class would be immensely accelerated and increased. With wages for all kinds of women's work at least thrice as high on the Pacific as in this quarter, and with larger opportunities for honorable and fit settlement in life, I cannot doubt that tens of thousands would annually cross the Plains, to the signal benefit of California and of the whole country, as well as the improvement of their own fortunes and the profit of the railroad.

3. Thousands now staying in California, expecting to "go

home" so soon as they shall have somewhat improved their circumstances, would send or come for their families and settle on the Pacific for life, if a railroad were opened. Tens of thousands who have been to California and come back, unwilling either to live away from their families or to expose them to the present hardships of migration thither, would return with all they have, prepared to spend their remaining days in the land of gold, if there were a Pacific railroad.

4. Education is the vital want of California, second to its need of true women. Schoolbooks, and all the material of education, are now scarce and dear there. Almost all books sell there twice as high as here, and many of the best are scarcely attainable at any rate. With the Pacific railroad, all this would be changed for the better. The proportion of schoolhouses to grogshops would rapidly increase. All the elements of moral and religious melioration would be multiplied. Tens of thousands of our best citizens would visit the Pacific coast, receiving novel ideas and impressions, to their own profit and that of the people thus visited. Civilization, intelligence, refinement, on both sides of the mountain—still more, in the Great Basin inclosed by them—would receive a new and immense impulse, and the Union would acquire a greater accession of strength, power, endurance, and true glory, than it would from the acquisition of the whole continent down to Cape Horn.

The only points of view in which a railroad from the Missouri to the Pacific remains to be considered are those of its practicability, cost, location, and the ways and means. Let us look at them:

1. As to practicability, there is no room for hesitation or doubt. The Massachusetts Western, the Erie, the Pennsylvania, and the Baltimore and Ohio, have each encountered difficulties as formidable as any to be overcome by a Pacific railroad this side of the Sierra Nevada. Were the railroad

simply to follow the principal emigrant trail up the Platte and down the Snake and Columbia to Oregon, or southwest-wardly from the South Pass to the foot of the Sierra, it would encounter no serious obstacle.

2. The dearth of timber on the Plains is the chief diffi-culty to be overcome; and this, with the prevalence of deep snows in and about the South Pass, will probably send the road considerably north or south of that famous and facile pass. I presume the shortest, most feasible, and best wooded route for a railroad from the Mississippi to the Pacific is one from Minnesota to Puget's Sound, leaving the Rocky Mountains, save some low spurs, on the south, and encoun-tering less formidable snows than those on the North Platte, South Pass, and Green River. Another pretty well-timbered and direct route, with but a moderate elevation at the pass of the Rocky Mountains, strikes westward from Dubuque to the Yellow Stone, follows one of the sources of that stream into and through the Rocky Mountains, and thence down a similar stream to the Columbia, and so through Oregon to Astoria. By taking this route, the timber of the Rocky Moun-tains could be cheaply rafted or floated to every part of the track on either side at which timber is naturally deficient. The routes which turn the Rocky Mountains and the Sierra Nevada by the south are necessarily longer than those above indicated (the earth's circumference being greater toward the equator than near the pole), traverse in good part a parched and sterile desert, and must encounter serious obsta-cles in the dearth of water and in crossing the Rio del Norte and Colorado. They would, however, rarely or never be formidably obstructed by snow.

In my judgment, however, the preferable, though not the easiest route for a Pacific road traverses the valleys of the Kansas and its Smoky Hill fork, crossing thence to the more northerly sources of the Arkansas, and passing with one of them through the Rocky Mountains, not far from the South Park, thence winding down some tributary to the Colorado, thence up a western fork or valley and down the Timpanagos or some such stream into Utah, and through that territory on or near Capt. Simpson's new road to the valley of the Carson, Truckee, or whatever stream should be found to proffer the least difficult way across the Sierra Nevada, to San Francisco. A railroad on this route would at once command a large and lucrative traffic from the Kansas gold region, from Utah, and from the newly discovered but rich and growing gold region of Carson Valley or western Utah —soon, I trust, to be the territory of Nevada. Thousands have recently been drawn to Carson Valley by the fame of these mines; and the fact being established that gold, silver, and other valuable metals are found in Carson Valley, it is at least strongly probable that they will be found elsewhere along the eastern base of the Sierra Nevada. A railroad on this route would have an immediate and large local traffic, both in passengers and goods, from California to Carson Valley, from Missouri and Kansas to the Rocky Mountain gold region, and from each to Utah. Its mails, too, would be heavier and far, far more beneficent, than if conveyed by any other route. I judge, therefore, that on this route the railroad is most likely to be built, unless future developments of mineral wealth north or south of it should change the whole aspect of affairs.

3. And now as to cost and the ways and means:

This road cannot be built cheaply, for provisions and all the necessaries of life must rule high along its line, and most of the laborers will have to be carried thither. Yet it is but fair to consider that many of the heaviest items of expense on most other railroads—land and land damages, timber, stone, etc.—will here cost nothing but the labor of preparing them for this use. Then the rock-cutting will, in the average, be light, and the bridging still lighter. For much of the distance, five thousand dollars per mile will grade and bridge a double track in the very best manner. Doubtless, there are miles that would cost $100,000, but these are comparatively few, while the Colorado is the only formidable stream to be crossed between the Missouri and the Sacramento. And, as the road would necessarily be commenced at each end and pushed toward the center, it would have a considerable traffic on the very first hundred miles that should be completed, and a large one on the first five hundred. Were it to be finished next April so far as Carson Valley from the west and Pike's Peak from the east, I firmly believe that those two sections would pay expenses and interest on cost forthwith. If so, what might not be hoped from the completed road?

Again: it is to be considered that, by building thus in sections, each portion, as finished, would be used to forward provisions, rails, timber, etc., for the next. If wheat be worth five dollars per bushel today at Denver, it by no means follows that it would cost half so much, with a railroad from the Missouri completed nearly or quite to that point.

I estimate that a railroad from the Missouri at Kansas City, Wyandotte, Leavenworth, Atchison, or St. Joseph, to San Francisco, must be nearly or quite two thousand miles long, and that it would cost, with a double track and fully equipped, seventy-five thousand dollars per mile, or one hundred and fifty millions of dollars. A sanguine engineer would probably reduce this to fifty thousand dollars per mile, or one hundred millions of dollars; but, as most works cost more than they were expected to, it is as well to begin with large figures, so as not to be disappointed. More than a third of this road would build itself—that is, so much of it as lies in California, or within the boundaries assigned herself by the new state of Kansas, would readily be built by private

323

enterprise, if the connecting link were certain to be perfected in due season. It seems advisable, however, to have a single road, under one direction, from the Missouri to the Pacific, and thus make the certain profits of the extremities contribute toward the construction and support of the less promising center.

But, supposing the cost of a Pacific railroad to be one hundred and fifty millions of dollars, or even one hundred millions of dollars, how is so large an amount to be procured?

I answer—not wholly by individual subscription, or voluntarily associated enterprise. The amount is too vast; the enterprise too formidable; the returns too remote and uncertain. In the present depression of railroad property and interests, an attempt to raise such a sum for any such purpose, would be madness. One railroad to the Pacific would probably pay; but what assurance could an association of private citizens have that, having devoted their means and energies to the construction of such a road, it would not be rivaled and destroyed by a similar work on some other route? No hundred millions can be obtained for such an undertaking without assurance of government aid.

But neither will it answer to commit the government unqualifiedly to the construction of such a work. Its cost, in the hands of federal functionaries, would be incalculable; it would be an infinite source of jobbing and partisan corruption; it would never be finished; and its net revenues would amount to nothing. And then the question of location—the conflict of rival interests—would alone suffice to prevent the construction of the work by the federal government.

But let that government simply resolve that the Pacific road shall be built—let Congress enact that sealed proposals for its construction shall be invited, and that whichever responsible company or corporation shall offer adequate security for that construction, to be completed within ten years, on the lowest terms, shall have public aid, provided the amount required do not exceed fifty millions of dollars, and the work will be done, certainly for fifty millions' bonus, probably for much less. The government on its part should concede to the company a mile in width, according to the section lines, of the public lands on either side of the road as built, with the right to take timber, stone and earth from any public lands without charge; and should require of said company that it carry a daily through mail each way at the price paid other roads for conveying mails on first-class routes; and should moreover stipulate for the conveyance at all times of troops, arms, munitions, provisions, etc., for the public service, at the lowest rates, with a right to the exclusive possession and use of the road whenever a national exigency shall seem to require it. The government should leave the choice of route entirely to the company, only stipulating that it shall connect the navigable waters of the Mississippi with those of the Pacific Ocean, and that it shall be constructed wholly through our own territory. Payment of the national bonus to be made, say, one-twentieth as soon as one-tenth of the road shall have been finished and approved, and at this rate until one-third of the road shall have been built, when the remainder of one-fourth of the bonus shall be paid; when half the road shall have been built, the payment of bonus shall be increased to one-third; when the work is three-fourths done, what remains of five-eighths of the bonus shall be paid; and when the work is done and accepted, all that remains unpaid of the bonus shall be handed over to those who will have so nobly earned it.

By adopting this plan, the rivalries of routes will be made to work for, instead of working against, the construction of the road. Strenuous efforts will be made by the friends of each to put themselves in position to bid low enough to secure the location, and the lowest rate at which the work can safely be undertaken will unquestionably be bid. The road will be the property of the company constructing it, subject only to the rights of use, stipulated and paid for by the government. And, even were it to cost the latter a bonus of fully fifty millions, I feel certain that every farthing of that large sum will have been reimbursed to the treasury within five years after the completion of the work in the proceeds of land sales, in increased postages, and in duties on goods imported, sold, and consumed because of this railroad—not to speak of the annual saving of millions in the cost of transporting and supplying troops.

Men and brethren! let us resolve to have a railroad to the Pacific—to have it soon. It will add more to the strength and wealth of our country than would the acquisition of a dozen Cubas. It will prove a bond of union not easily broken, and a new spring to our national industry, prosperity and wealth. It will call new manufactures into existence, and increase the demand for the products of those already existing. It will open new vistas to national and individual aspiration, and crush out filibusterism by giving a new and wholesome direction to the public mind. My long, fatiguing journey was undertaken in the hope that I might do something toward the early construction of the Pacific railroad; and I trust that it has not been made wholly in vain.

INDEX

i

A Note on the Type

THE TEXT of this book is set in *Monticello*, a Linotype revival of the original Binny & Ronaldson Roman No. 1, cut by Archibald Binny and cast in 1796 by that Philadelphia type foundry. The face was named Monticello in honor of its use in the monumental fifty-volume *Papers of Thomas Jefferson*, published by Princeton University Press. Monticello is a transitional type design, embodying certain features of Bulmer and Baskerville, but it is a distinguished face in its own right.

Composed, printed, and bound by
The Haddon Craftsmen, Inc., Scranton, Pa.
Typography and binding design by
VINCENT TORRE